ALONE
AND UNAFRAID

Patriot Defense
and Survival Guide

JASON HANSON

S0-ATV-403

Copyright © 2018 by Laissez Faire Books
All rights reserved.

Published by Laissez Faire Books, 808 St. Paul Street, Baltimore, Maryland

www.lfb.org

Cover and Layout Design: Mena Sugg
Managing Editor: Shane Ormond & Barbara Hauck

TABLE OF CONTENTS

CHAPTER 6:
DISASTER PREPAREDNESS: HOW TO SURVIVE ANY CRISIS   261

CHAPTER 7:
EMERGENCY MEDICINE: THE BASICS OF FIELD MEDICINE   **421**

CHAPTER 8:
SURVIVAL AND SPY TRAINING: THE NEXT LEVEL   **463**

INTRODUCTION

I learned a lot more than spy and survival tactics during the almost decade I spent working for the CIA.

I learned that most folks take their safety for granted, rarely giving a second thought to their survival until it's too late. I discovered that the world today is more dangerous than most people ever realize. And with terrorist attacks, mass shootings and large-scale disasters, it's only getting worse by the day.

But more than anything, I realized that only you can take responsibility for your and your loved ones' safety.

If an intruder breaks into your home, you and I both know the police can't get there quickly enough. If a thug stops you in the street, no one is going to come to your rescue. And during a flood or an earthquake, you can be waiting for aid — and wasting critical time — for up to 72 hours or more.

That's why I always choose to act instead of wait.

If you're already reading this book, then you're probably like me. You'd rather have the tools and knowledge to take matters into your own hands than wait for someone else to arrive just a few moments too late. You sleep better at night knowing that you've already taken the necessary precautions to protect your family. And you're done with being afraid.

Now don't get me wrong: I'm not Mr. Doom and Gloom.

Far from it, in fact. Knowing that I'm prepared for the next flood or blackout… that my family's home is safe and secure… or how to handle myself when attacked… gives me the peace of mind and confidence to enjoy every day with my loved ones to the fullest.

As I always say, "Hope for the best, but prepare for the worst."

And if you can take care of hoping for the best, then this book will prepare you for the worst. In it, I've adapted many of the spy and survival techniques I've learned over the years —

on escape and evasion, self-defense, survival and much more — for use in everyday life.

By the time you finish this book, you'll know how to survive in a prolonged blackout, be able to turn your house into a secure fortress and learn a powerful self-defense technique anyone can master — as well as dozens of techniques for making your everyday life safer.

Of course, I couldn't have put together this massive tome of knowledge on my own. When you're in the intelligence business, you learn that there's no place for ego when people's lives are on the line. To get the job done, you have to surround yourself with the "best of the best" and know when to tap the talents of other "A-players."

That's why I've enlisted the aid of former Navy SEAL Cade Courtley, Special Operations Physician Dr. Omar Hamada (a 14-year veteran of the U.S. Army) and an ex-CIA operative known only as JAVELIN to protect his identity. Together — along with contributions from experts on self-defense, survival and guns — they form an unbeatable dream team of spy and survival knowledge… and it's all in here.

By the way, feel free to read this book however you like. It's made so you can read it back to front or dip in and out, cherry-picking your favorite subjects first. (If that's your style, I recommend checking out *Trident: A Simple Self-Defense Technique That Anyone Can Master* on Page 183 or *How to Survive North America's Most Dangerous Animal Attacks* on Page 391.)

Enjoy this book and don't allow yourself to become a victim. Your safety is in your own hands.

Best,

Jason Hanson
Former CIA officer
Safety and survival expert

CHAPTER 1:

SPY TECHNIQUES: COVERT OPERATIONS TRAINING

THE SINGLE-BEST WAY
TO HELP YOU DETECT LIES

We'll call her "Lindsay." She was a young woman, about 25 years of age, and she was sitting in my office for a job interview. Her résumé was solid. She looked like the perfect candidate for the opening I had at my company.

But in a matter of moments, after asking her my two favorite questions that I use to determine the quality of a potential employee, Lindsay would flunk out.

Now, I understand you might not be an employer, but this method of questioning can be used anytime you need help determining if someone is being honest with you or not.

Establishing a Base Line

When Lindsay first came in, we were chatting about less serious topics: the weather, where she was from, where she heard about the job, and so on.

In addition to getting to know her better, the purpose of these first few questions was to establish her "base line." What this means is that I was watching her verbal and nonverbal reactions to see how she responded to questions she had no reason to lie about.

After several of these questions, I was able to determine her base line and how she reacted when she was in her comfort zone. Now that I knew her comfort zone, it was time to move on to more serious questions to find out if she really was the right person for the job.

My Two Favorite Questions

The first question I asked was, "When is the last time you stole something?"

She sat in her chair for a second, got an uncomfortable look on her face, and was clearly taking as much time as she could before she answered me.

Finally, after several seconds, she informed me that she used to work for a bookkeeper a few years ago when she was right out of school. She had stolen several office supplies so she could quit that job and start a competing business.

Clearly, after I heard her answer, I knew I would not be hiring her for the position. But I proceeded to my next question since I treat all interviews the same and ask everyone the same set of questions.

The next question was, "When's the last time you did drugs?"

Again she got that awkward look on her face and was stalling for time before she answered. She ended up admitting that she still does drugs, smoking marijuana almost on a daily basis. At that point, I asked her a few other questions and then thanked her for her time and concluded the job interview.

To Get the Truth, Ask a Presumptive Question

So why are these my two favorite questions to ask of potential employees?

Well, I ask the first question about stealing because almost all of us have stolen something in our lives. When many of us were in elementary school, we would steal candy from the supermarket.

Obviously, I realize we were all kids once and I don't care if someone stole a Snickers when they were in fifth grade. However, if someone is stealing from their employer as in the story above, that's definitely not someone I'm going to hire.

I ask the second question about doing drugs for the same reason as the first. I know many people tried drugs in high school or college, and I don't care about that. I just want to make sure they're not doing drugs today.

Both of these questions are known as "presumptive questions," meaning I am presuming that someone has done them. I am presuming they've stolen, and I am presuming they've done drugs.

When I ask these presumptive questions and a person has never done drugs before, they just immediately tell me no and their base line remains the same. I know they're telling the truth. In other words, I don't get a pause from them or an awkward look on their face, because they don't feel guilty about the question and so have nothing to hide.

To get the truth, all you have to do is ask a presumptive question about whatever it is you'd like to know.

Versatility of Presumptive Questions

For instance, let's say someone knocks on your door trying to sell you a vacuum. This is a trick of many criminals: They'll pose as salesmen because they're trying to case your house to see if there's any reason to come back and rob the place when you're not home.

To find out if the salesman is legit, you could ask him, "When's the last time you sold a vacuum to someone?" An honest person will have an immediate answer because they have nothing to hide. However, if the salesman stutters or buys time, that could mean he's never sold a vacuum and he's not really a salesman. In which case, you should write down his license plate and perhaps notify police.

Or say you have kids, like I do. If you've got a teenager who came home extra late one night, you could ask them, "You told me you were going to Rob's house. How come you didn't tell me where you were really going?" If the kid is truthful, they'll likely have an instant answer such as, "What are you talking about, Mom? I was at Rob's house all night."

But if the child hesitates and you see that guilty look on their face, you know you need to do more digging to find out where they really were.

The bottom line is it's easier to detect deception than most people realize. By using a presumptive question, you can quickly ferret out honest people from dishonest people, saving you a lot of headaches in the future.

Also, remember to be creative, because there are many situations where you can use a presumptive question, including if you're a single man or woman on the dating scene. In fact, when I was single, I used to ask women (in a joking tone with a smile), "When's the last time you slashed an ex-boyfriend's tires?"

And yes, one time, a girl did tell me she vandalized an ex's car, so I certainly didn't go on a date with her!

BECOME A PROFESSIONALLY TRAINED HOSTAGE

In 1989, an American by the name of Kurt Muse was living in Panama with his family. Though he loved the country and people of Panama, Kurt was horrified by the brutal acts of dictator Manuel Noriega.

So to help the country he lived in, Kurt set up underground radio broadcasts urging the citizens of Panama to fight for their God-given rights. Eventually, Kurt was discovered as the perpetrator of the broadcasts — and was promptly arrested and imprisoned by Noriega's men.

For months, he suffered things you and I couldn't imagine, until a harrowing rescue took place by operators of Delta Force.

On the night of Dec. 20, 1989, a helicopter dropped the operators onto the roof of the infamous Modelo prison where Muse was being held.

One operator was given the task to drop outside his window and shoot the guard whose job it was to kill Muse in the event of a rescue attempt. That guard wasn't there; instead, he was taken out by another operator as the rescuers rushed through the prison to Muse's cell.

Once there, they blew off the door and gave Muse a bullet-proof vest, a helmet, and goggles for his protection.

After making it safely to the roof, they were picked up by a helicopter, but they sustained heavy gunfire and crashed a few minutes later. Thankfully, nobody was seriously injured, and the operators were able to form a secure perimeter at the crash site until an armored personnel carrier could rescue them.

Incredibly, this Delta Force team became the first counter-terrorist unit ever to rescue an American hostage from enemy's hands.

The FBI's Secret Weapon

Of course, not all hostage rescue attempts go as well, and not all of them occur overseas. When someone is taken hostage here in America, the job of rescuing them falls to the FBI's Hostage Rescue Team (HRT).

For example, you may remember in 2013 when a man named Jimmy Dykes stormed a school bus in Alabama.

Dykes shot the bus driver five times, killing him, and then kidnapped a 5-year-old boy, taking him to an underground bunker that was booby-trapped with explosives. After a six-day standoff, the FBI's HRT raided the bunker, killing Dykes and saving the life of the boy.

Obviously, the chances that you'll ever be kidnapped and held hostage by a madman are rather slim. However, if, heaven forbid, you were to find yourself in this situation, you could significantly increase your chances of being rescued by becoming a "professionally trained hostage."

Very few people have had the training or knowledge I'm about to share with you, so please spread the word to your friends and family, because this information has and does save lives.

How to Be a Professionally Trained Hostage

In the kidnappings mentioned above, it was obvious who the captors were and where the individuals were taken. However, this is often not the case.

This is why if you're ever kidnapped, you want to leave as many clues as possible to your whereabouts, so you're easy to track by the police and FBI.

The trail of evidence begins with you sticking your finger down your throat so you force yourself to throw up. I know, this sounds highly unpleasant — but it's evidence that could be the key to finding you.

You also want to cut yourself and leave blood if you can.

For example, if you were kidnapped and transported to a room, you would want to find anything that could cut your finger and draw some blood. You would then wipe this blood in areas that are not obvious.

In other words, you wouldn't wipe the blood on top of a table, because your captors could see it and quickly clean it up. Instead, you would want to leave blood evidence under a table, in a corner, on a piece of carpet, or on the wall in a less obvious place.

Keep in mind I'm talking about making a small cut to leave blood evidence. Don't create a huge gash that's going to require medical attention and weaken you.

Also, if you can, leave footprints or scrapes with your shoes or boots on walls or floors. Again, don't make these marks super obvious. Put them in more discreet places.

The reason you're doing this, leaving as much evidence as you can, is because that way your family or friends can tell the police you've had training and you know to leave clues.

This means the police won't just walk into the supposed place you may have been and spend a few minutes walking around. Instead, they'll be looking at the walls, under tables, pulling up corners of the carpet, and spending a lot more time looking for clues.

If you've left these clues discreetly, you'll make the police's job easier and you'll significantly increase your chances of survival.

A Final Tip

If a rescue attempt does happen, make sure you're low to the ground when it takes place.

The last thing you want to do is to stand up, waving your arms as law enforcement bursts through the door, because anyone standing up is a threat to them.

So to avoid being accidentally shot, lie flat on the floor and don't move at all. They'll eventually get to you after a (hopefully) successful raid.

THE WALKIE-TALKIE SPY TRADE TRICK

Modern cellphones are incredible communication tools. But sometimes, there are situations where a more low-tech device is actually better.

The trusty walkie-talkie is a perfect example.

No, not the cheap kind you find at RadioShack that kids play with. I'm referring to a unique walkie-talkie that has literally saved lives in the intelligence business.

Below, I'm going to divulge one of the tricks of the spy trade to show you how powerful this simple device can be. Pay attention, because in a crisis situation, you can use this technique in a similar way to keep you safe.

Your Mission, Should You Choose to Accept It...

Imagine you're a government operative who was just handed a top-secret mission in Belarus.

Your job is to locate a scientist who has a flash drive with some critical information about nuclear weapons. Since this scientist is so well-known, it's not easy to get into his office, but you just found out he's giving a presentation at a conference.

The conference takes place in a week, so you hop on a plane to Belarus to exploit this small window of opportunity. When you land in Belarus, you know that you have to be extremely careful, because the Belarusian government knows people want access to this scientist.

In other words, they know the conference is coming up, so the Belarus intelligence services are on high alert for anyone in the area who looks suspicious.

Your legend (cover) for this mission is that you work for a think tank that studies nuclear and biological weapons. As soon as you get off the plane, you head to your hotel and check in under your alias, Alan Bowen.

Because this is such a dangerous mission, as soon as you get to your room, you pull out your special radio.

The radio is fully charged, so you turn it on and tape down the "talk" button so that the radio is constantly transmitting. You then take out a second radio and turn it on, making sure that you can clearly hear what's coming from the first radio.

Once you've determined the radio with the button taped down is working properly, you then put it close to the door under a small pile of clothes.

Next, you use the room phone to call the front desk, telling them that you've got a friend checking in and that they prefer a room on a lower level.

You're on the sixth floor, so you ask them if they have anything available on the third floor, which they do. You then go down to the front desk to get the room key for your "friend" — and then you check into that new room on the third floor.

You leave that second radio on all the time so you can hear if someone raids your original room, in which case you've been exposed and it's time to escape to safety.

The Versatility of a Good-Quality Radio

The key to making this spy trick work is, of course, the good-quality radios. The ones that I prefer are the Baofeng radios.

Baofeng Radio: **http://amzn.to/2gMiPZO**

Baofeng radios have a multiband FM transceiver with an extensive frequency coverage, which means you won't have a problem finding a channel and getting them to work. They're also very inexpensive, at only about $35 each, and are

Baofeng Radio

great for bug-out bags and home invasion protection purposes.

I have a friend who lives in a rural area of Alabama and doesn't get any cell service. He leaves his radio on all of the time, and a neighbor does the same. If there's ever an emergency, he can just key up his radio to let his neighbor know what's going on.

You can also use these radios in place of a "nanny cam." Simply tape down the talk button on one of the radios and leave it in the room of someone you wish to record and you'll hear everything they say.

I've even heard of instances where these were taped underneath a restaurant table to hear the conversations of some guests who were being investigated.

I'm sure you can think of several more uses for the Baofeng radio. But my point is during a crisis situation, cellphone towers will likely be down, just as they were during the Sept. 11 attacks, when nobody could get calls through. So since none of us knows when the next natural disaster or terrorist event is going to take place, I would consider getting a set of radios, such as the Baofeng, today.

DISAPPEAR FROM UNWANTED SURVEILLANCE

A couple years ago, while teaching a seminar in Las Vegas, a man approached me and asked to speak privately. The reason for his discretion became clear once we'd stepped away from the group: "I've had multiple wives cheat on me — and I think my current wife is cheating on me too."

Awkward as this was, I felt sorry for the guy and asked how I could help.

He admitted he wasn't 100% sure. He just suspected his wife was lying when she claimed to be going to the gym and on other errands. He wanted my advice on how to follow her so he could discover the truth.

I laid out two options for him. The first was to hire a private investigator to tail her for a week. This, however, would be rather expensive. So option two would be to buy a GPS tracking device, pop it on her car, and check the data after a week to find out where she'd been going.

He went with the second option.

A short while later, I heard back from this gentleman and, unfortunately, among other things, the tracking device showed that his wife had driven to a local hotel, where she'd spent about an hour. He confronted her about this, and she told him she went there to smoke marijuana with a friend.

Turn Your Smartphone Into a Motion Detector

Perhaps you're in a hotel room and you want to ensure nobody enters your room without you knowing. Or maybe you've got a child or grandchild in college and you want to protect their dorm room from unwanted visitors.

Well, there's a simple app that solves this issue by turning a spare smartphone into a motion detector.

All you have to do is place the phone in front of a hotel room door, for example, and when someone crosses the path, the phone will begin recording a video that's uploaded live to the Internet. You can even have the phone set off an alarm too if you want.

You can also use this app in a two-phone set up: One phone is used as the motion detector, and then you use your other phone to monitor in real-time what's taking place on the first phone.

This clever app is called Presence and is the brainchild of a fellow named Gene Wang. Gene's mother had her home broken into twice in one year, so Gene developed the app as an inexpensive security system to monitor her home.

The app is available for both Apple and Android devices and can be downloaded for free.

Download Presence: **www.presencepro.com**

In the nicest way possible, I pointed out that she probably wasn't just smoking marijuana. That was the end of our conversation, and I never heard back from the guy to see what happened with his marriage.

Obviously, I hope you never have to track a spouse because you've grown suspicious about their fidelity. But the fact is that technology today has made it incredibly easy to track and follow another person.

And when you consider that this technology could be turned on you, that's a scary thought. The good news, however, is that it's also very easy to keep yourself undetected, and it requires no fancy equipment.

Disappear Like Jason Bourne

For those in the "intelligence business," a common trick is to "tag" a car so that it's easy to follow. These tags can include a sticker on a taillight or a piece of tape on the bumper.

To protect against this, you're trained to discreetly walk around your car before getting in to ensure you haven't been marked by a foreign adversary. In a high-threat situation, intelligence agents will also pretend to drop their keys on the ground so they can take a quick look under the car to make sure there are no tracking devices.

Since you probably don't have any need to be discreet, I'd recommend you simply kneel down to look under your car anytime you feel the need to check for a GPS.

The average GPS device is a small black box about 3 by 3 inches in size. Most come with a magnetic case and easily attach to the metal frame of the car. So if you glance under the car, you'll want to quickly scan the outer edges of the vehicle, where the device is most likely to be placed.

If you did find a GPS, you could have some fun and put it on someone else's car so the folks trying to follow you get sent on a wild-goose chase.

Another simple way to keep yourself safe is to turn off all tracking features on your cellphone.

That way, no one can use your phone's GPS or your social media accounts against you. I'd recommend everyone with a smartphone take this step.

For those with an iPhone, you can do this by going to Settings: Privacy: Location Services.

There, you'll see any apps that have access to your location. Slide them all to "off."

If you're really worried, the best way to ensure your phone can't be used to track you is to remove the battery completely or, better yet, purchase a "faraday bag."

A faraday bag (the name comes from the great English scientist Michael Faraday) is a special type of bag that blocks electric fields. This means that anything you place inside it that emits a signal — such as a cellphone or GPS or key fob — will be blocked.

The one I recommend is made by a company called Mission Darkness, and you can buy it on Amazon for $30.

Mission Darkness Faraday Bag: **http://amzn.to/2gFI6kB**

As technology continues to get better, I believe the average American is going to need to be a lot more vigilant to ensure they can't be easily located or followed. By taking the steps above, you'll be ahead of the game.

HOW TO COUNTER FACIAL RECOGNITION TECHNOLOGY

The most wanted terrorist in the world lay dead with a bullet in his head. However, the Navy SEALs who killed Osama bin Laden needed to be 100% sure this was their man.

After all, the president of the United States would soon announce to the country that after several long years we had finally tracked down and killed the man responsible for the Sept. 11 attacks.

To verify bin Laden's identity, the SEALs used a variety of techniques, including photographs, a DNA sample, and fingerprints. In addition, they carried with them a unique hand-held device used for facial recognition, which helped confirm once and for all that Osama bin Laden had been eliminated.

Designed to Trap Criminals at Home and Abroad

The first facial recognition software was developed by the CIA in the 1980s. At the time, it was crude and didn't do much, but the agency was well aware of the potential in using it to help identity threats across the world.

Today, the agency still uses their venture capital firm called In-Q-Tel to invest in private companies currently developing the most advanced facial recognition software to date... and trust me, it's come a long way.

Of course, the CIA isn't the only group using facial recognition to catch people. The FBI and police often use it to catch criminals right here in the U.S.

For instance, in 1996, a Pennsylvania man named Lynn Cozart was convicted of sexual assault of his three children. Two months before his sentencing, he disappeared and remained on the run for 19 years.

During his time on the run, Cozart took an alias and obtained a new driver's license and Social Security number. This horrible criminal was well-known, even featured on the TV show America's Most Wanted and listed as one of Pennsylvania's most wanted fugitives. Despite all of the publicity, he went free until last year, when he was captured in Muskogee, Oklahoma. He was comfortably working at a Wal-Mart under the alias of David Stone.

The FBI used facial recognition technology to catch him. In short, they uploaded his photo to a database that searches for facial matches among driver's licenses, military IDs, passports, and law enforcement mug shots all over the country.

Cozart was caught when the facial recognition database matched his mug shot to a driver's license in another state.

Keeping Us Safe... or Tracked?

Obviously, guys like Cozart deserve to get caught, as do terrorists, so facial recognition software certainly has its benefits. However, you and I both know that like all technology, facial recognition could be used for evil purposes.

The government could easily use it to spy on ordinary Americans who aren't fugitives on the run.

In the U.K., facial recognition technology called NeoFace was used on over 90,000 ordinary people attending a music festival in Leicestershire last year. Police claimed that it was part of their security measures, used to scan for potential terror threats, but the festival attendants were not made aware of its use.

Or what if an ex-spouse or ex-lover had access to this software and were using it to stalk you?

In these cases, you might want a way to avoid getting picked up by this software.

Facial recognition can be defeated, but it's not as simple as the movies make it out to be. Sure, you could wear a ski mask, but in most cases you'd draw attention to yourself and look like a criminal or crazy person.

Instead, let's look at a few ways you can stay safe from facial recognition and not stick out in your everyday life.

Disappear in Plain Sight

One of the simplest ways to reduce the chances of being caught by facial recognition is to disguise your face. This is done fairly often in the intelligence business. Stick to simple techniques — you could wear big sunglasses and a hat or wear your hair so that it covers your face a little. You could even put on fake facial hair such as a beard or mustache, which I've done before.

Those are pretty basic disguises, more for everyday use. If you are truly worried about the government spying on you and want to do everything possible to cover your face, you could purchase clothing or accessories that have NIR LED lights.

These lights work by overloading the light sensors on cameras, causing any pictures taken to appear blurry and your face to be unrecognizable. These lights can be worn on glasses, T-shirts, and other clothing you can wear on a daily basis. The good thing about some of these lights is that they are not easily noticeable to the naked eye. The lights will be apparent only through a camera lens.

A third option for staying safe from facial recognition is to wear a prosthetic mask. This is an extreme measure, which would take your disguise to another level. I don't mean some cheap mask you bought at the Halloween store — remember, you don't want to draw any attention to yourself. You can actually purchase realistic-looking prosthetic masks for around $500.

From a distance, these masks look very real and appear to be a normal face. If you're up close, you can see the holes on the mask for the eyes, but that's the only feature of your actual face that's exposed.

A few of these techniques are certainly extreme, but they can help you stay safe from facial recognition. However, we all know technology is constantly increasing. We're going to continually have to come up with ways to defeat this and protect our privacy as it becomes more widespread.

HOW TO SHAKE A TAIL IN THREE EASY STEPS

Each day when I leave to go to my office and when I return home, I always check my mirrors to make sure I'm not being tailed. At this point, I don't even really think about it; it's just second nature.

The other day while I was driving home, I noticed a red sedan following me. There was nothing unusual about this particular vehicle, and nothing immediately set off any alarm bells.

But after several turns the red sedan was still behind me — which was highly unusual because I take a shortcut to get to my neighborhood that not many people know about.

The Long Way Round

Since the sedan was still following me, I passed my street and kept going. I took a left a few streets later, and sure enough, the red car turned after me. My heart started to race — at this point the chances were pretty slim someone else would be driving the exact same route I was.

I made one last turn and the red car followed. I had reached the end of a cul-de-sac and was planning to turn around to face the pursuing vehicle so I could get a good look at the driver and the license plate. (It was a sunny day and the glare prevented me from seeing much in my rear-view mirror.)

But guess what? Before I could spin my car around, the red sedan pulled into the driveway of a nearby house. The driver — a woman who looked to be in her seventies — got out and went inside. She didn't notice me at all!

I sat and had a good laugh to myself. This was one of those rare instances when it was all just a big coincidence. But I'm glad I didn't take any chances.

A Hard Act to Follow

This brings me to my first tip if you think you're being tailed: Don't drive directly to your house. You certainly wouldn't want to lead a criminal straight to where you lay your head at night.

Here's my second piece of advice: Make as many turns as necessary to determine if you are indeed being followed. If you make eye contact with the other driver and it's obvious you're trying to get their license plate, that's perfectly OK.

If you're truly uncomfortable or feel like you're in immediate danger, do this: Head directly to a police or fire station to get help. I don't recommend doing what I did — going to the end of a cul-de-sac to spin around. The last thing you want to do is get yourself cornered.

Keep It Casual

As I mentioned, it's all right if your attempts to shake your tail are obvious. In the world of espionage, the person following you is likely with another intelligence service. If you are clearly trying to lose them, they'll know you're a spy because only a spy would do that.

In that case, you'd want to drive naturally and do nothing to arouse suspicion so they'd eventually leave you alone. The goal is to lull your pursuer to sleep because you're so boring and normal.

Thankfully, you don't have to worry about evading a foreign intelligence service, so you can drive in as many circles as necessary to ensure nobody is following you.

Always put your safety first. That way, the worst thing that will happen is that you'll be laughing to yourself as you watch a perfectly nice stranger pulling into their driveway.

CONCEALING SPY GEAR WHEN YOU TRAVEL

I was 30,000 feet in the air on my way overseas. I was going over the checklist in my mind to make sure I had all of my gear and that it was properly concealed. The truth is it doesn't matter how many times you head overseas — you never let your guard down. To this day, I obsessively double check everything.

For instance, as I was sitting on the plane that day I was wearing my Escape & Evasion Gun Belt. This is a solid leather belt that has three hidden zippered pockets inside of the belt.

In the first pocket, I had $40 in cash because it's always a good idea to have extra cash when traveling.

In the second pocket I had a small lock pick set. If you don't know how to pick locks it's something you can learn very easily.

In the third pocket I had a bobby pin, hair barrette and a handcuff key. Overseas, you're more likely to run into corrupt police who will use handcuffs to restrain you. The bobby pin and hair barrette would allow me to escape handcuffs if that situation arose, as would the universal handcuff key I was carrying.

Escape and Evasion Belt:
http://bit.ly/2xNU1o9

If you're traveling to more dangerous areas of the world, having escape gear on your belt is just the beginning of the preparations you should be making.

There are additional steps you can take once you've arrived, to keep you safe as you travel around.

1. One good, yet painful way to conceal items on your body is by using a piece of Gorilla Tape. This is a great way to carry small items that could come in handy, such as a razor blade, a handcuff key or lock picks. Simply place the item in the middle of the Gorilla Tape and stick it somewhere on your thigh or leg.

   If you're wearing shorts, put the tape lower on your leg. That way, when needed, you can just lift up the bottom of your shorts to tear off the piece of tape to access the gear. If you're wearing pants, fasten the tape up higher around the waistline so you can easily access it with your hands. Ripping the tape off your skin might be uncomfortable, but in a life-or-death situation you won't think twice about doing it to get to the tools to keep you alive.

   (A pain-free version of this tactic is to wrap your arm or leg in a bandage to make it look as if you've been injured. Underneath the bandage, you can have your escape gear, essentially allowing you to hide the items in plain sight.)

2. If you wear pants with a button closure, you can hang survival items on the button. Simply take a piece of string and loop it around the button with the string hanging down inside your pants. On the end of the string, you can tape a handcuff key, hair barrette or bobby pin.

I wouldn't hang a razor blade or anything sharp using this method because it would be too easy to cut yourself.

Upgraded Hotel Safety

When checking into hotels, always ask for two keys. That way, anyone who is watching you check in will think there's more than one person staying in the room. If you're clearly staying alone, criminals will think you're an easy target. After all, if they're planning on breaking into your room, one person is much easier to handle than two.

Use a door stop alarm in front of your hotel room door. A door stop alarm is a wedge-shaped device that acts as a security system. If someone tries to open your door, a very loud alarm goes off. Door stop alarms are inexpensive and you should never travel without one.

GE Door Stop Alarm: **http://amzn.to/2wFhc5q**

Don't stay higher than the sixth floor. A lot of the places in the world don't have fire codes and you don't want to have to run down 77 flights of stairs to get to safety. What's more, even if your hotel has smoke alarms and is up to code, most firetruck ladders only go as high as the sixth floor.

3. One of my favorite ways to conceal gear on my body is by using a safety pin and a small plastic bag. First, take the small plastic bag and fill it with whatever items you wish — cash, handcuff key, copy of your passport — and then clip the bag to the inside of your pants using the safety pin. You can even clip one set of gear to your front and one to your back since you don't know if you'll end up restrained with your hands in the front or back.

4. A final way to conceal gear is by using your shoes. On the tip of the laces on my shoe is a small handcuff key that is secured to the laces. Unless you know what you're looking for you'll never see it. You can also tape items to the inside of your shoes or under the tongue of your shoes.

These are just a few of my favorite ways to conceal my

escape and evasion gear. Your chosen method should vary according to the threat level of the country to which you're traveling. If you're going to Bora Bora, you probably don't need to be decked out head to toe in evasion gear, but if you're going to Iraq you better be well equipped.

A PRACTICAL GUIDE TO DISGUISING (AND PROTECTING) YOUR IDENTITY

By JAVELIN | *Ex-CIA Operative*

Through a chance encounter with a member of the Japanese Triad, I found an opportunity to gain intel on government telecommunications. So with plenty of support from Uncle Sam, I set out to recruit this Triad member.

To ensure a favorable outcome — and to protect us both in the developmental stage of the operation — I chose to wear what I call my "Colombian drug lord" disguise, which included a long, light-brown wig tied into a ponytail at the base of my neck and reaching the small of my back. I also had a thick walrus mustache to match, a tailor-made Italian suit and thick, gaudy glasses.

In the beginning stages, our PMs (personal meetings) were set up on his turf, in a very dangerous part of Tokyo where he felt more comfortable. If there was a deal to be made, this is where it would all go down. Blending in was critical to the success of the mission, and the slightest mistake could prove deadly for me.

Start With a Blank Slate

The average citizen might think wearing a disguise is easy, but there are many challenges to executing a successful disguise. First, you need to ask yourself: For whom are you wearing the disguise? What is the weather like? How do the locals dress? How long are you expecting to remain in disguise? Is this a long- or short-term situation?

Next, when choosing a disguise, select one that is opposite from your typical appearance and completely own your new persona. You must be meticulous. Don't half-ass anything. In this case, my disguise had to be absolutely perfect, because my life was on the line.

Keep Up Appearances

Here's a list of the items I carry in my disguise kit:

1. Mascara in several shades for quick root touch ups to match my natural hair to the color of my wig

2. Alcohol wipes to remove makeup quickly and effectively

3. Good facial adhesive to apply facial hair in a different color. Keep in mind this is difficult and dangerous to work with when heat and perspiration come into play.

4. Wigs in a variety of colors and lengths. If you have long hair, using a wig might be too much trouble. If this is the case, consider cutting your hair short

5. Makeup that can be used for minor to major changes

6. Several sets of glasses. Glasses help to break up your face drastically. This application works better when you don't normally wear glasses

7. A small mirror to aid in quick changes when a full-length mirror is not accessible. Catching a flaw in your disguise

before the enemy does will protect your cover and can save your life.

Change Your Stripes

For quick disguises when the threat of discovery isn't as severe, you can use coverings like hats and coats that can be slapped on and quickly removed. The simplicity of changing colors by adding or removing articles of clothing can do wonders in helping you lose a surveillance tail.

If you find yourself trying to shake off a tail, take it to the next level by changing your shoes. This simple change is notorious for being the hardest to affect with any disguise, but can easily throw off even trained surveillance. The key is to change your gait as well.

It's imperative to be comfortable in your disguise and adept at applying it. The purpose of a disguise is to take on another persona to protect your true identity, family, friends, etc. Immerse yourself in the persona to avoid blowing your own cover. Grow your confidence and comfortability and practice, practice, practice.

The good news is you probably won't be meeting with a Triad gang member in Tokyo, so you don't have to put as much effort into a disguise as I did. But a quick change of a hat and jacket will do a great job of helping you escape a dangerous situation when you want to ensure you're not noticed.

LEAVE THESE ITEMS AT HOME AND YOU MIGHT NOT RETURN

Keys? Check. Wallet? Check. Phone? Check. Gun? Knife? Lock pick set?

Whoa, whoa, whoa. What?

Yes, you read that correctly. And that's not all.

Every time I walk out my front door, I carry certain items on me. Items I can use to protect myself and my family or to get out of a sticky situation.

Below is my list of everyday carry (EDC) items. Hopefully, this list will give you the means to keep you and your family safer:

1. Gun — I realize not everyone wants to carry a gun, but I think it's wise. These days, I carry a Sig Sauer P238 in my front pocket. I carry it in a Kydex holster that allows me to easily draw the gun from my pocket without the holster coming with it. At times, I also carry a Springfield 1911 inside the waistband at the four o'clock position on my hip. The ammunition I use for my guns is Speer Gold Dot.

2. Knife — If I'm just running errands around town, I'll

have a folding knife clipped to my pants pocket. It might be one made by Spyderco or Benchmade. If I'm going up in the mountains or out in the middle of nowhere, then I always have the fixed-blade NOC Knife with me.

3. Flashlight — A small flashlight is a must-have. Especially if you work a job that requires you to leave late at night. Don't forget, a flashlight can also be used as a self-defense tool, as evidenced from this newspaper excerpt:

   A Seattle, Washington, nurse was walking through a hospital parking lot to begin her 5 a.m. shift when she noticed a man following her. The man grabbed her purse and arm to pull her away. She let go of the purse but he continued to grab and pull her arm. The nurse was carrying a tactical flashlight in her hand and struck the man in his head, causing him to drop to his knees. The man was caught by police and required 43 stitches to repair the gash in his head. The suspect had been arrested four previous times for assaulting women.

4. Belt — I always wear a gun belt because it can be used in many different ways in addition to its intended purpose. See this month's article about seven ways your belt can keep you alive.

5. Lock pick set — I know most people won't want to carry a lock pick set around either. But I've found them very useful over the years, from helping neighbors get into their homes to helping someone get into a filing cabinet when they've lost the key.

6. Cash — It seems that you can use a credit card to pay for almost everything these days, but that doesn't mean you shouldn't always have emergency cash on you. I've been in two situations in my life when having cold, hard cash got me out of a nasty jam. I personally carry at least $300

in cash on me — with one $100 bill — every day.

7. Paracord keychain — These days, you can find paracord — also called parachute cord — almost anywhere. Even kids use it to make bracelets and necklaces and belts. I carry paracord because it has amazing escape uses and can saw through duct tape, zip ties and rope.

8. Cellphone — I'm pretty sure this is the one item that everyone can agree on. If a crisis occurs, you want to be able to dial 911 as quickly as possible.

9. Handcuff key — This is another item you probably won't need to carry unless you're traveling to more dangerous areas of the world. I carry one because they're lightweight, don't take up much space, and I can legally carry one almost anywhere.

10. Tactical pen — This is my favorite self-defense tool. It goes with me everywhere, whether I'm entering a highly secure government building or I'm on an airplane. In addition to using it for self-defense, I also use it to take notes throughout the day.

EXTRACT TOP-SECRET INFORMATION LIKE A CIA OPERATIVE

By JAVELIN | *Ex-CIA Operative*

"We are back in the business of stealing secrets."

At this declaration by CIA Director Mike Pompeo, spies' ears everywhere perked up. Although, the truth is some of us never stopped.

In my years of undercover work, I have never once lost a target. Which is why they kept me in the business so long. For me, it was easy — like breathing.

To be clear, my line of work isn't your run-of-the-mill sifting through trash and questioning the neighbors. It's much more intricate.

Man on a Mission

To start, I rarely know who my target is. You see, if any old investigator could find you, they wouldn't be calling me. No — my assignments begin with an objective. Once for almost for two years, I was out on an assignment you could write on one line:

"Find out how Russia is getting railgun information out of Korea."

And they wanted names. First, I found a list of railgun experts in Korea and sent the names to a foreign technology center. I had the center help me sift through the names to find a senior researcher — someone with a heavy amount of published work on railguns.

Now, researchers usually list collaborators on their published work. I noticed one researcher, Armano, listed the same two collaborators on each publication. And his collaborators were Russian. It could have been a coincidence, but it almost never is.

So I followed Armano for a few days. Generally, when I start following a target, I'm looking for body language. Are they confident or meek? Tense or relaxed?

And I look for routine. When do they leave work? What route do they take? Where do they like to eat?

I can learn a lot from surveying a person's normal behavior. Following Armano, I knew he wasn't meaningfully leaking information. Which meant his Russian collaborators were stealing it.

Keep Your Friends Close

The only way I could get close to the Russians was by getting close to Armano. I knew the Russians would be watching him, so I couldn't get too close too quickly.

I found a job where Armano's best friend, Jin, worked and made sure we became friends — in fact, Jin and I are still good friends to this day. We would go swimming and play tennis on the weekends. Then Jin introduced me to Armano.

After spending time with Armano, it was crystal clear he had no idea the Russians were using him. But I couldn't just come out and say this. I had to spend months building rapport with Armano to gain his trust.

When I'd built up this trust, I was able to convince Armano that the Russians were planning to take his research and develop deadly weapons to use against the world.

I was so successful in convincing Armano, he immediately went to the Korean government and explained what was going on. The Russians were exposed and their operation was shut down.

These types of operations — where covert operatives work to keep critical research and technology out of the bad guys' hands — still go on every single day, although you'd never know it.

Most of the time, our enemies get information the same way they tried to get it out of Armano. They befriend their targets — and the mark usually has no idea they're giving away valuable secrets.

The Bottom Line

My point is that 99% of people in this world are good and honest, but you can never let your guard down. There's a Russian proverb (often misattributed to President Reagan) you should keep in mind:

Trust, but verify.

Always be alert and pay attention to what is going on around you. That new co-worker could be up to something, or that strange van in your neighborhood might not be the cable guy. Remain vigilant and don't be afraid to question people before divulging too much information.

THE ART OF LOCK-PICKING

The majority of locks in homes are the cheapest a homebuilder can buy. Once you understand how easy it is to open the locks securing your home, I hope you'll change them out with a better quality lock, such as a Medeco or Schlage.

You also won't have to worry if you ever lose the key to a filing cabinet or a desk drawer.

Tools You'll Need

To open a standard lock, you'll need two tools: a tension wrench and an L rake. A tension wrench is a tool with a 90-degree angle that's used to apply pressure to the lock. Once the lock is picked, the wrench turns the lock, opening the door. An L rake is designed to push the cylinder pins into the correct position.

Household Items for Picking Locks

Most people don't realize how many common household items you can use to pick locks — like bobby pins, hairpins, bits of wire and paperclips. In fact, it takes just two paper clips to pick a standard lock. Simply straighten them out and bend one in a 90-degree angle — this one is your tension wrench. On the other paperclip, create three wavy ridges totalling about ¾". This pin will act as your raking tool.

How to Pick a Lock

Lock-picking is a handy skill to have and a fairly easy one to learn. That being said, it's probably easier to show you how to pick a lock than it is to tell you. Which is why I've prepared this video to show you how to pick a standard lock in 60 seconds or less.

For a more detailed guide check out my step-by-step lock-picking video: **http://bit.ly/2w62wsL**

Is This Legal?

People constantly ask me if carrying a lock pick set or picking locks is legal. To be clear, you should only pick locks of your own property, unless you have permission from the owner. As long as you aren't using the lock pick set to break into somewhere or something that's not yours, you shouldn't worry about carrying these tools. I always carry my lock pick set — I've been all over the world with it — and I've never had an issue.

AVOID BEING WINED, DINED AND DUPED

I saw her check my hand for a wedding ring before she introduced herself. In her eyes, I was a single man out to lunch — and I wanted to keep that image.

After a brief introduction, we were enjoying a meal together. She was a Chinese woman, approximately 5'4", dressed in business casual. She blended in perfectly with the surrounding crowd and seemed relatively harmless.

But then again, so did I.

I was on an intelligence-gathering operation that day, but we spies have to eat, too. So I made a brief stop for lunch. This woman who approached me could have been anyone — including a foreign spy.

The fact is, women are extremely effective case officers. They utilize their allure to gather information, penetrate organizations and recruit informants.

In many cultures, women are viewed as delicate, gentler and more innocent. Their strength and intelligence are constantly underestimated. But trust me when I tell you that female case officers are well aware of their faculties and cunningly use them to their advantage.

Which is why I was especially wary of my lunch companion — she could have easily been an enemy agent. She also could have simply been looking for company during her lunch break.

Regardless, I made sure I was careful. I didn't allow myself to offer up any information that could hurt me in the long run. If she were a spy, she would want my guard down. And I wasn't about to play into her hands that easily. I made sure I came across as a typical businessman. We shared a polite, casual lunch, and then I departed — leaving her with nothing worth reporting.

Not everyone is this careful.

In 2014, retired Lt. Col. Benjamin Pierce Bishop, a defense contractor at the U.S. Pacific Command, plead guilty to supplying classified information to a Chinese woman he was dating.

As with many of our opposing intelligence agencies, many of China's most effective case officers are females. Not only do they purposefully create "chance encounters," some even join our intelligence agencies as American citizens.

At this very moment, I can name over 10 Chinese-Americans recently discovered to be double agents working for the Chinese government. All of them had even passed polygraphs to supplement their TS/SCI (Top Secret/Sensitive Compartmented Information) clearances. All of these uncovered agents had been tasked with obtaining U.S. war plans and military strategies from the Pentagon.

The Chinese may well have the most extensive network of cooperating sources at their fingertips, and their intelligence activities have significantly increased in the last decade.

One tactic is utilizing Chinese scholars studying at American colleges as passive collectors. These students are pre-briefed before their journeys, and then debriefed upon return to their homeland.

If someone appears to have developed facile access to

intelligence-related information, they'll be contacted by a case officer to work a collection-type operation. This is known as the "saga of the visiting Chinese student."

The bottom line is you should always be wary if a stranger randomly wants to have a drink with you at a bar or a meal with you at a restaurant. The beautiful woman talking to you may not be a foreign spy, but she could be gauging to see if you're worth pickpocketing... worth following home... or worse.

There are, of course, chance happenings in life. But regardless of what you see in the movies, such coincidences are rare.

So keep your head up, your wits about you and your cards close to your chest.

BE AWARE OF TRAITORS IN OUR MIDST

By JAVELIN | *Ex-CIA Operative*

Recruiting a double agent is the hardest task you will ever come across as a case officer.

During my time in Asia, I became involved with a famous scientist who was conducting weapons research. It wasn't known to many, but he was working closely with Soviet weapons. My assignment was to recruit him as a double agent for the U.S. My efforts proved to be successful, and he quickly became a valuable resource in providing information on Soviet weapons research.

Just as I traveled the globe looking for those — like the famous scientist above — who could work in favor of the U.S., foreign operatives are scouring the U.S. in search of weak Americans to work against us.

Spies Among Us

In our industry, we refer to these recruiters as Hostile Intelligence Service Operators, or HOIS Operators. Years ago, I caught wind of HOIS Operators working out of a college in

New York. I booked the next flight out.

Soon I found myself in the school's administrative offices in search of a trustworthy spotter. A "spotter" is shop talk for anyone with an inside knowledge or access. HOIS Operators are well hidden — and they work hard to keep it that way. I knew if operators were recruiting at a college, they would be looking for candidates interested in government positions. So I started making files for any student applying for a government job.

Cameron's file caught my attention right away, although to anyone else, it would have seemed harmless. I kept every piece of information I could find — from phone numbers to traffic violations — but the only thing I had on Cameron was an immigration form.

The scarcity of information was a red flag.

I worked with the school to see if there was anything more I could learn about him. Nothing. At least I had his job application, and I used it to set up an interview. The interview was just what I expected. I asked Cameron for his birthday and birthplace. He responded calmly with a date and location, but the information did not match his file.

He was lying.

He was a good liar, but he was also sloppy. HOIS Operators don't make that kind of mistake. I knew Cameron wasn't an operator, but he was exactly who operators would be looking for.

Easy Targets

I narrowed down my list to 10 students who would be primary targets for HOIS Operatives. I watched them closely while staying under the radar myself, and turned their names into Washington. Even if the recruiters didn't go after these students, they were unfit for government employment.

Ultimately, there were six HOIS Operatives working out of that school. While it's good to see six operatives out of commission, you have to wonder about the situation before I arrived. How many students had been influenced by foreign intelligence? And how many government employees already work as double agents for our enemies?

Recently, Germany exposed a double agent within their intelligence service. The agent had gone through extensive interviews and training without so much as raising an eyebrow. He was ultimately discovered through a fake name online and turned over to prosecutors. German officials believe they caught the double agent before any damage was done, but only time will tell.

The German Federal Intelligence Service (Germany's equivalent to the CIA) discovered a weakness within their own walls. U.S. government personnel are trained to do the same.

Upon employment, every new hire is briefed to be watchful of their colleagues and report any unusual — even cavalier or sloppy — behavior. Most people might not consider a sloppy government employee a significant terror threat, but they can be.

Be Careful Who You Trust

Double agents and HOIS Operatives are out there right now, threatening our national security. As citizens of the United States, it is our responsibility to be actively looking for anything — or anyone — that could threaten our way of life.

We all need to be more careful. Don't let yourself dismiss anything out of the ordinary. Better yet, don't even dismiss the ordinary. Be observant. Always take all details into account and help keep America safe.

HOW TO HANDLE AN INTERROGATION LIKE A PRO

By JAVELIN | *Ex-CIA Operative*

In a particularly perilous country — I can't say where — I was nervously heading to the airport. It was my last stop before home, but also the most dangerous. You see, in this country, if I was suspected of being a spy, I would be detained. And if I was detained, I would be tortured and most likely killed before the week was out.

My training taught me how to keep my nerve at times like this. And ultimately, what it really boils down to is confidence. What one man can do, another can do… and I can do it better. I've watched a lot of good people drop out of training because they didn't have the confidence to push through.

Think about it. Knowledge is an important part of any job. But if you don't have the confidence to act on what you know, you might as well know nothing. Going to the airport, I remained confident — then security flagged me for questioning.

Keep Your Cool

This interview was a life-or-death situation for me. To keep my fears in check, I had to isolate and identify the problem. What was I actually afraid of? I was afraid of losing my life. What would cause that? If security discovered my true identity. What would it take to keep my fear from becoming a reality? If my interrogators believed my assumed identity, I wouldn't be detained and I would live. Once the problem was identified, the solution became clear.

The interview was pretty basic. Airport security questioned me and accused me. So I acted like anyone else would under the circumstances. I was cooperative and showed obvious signs that I was scared and confused. Of course, I had abandoned my actual fears — this was all an act.

I was questioned for about 25 minutes before I was free to leave. But I knew I wasn't out of the woods yet. I knew enough about customs to know I would be subjected to a second interview before my flight. I found an ugly green bench and sat for a moment to calm my nerves.

Know Your Weakness

The second key element to keeping your wits about you is knowing your weaknesses. Part of training is learning how to function while fatigued. I'm talking no sleep, little food and utter physical exhaustion.

During my training, once I was so tired I could practically sleep standing up, the trainers would put me in an interrogation room for hours. The U.S. would hire retired foreign nationals to do the questioning. The idea was to practice getting through foreign security.

As you can image, interrogation is a terrifying experience even when it's only training. After my first interrogation drill, I watched the recording over and over again, looking for any unconscious actions that gave away that I was lying. This is what's known as a "tell." Some people shuffle their feet, touch their face or blink faster when they're not being truthful. As a spy, these involuntary behaviors can get you killed.

But rather than completely covering up your tells, you can simply approach them with a countermove. If you touch your face a lot when you lie, purposely touch your face the same way when you are telling the truth. If you blink faster when you lie, focus on blinking normally through at least half of your lies.

That way, you won't panic if you slip up occasionally, and you'll throw your interrogator off the scent. Watching my interrogation training, I noticed that I blink less when I lie. And it's easy enough to counter that.

Get Ready for Round Two

I was staring at the ugly green bench, mentally preparing for a round two with security. I consciously swallowed my fear for my life. Feeling afraid was a waste of my energy. I had already isolated the problem, so I needed to remain focused on the solution. Sure enough, security "surprised" me with a second interview.

Second interviews are usually more intense. On this occasion, they kept me locked up long enough to miss my flight before they started threatening me. Now, the average person traveling for leisure would be upset that these people were wasting their time with ridiculous allegations.

So I started showing frustration about missing my flight and demanded to be reimbursed. The money really didn't matter to me, but it would matter to someone who was innocent. After a few more hours of interrogation, I was released and put on a plane.

The lesson here is that fear is healthy. Fear helps keep me alive. If I conducted my work with a fearless mentality, I would quickly become careless — and carelessness gets you killed. But I don't let my fear control me. I'm the one in control of my fear.

Whenever I'm faced with fear, I isolate it, identify the problem at the root of my fear and figure out a solution. It's that easy.

HOW FOREIGN SPIES LIVE AMONG US

By JAVELIN | *Ex-CIA Operative*

On a warm June day in 2010, FBI agents arrested a couple known as Donald Heathfield and Tracey Foley on suspicion of being part of a Russian espionage ring tasked with gathering information on nuclear weapons, American policy toward Iran, CIA leadership and congressional politics, among other topics.

The KGB had recruited the couple in their early twenties and directed them to Canada, where they assumed their new identities. After the birth of their first son, the family moved to the U.S. They joined our society as Canadian-Americans with the knowledge and language skills necessary to blend in with their surroundings.

This FBI operation, known as "Ghost Stories," led to the arrest of 10 Russian spies living in the U.S. These agents were part of an ongoing, deep immersion program that was believed to be shut down until a Russian spy betrayed his comrades.

It's rare to find an undercover operation running this long. These spies had been hiding for 20 years to build up their cover stories — which is no easy task. As someone who's had numer-ous legends (cover personas), I can tell you there are three vital elements a spy considers when creating a cover persona:

1. Find a job that will provide access to the target or mission. You want a job that will carefully and slowly ease you into the situation to avoid raising any suspicions. Any posi-tion too close to the subject that you assume too quickly will draw unwanted attention. On the other hand, a job that provides more distance could become a loss.

2. Find a job you can assume quickly. This requires an ac-curate self-analysis of your job skills — both strengths and weaknesses. It's vital to build a persona that matches your strengths with the target's vulnerabilities. The Fo-leys had an extended timeline, which allowed them to attend universities in the U.S. Most jobs don't allow you that much time. I've had assignments where I spent over 18 hours a day preparing for a new role.

3. Study and predict any risks involved with the cover you are assuming. Mrs. Foley worked as a realtor, which is a low-risk job, and Mr. Heathfield in a consultancy firm in Boston, which gave him access to high-profile clients. Understand a spy is looking for a cover position requiring little know-how and little attention but plen-ty of access to valuable information.

Once in Japan, I created a cover persona to get close to a highly targeted Russian scientist. Many Russian scientists are either a spy or working for one, so my mission was to obtain information from this scientist who was doubling as a spy working with biological weapons.

Now, I can't give too many details, but here's what I can tell you. In order to build up my persona, I posed as a college pro-fessor in Osaka to gain access to instruction manuals and study guides. Of course, anyone working with biological weapons is a valuable target. A target of this caliber draws the attention of spies from across the globe. After discovering their objectives were identical to mine, I recruited two foreign female spies to assist me. Our combined efforts netted some of the most valuable information on Russian biological warfare ever obtained.

In America, Russian spies also assume the cover of scientists, as well as researchers and diplomats. The use of diplomatic cover is well-known to U.S. intelligence agencies. Our agents build relationships with the known Russian spies to obtain valuable information on targets of mutual interest. This orchestrated dance is a careful waltz of trading information back and forth without causing any damage to either side.

Based on my experience with Russian intelligence, there's little doubt that Russia was behind several of the most recent hacks on our internet systems and will continue to be a threat in the future. But Russia is a potential superpower, and we need to maintain positive relations to remain allies. The waltz continues…

CHAPTER 2:

ONLINE SECURITY: SURF LIKE A SPY

SAFEGUARD YOUR SECRETS AGAINST DATA THEFT

"One of the largest thefts of government data ever seen…"

That's how *The Wall Street Journal* described the data breach in which Chinese hackers broke into the federal Office of Personnel Management (OPM) database, stealing the records of over 21 million government employees.

The hackers made off with everything from Social Security numbers to all kinds of personal information which the OPM obtains on people during their background investigations.

Since I used to work for the CIA and had a top-secret security clearance, the security clearance files the OPM had on me contained every bit of private information.

And I know the hackers obtained my files because I received a letter from the OPM saying exactly that.

But the threat of identity theft is just part of it. To make matters even worse, a friend of mine who's also ex-CIA told me:

"If you traveled to any foreign countries in true name or in alias while you were an officer, then that country — if you went back — could pick you up while you're overseas and hold you for espionage based on previous travels and activities that they suspect you committed. Also, we already know that the Chinese have sold those lists of information to several other countries, such as North Korea, Iran, Afghanistan, Syria, etc."

I'm not going to lie. I certainly wasn't happy hearing the government lost my security files to the Chinese. But the truth is I'm also not that worried about it.

Why not?

Because for years, I've taken various measures to protect my identity and privacy, so a lot of the information they have on me is practically useless. Below, I'll share some of those measures with you so that you can start implementing them and better protect your identity and personal information in 2016.

Is Your Home Address a Mystery?

One of the first things I recommend is to take your home address off of your driver's license. Too many people can hack that database and find out where you live.

In fact, a friend of mine was the victim of a home invasion after someone at the DMV gave criminals his home address. (My friend got in a shootout with the intruders and was thankfully unharmed and the intruders were captured.)

In the state of Utah, where I live, you have to have a physical address on your license, so I just use a UPS Store mailbox as my address. When I lived in the state of Virginia, I was allowed to have a PO box on my license.

Also, not only do I have my UPS Store address on my license, I also have it on my car registration, and everything else I own is registered to that address too.

Another benefit of having a UPS Store type of box is that you don't have any mail coming to your home, so you don't have to worry about criminals stealing credit card applications or other important documents from your mailbox.

You can get set up with a UPS Store mailbox of your own at **http://bit.ly/2w6bLcm**.

Putting Your Credit on Ice

The second thing I recommend you do is put a freeze on your credit report.

This is one of the best ways to protect yourself from identity theft, as it prevents someone from taking out a mortgage, car, or any other type of loan using your credit.

"Putting a freeze on your credit report is one of the best ways to protect yourself from identity theft."

All you have to do is go to the three credit bureaus — Experian, TransUnion, Equifax — and freeze your credit. It only takes a few minutes to do. I've had my credit freeze in place now for over 15 years.

In fact, right before I appeared on the ABC TV show Shark Tank, I got a call from one of the producers saying they were trying to check my credit to be on the show and they weren't able to access it.

This was a good reminder that the freeze keeps people out of your credit, and so when someone does need to access it, you can easily lift the freeze, which is what I did for the Shark Tank producer.

Freeze Your Credit

Experian: **http://bit.ly/2eETA7a**
TransUnion: **http://bit.ly/2eKADn1**
Equifax: **http://bit.ly/2l9cF6J**

Upgraded Shredding

Another simple measure you can take is to get a quality shredder for important documents. But not just any shredder.

A lot of folks own older shredders that simply cut the paper into long strands. However, these long strands of paper can be put together using a simple device that my team happens to own.

Instead, you want to buy a crosscut shredder, which is sometimes referred to as a "popcorn" shredder because it crosscuts the paper into tiny balls. While there are many of these crosscut shredders on the market, I would check out the Fellowes 79Ci.

Fellowes Powershred on Amazon: **http://amzn.to/2w6ia7n**

The Ultimate Hard Drive Eraser

Here's something else you'll want to do this year. If you're like me, you have old laptop or desktop computers that are sitting in a closet somewhere but need to be thrown away.

Before you get rid of any computer, though, you need to make sure that all of your personal information is removed.

"If you go to Starbucks and hop on their free Wi-Fi, you are putting your personal information in danger."

People claim there's software that can erase your hard drive, but the only method of truly ensuring no one can ever access your data is to follow this four-step process:

1. Remove the hard drive from the computer.
2. Boil it in water for 10 minutes.
3. Smash the hard drive into pieces.
4. Throw the pieces away in separate garbage bags and dispose of the bags in multiple different trash cans.

While this might sound like too much work, I guarantee there's a young person in your life who would be thrilled to remove a hard drive and smash it into a million pieces.

Secure Internet... At Starbucks

The last nugget I want to share with you is about getting a virtual private network (VPN). Though it doesn't provide you with true anonymity on the Internet, it does provide you with an extra layer of security when connecting to unsecured networks.

The fact is if you go to Starbucks and hop on their free Wi-Fi, you are putting your personal information in danger. Someone can easily hack that free Wi-Fi and locate your passwords and bank account information.

But if you have a virtual private network — a technology that uses an encrypted connection over an unsecure network — then you can surf free Wi-Fi all day long and be protected.

The VPN that I use is called TunnelBear, and all you have to do is download it from their site and install it and it'll be up and running, allowing you to surf the Internet as usual.

TunnelBear: **www.tunnelbear.com**

The bottom line is while you probably won't have your information stolen by the Chinese like I did, you still don't want to open yourself up to other hackers out there, so take the steps above to protect yourself.

HACKING THE DIRECTOR OF THE CIA IS EASIER THAN YOU THINK

Recently, the personal email account of the director of the CIA was hacked. His personal information was stolen, along with numerous confidential emails.

He wasn't hacked, however, by a foreign government or organized crime syndicate — he was hacked by an American high school student.

"The reason this type of 'hacking' works is that we live in a high-trust society where most people believe in being honest and polite."

How did the kid do it?

The same way I would've done it: through psychological manipulation.

It's far easier to gain access to confidential information through elicitation, better known as "social engineering," than through brute force or computer wizardry.

This is why it's vitally important to be aware of how this kind of manipulation gets deployed.

Through some simple awareness of the principles involved — and by taking a couple practical steps — you won't be so easy to be taken advantage of.

A Step-by-Step Guide to Performing a Hack

So if you want to hack the director of the CIA, where do you start? Here's how the American high school student did it.

First, he went online and did a reverse lookup of the director's cellphone number and discovered that he used Verizon. Next, he called Verizon and pretended to be one of their technicians who needed help with a customer's cellphone.

The Verizon customer service representative then gave the "technician" the director's four-digit pin, his email address, and the last four numbers on his credit card.

Once the high school kid had the director's email address, which belonged to an AOL account, he called AOL customer service and told them he'd forgotten his password and needed it reset.

AOL customer service asked a series of questions, such as the last four digits of his credit card, and because he could answer them correctly, the teen hacker was able to reset the director's email password — thereby gaining access to his email account.

When you want to find out all sorts of private details about a person's life, this is the most reliable way of doing it. This is how it's done in the intelligence business and in the criminal world.

Why is this method so effective?

The Vulnerability of Trust

The reason this type of "hacking" works is that we live in a high-trust society where most people believe in being honest and polite.

Criminals know this, and they like to take advantage of it.

It's why so many people are fooled by phone and Internet scams. We take others on their word and often don't question people enough, as we're afraid to offend them.

But if we're to avoid being swindled, we need to challenge people when they're asking too much information from us. If you find yourself in a situation where someone is poking around and asking you a bunch of personal questions, don't be afraid to walk away or straight out tell them it's none of their business.

What to Do

However, as noted in the story above, when it comes to the Internet, sometimes you can get hacked without having anything to do with it.

This is why you want to create a separate email address that you only use for businesses such as the cellphone company, Internet company, cable, etc. That way, if that account gets hacked, none of your personal emails will be exposed because they're on another account.

To be extra safe, I would use the email service provider Hushmail, which encrypts your emails.

Hushmail: www.hushmail.com

Another thing you may want to consider is to have a separate cellphone number that you give out to businesses. You can easily buy a flip phone from Wal-Mart for $10 with a plan that costs only a couple of dollars a month.

What you don't want is to have your smartphone details given out, because most people keep pictures, passwords, and other personal information on them. We've seen how dangerous this is when celebrities' cellphones have been hacked and nude photos have been exposed.

The bottom line is if you set up a Hushmail account and get an inexpensive flip phone, you'll be more secure than the vast majority of Americans.

Just don't forget to keep tight-lipped if someone comes around asking you unusual questions, because that's still the No. 1 way to "hack" someone.

10 WAYS TO PROTECT YOURSELF FROM SOCIAL ENGINEERING HACKS

We saw in the last chapter how — with very little information — hackers easily exploit social engineering skills to extract information from banks, utilities, email providers, online retailers, social media companies, even government agencies.

The truth is the CIA director got off easy. The hackers could have used his Verizon account information to have his number ported to another device. This means every phone call or message sent to Brennan's cellphone would instead go to a phone in the hacker's possession. And unfortunately, there's no way for service providers to block the porting of cellphone numbers.

Now let's say the hackers want to get into your online bank or Gmail account. They would simply go through the "I forgot my password" process, which often entails a call or a text with a code to reset the password. This ploy can be used to hack into accounts for major sites like Facebook, iCloud, Dropbox, PayPal, even online banking websites.

Think about how many accounts use your phone number for security purposes. Every single one of those accounts is vulnerable to this kind of social engineering attack. And companies are doing little to prevent this from happening. Yet another reason why the burden of protecting your online security rests on you.

If you follow these 10 steps, you'll achieve the highest level of protection possible when it comes to your online accounts:

1. Have a passcode on every account. This is pretty basic, and many companies already require a four-digit security pin that you set up when you first create your account. Obviously, make sure this number isn't similar to any other number, such as your SSN or address, and use a different pin for every account you have.

2. Use a separate email address for your cellphone account. Create a new email address and use it only for contact with your cellphone carrier. This may be inconvenient, but you don't want this email connected to any other websites. Right now, you probably have your phone number and primary email address tied to several different accounts. If one account is breached, the hackers can easily gain access to your other accounts.

3. Block online access to your cellphone account. This removes the ease of viewing your account online, but it's another way of stopping hackers from stealing your information. You'll have to go into a retail store to access your account or change information, but it's worth it to keep your account secure.

4. Ask your cellphone provider to require photo ID to alter your account. This is just an added layer of security. The more the better when it comes to preventing fraud.

5. Use Google Voice. A Google Voice number can't be ported to another device, meaning a hacker couldn't reroute your communications to their phone. Let's say you want to use Google Voice, but don't want to get new phone

number. You can set up Google Voice with your existing cellphone number.

Then go to your cellphone provider and ask for another number for a second line. Your old number is your Google Voice and you have a new number from your cellphone carrier. Don't share the new number with anyone. Have all calls to your Google Voice (old number) forwarded to your new number (the number only you know).

You can also set it up so that all calls or texts from your new number (the number only you know) will appear to come from the old number. And remember, never share your new number.

6. Option No. 2 with Google Voice. The only drawback to the step above is that you'll be paying your cellphone provider for two lines. If you don't want to pay for two phone lines, you can just set up a new number through Google Voice.

Set up a new Gmail account, but don't provide any back-up email address or backup phone number. You don't want anything tied to this new Gmail account. Set up Google Voice with your new email address. Select a phone number for this Gmail account — you can even have a random area code.

Use your Google Voice number for all your important online accounts — banking, Facebook, Twitter, etc. This way, you won't have to worry if your cellphone number is hacked, as none of your important accounts is tied to your real number. If you choose this option, make sure your new Gmail account has a very strong password, since it will be connected to your other online accounts.

7. Create strong passwords. Even if you think you have strong passwords, you should revisit them. Make sure

each one contains random numbers, upper- and lowercase letters and special characters. Passwords should be at least 10 characters long and random enough that they only make sense to you. Be sure to invent a different password for each of your accounts.

8. Give different answers to security questions. I'm sure you've forgotten your password to a particular website at one time or another and gone through the reset process. You're usually prompted with security questions such as, "What was the name of your first pet?" The problem is when hackers steal information from a website, that information usually includes the answers to your security questions. I recommend giving dissimilar responses on each website, so if your answers are stolen, a hacker can't easily go to another website and use them to get into a different account.

9. Purchase a security key. The YubiKey, for example, is a security key you plug into your USB port. When you open a website, simply enter your login information, and then put the USB key into the port and press the button on the key. Each security key has a unique chip that completes the security process when you push the button.

   In other words, the physical presence of the key is required anytime you want to log in to your accounts. This prevents anyone who doesn't have the key from logging in. If you decide to use this key, you need to verify the websites you want to use it with support this protocol. Currently, a lot of websites — Gmail and Dropbox, for instance — offer this security.

10. Biometric Authentication. This type of verification requires a fingerprint, eye scan or voice verification to access your account. This only works with mobile de-

vices that recognize one of these biometric readings. However, most new cellphones offer some type of bio-metric security, and popular websites are adding it to their log-in options. Biometric authentication can still be hacked by very sophisticated criminals, but it's incredibly costly and time-consuming, so it's not likely to happen on a large scale.

The 10 steps I've outlined here will take time to implement, but if you follow them, you will be infinitely better protected from hackers looking to steal your information and access your online accounts.

If hackers can get information from the director of the CIA, they can get it from you. Don't make it any easier.

HOW CYBER THIEVES ARE HOLDING YOUR COMPUTER (AND YOUR DEEPEST SECRETS) HOSTAGE

Recently, the University of Calgary received dozens of complaints that the school email system and wireless network weren't working. Students couldn't properly access their school email and were being repeatedly kicked off when they tried to login to different school sites.

Email and the student-focused websites are vital to campus life, so this had a huge impact on the school's day to day operation.

Shortly after the problems began, the issue became clear. The school received a ransom notice stating that hackers broke into the school server and had infected it with ransomware. The hackers told the school that if they ever wanted to access to their servers again, they would have to meet their ransom demands.

Against better advice, the University of Calgary paid a ransom of C$20,000, which is about $15,000 in U.S. dollars. The school agreed to pay the ransom with the digital currency Bitcoin so the hackers could make sure the payment couldn't be traced back to them.

Ransomware: Cyber Criminal's' Best Friend

Taking over an organization's computer system and holding it for ransom is becoming one of the most popular ways for cybercriminals to make money.

In February of this year, Hollywood Presbyterian Medical Center in southern California paid a $17,000 ransom to regain access to their computer system. The hackers had blocked all access to the Medical Center computer system, forcing employees to do record keeping with pen and paper and hampering the efficient care of patients.

For some reason, the hospital didn't contact law enforcement until after they had paid the ransom. The entire ransom was paid in Bitcoin, again ensuring that it would be nearly impossible for the FBI to conduct a trace.

As you can see, Ransomware is no joke, and it's becoming more common every day.

By understanding the details of how Ransomware works, you'll be better able to protect yourself against this cybercrime.

Ransomware has been around since 1989. That year, a man named Joseph Popp created a virus that would pop up, telling the computer user that their software license had expired and that they needed to pay immediately in order to reactivate it. It was designed to lure the user to click on the message and enter payment information, shutting down their computer in the process.

Ransomware is a type of malware (think, bad software) virus that disables your computer by restricting access.

Once they have control over your computer, they'll then try to extort you for money — in other words, they're holding the computer or larger network for ransom.

There are two main ways that hackers usually restrict access. They either lock you out of your computer entirely, or they block access to certain computer files. Then, when you attempt to log in to your computer or access those specific files, you will receive a notice that tries to intimidate and extort money from you. Often, these notices will claim to be from the FBI or the Department of Defense.

There are a number of other ways that these criminal hackers infect computers.

One popular method is to send an email with an enticing offer, tempting you to open an attachment. The attachment would then release the virus, and infect your computer.

It's also common to disguise malware as advertisements or giveaways. For example, you may see an advertisement that says, "Click here to enter for a chance to win" — but when you click on the ad, it takes you to a website that will infect your computer or trigger a file download.

Hackers will also put a time-sensitive date on many of the emails and websites, further enticing the average person to click on the link or download the attachment. None of us want to miss an important notice, after all.

Protecting Yourself from Hackers

The first rule in protecting yourself from a cyberattack is really common sense. Never open suspicious emails or apply for contests that don't appear legitimate.

But what happens if you do find yourself a victim of ransomware? What are the best steps to take?

First, you'll want to alert local law enforcement. Unfortunately, there is little they can do, but you should always notify them of the crime in order to create a paper trail.

You should also disconnect your infected computer from your network and immediately turn the computer off. This is vital. If you remain on the network you could potentially infect other computers. I doubt you want to be the person explaining to your boss that you crippled the company's entire network by clicking on a free vacation giveaway.

After you turn off the computer you need to decide if you will pay the ransom. I highly recommend never paying a ransom. You'll be dealing with criminals who probably won't honor their word. If you choose to pay the ransom you will likely be forced to pay with Bitcoin, which makes tracing the money impossible. Also, if you do cave to their demands and pay the ransom, it's no guarantee that the problem is over. They could very well return to access your computer again down the line, and hold it for ransom again since they know you're good for it.

Instead, be sure that you regularly backup the data on your computer. That way, if your computer is hacked, you'll still have access to everything you need without having to give into ransom demands.

I backup my information in two ways, using a physical hard drive and also a cloud-based service that automatically backs up my data.

These cyberattacks continue to grow in frequency and severity on a daily basis. Studies from Norton AntiVirus show that hackers can easily earn $30,000 a day by infecting thousands of computers. On average, only 2.9% of victims will pay the ransom.

However, if a criminal is infecting 5,000 computers a day (which is common) then they will make a large amount of money. So the next time you see that free vacation give away, think twice before you click on it. And, most importantly, always remember to backup your data.

THE SECRECY APP USED BY SENATORS AND SUICIDE BOMBERS

November 13 2015. Terrorists attacked six different locations around Paris, killing 130 people and wounding hundreds more. The city was attacked by terrorists armed with assault rifles and explosives. ISIS claimed responsibility for the carnage.

The attacks started with multiple explosions in different areas of the city at 9:20 p.m. local time. Around 9:25 p.m., men armed with rifles killed 15 people at a popular bar in the city. At 9:40 p.m., three terrorists stormed a concert venue, gunning down 89 people.

About a month after the tragedy, French investigators revealed that the terrorists were communicating with smartphone apps that use encryption to hide their conversations.

One of the apps specifically used by the terrorists was Telegram, which is one of the more popular encrypted messaging apps. Russian developers Nikolai and Pavel Durov included multiple security measures when creating the app in the hopes of preventing eavesdropping — whether by hackers or the government.

The app is designed with end-to-end encryption, which

means only the people sending and receiving messages can read them. In fact, all data (including media and files) that you send and receive via Telegram cannot be deciphered if intercepted.

The app also allows you to choose if you want the messages to self-destruct after a certain time period. And you can use an image encryption key that you compare with the other user to make sure the conversation is secure.

Criminals aren't the only ones who use these encryption apps. Many lawmakers use similar apps when conducting personal business. Now, lawmakers aren't using these apps to share government information. Instead, they're using them to communicate with their families and friends.

Foreign criminals love to target high-profile people and steal their personal information, and we've seen repeated email hacks confirming this. Kansas congressman and candidate for CIA director Mike Pompeo said he uses apps like Telegram because he wants to do everything in his power to protect his personal information as an elected official.

If terrorists and members of Congress use these apps, should you?

Let's be honest: Most of us probably send text messages we want to remain private. Even though the majority of hackers don't target average citizens, in this day and age of constant security breaches, it's a good idea to use an encrypted app.

In addition to Telegram, there are two other apps you should check out to protect your privacy:

1. Wickr — This app was one of the first to offer end-to-end encryption as well as self-destructing messages. Wickr contains multiple layers of encryption and is built on the industry standard calculations for security. Best of all, Wickr is free in the App Store.

2. WhatsApp — This is the most popular messaging app on the market, with over a billion users. WhatsApp provides

similar encryption to the other apps mentioned here, but it also uses secret keys to verify the authentication of messages. This app is also free in the App Store.

Of course, cybercriminals are constantly looking for ways to crack these security measures. But unless you're a celebrity or government official, these apps should provide an adequate level of privacy to protect your personal information.

WHY YOU SHOULD THINK TWICE BEFORE POSTING ONLINE

Jackie Garner was a customer service rep who wanted an adventure. One day, she decided to quit her job and row the perimeter of Lake Michigan. Jackie had recently started a nonprofit organization for breast cancer awareness and thought this trip would be a great way to raise money for the group.

To prepare for her two-month journey, Jackie began a rigorous workout regimen. She rowed every day in the morning and attended CrossFit and yoga classes at night. A year after she began training, she purchased a 19-foot boat that would be her home during the trip. It was a small boat with no kitchen, but it had a sleeping area and a place to store food. Jackie spent time learning the mechanics of her boat so she would be prepared for anything. Or so she thought.

She set out from Chicago with a satellite phone, a GPS and a laptop so she could stay in touch with her friends and family. She posted daily updates to her blog and Facebook. Whenever she posted online, people could see her exact location from the GPS.

Erase Your Digital Footprint in Three Easy Steps

1. Delete or deactivate any and all social media accounts. This also includes online shopping accounts with various retailers. If you can't (or choose not to) delete an account, change any identifying information associated with that account.

2. Remove yourself from data collection websites. The easiest way to do this is to pay a reputable company to do it for you. But you can certainly do it yourself if you've got the time. You'll have to contact private websites individually. Or you can contact search engine sites and request to have the URL containing your private information removed from any searches.

3. Delete your email address. This should be the last thing you do, since you'll need a valid email address to complete Steps 1 and 2 above.

One night about a month into her trip, Jackie decided to dock at Seul Choix Point Lighthouse, a remote location on Michigan's Upper Peninsula. The area was desolate except for the lighthouse gift shop. Around 2 a.m., Jackie was awoken by her boat slamming into the dock.

She looked out the window and saw a man climbing aboard. He forced the door open and was inside before she knew it.

The man tried to grab her and pin her down. Jackie yelled and attempted to fight back. She managed to throw him off her and run to the lighthouse bathrooms, but the man chased after her. When he entered the bathroom, Jackie shoved him into a mirror, which fell over and shattered, giving Jackie time to run back to her boat and call 911.

At one point during the fight, the intruder had said to Jackie, "I know who you are and I knew where to find you." She told the police she had no idea how this man knew so much about her and how he could find her in such a remote area. Then Jackie realized he must have been following her blog and her updates on Facebook. With the information she freely posted online, this man was able to see exactly where Jackie was at any given moment. She was lucky to have survived the attack.

Ditch Your Online Identity

There are plenty of crazy stalkers in this world and not everyone is fortunate to survive such an encounter. That's why it's critical you protect your digital footprint so it isn't easy for people to find you.

One of the best things you can do is get rid of social media. I know, I know. But social media gathers a ton of information about you, and it's easy for other people to gain knowledge from social media. So the first step is to delete or deactivate your social media accounts. Make sure you delete them even if they contain old information. If you really don't want to delete your social media accounts, at the very least give misinformation. In other words, don't list your real birthday, your job or the anniversary of your marriage.

Next you need to delete all of your other online accounts, including your accounts on Amazon, eBay, PayPal, etc. If you can't delete or deactivate these accounts, I would again provide misinformation. Change the address or phone number associated with each account so they don't contain any personal information.

The second major step is to remove yourself from data collection websites. When you surf the web, information about you is constantly being gathered so advertisers know what sorts of products to target you with. How do you stop this data collection? Believe it or not, you can do it yourself, but it will take a good amount of time.

There are quite a few data collection companies and you would have to contact every single one directly to remove your information. Some data collection companies require you to submit paperwork to make it as big a hassle as possible. So I recommend finding a company that will do this for you.

A company called Abine provides a service called DeleteMe. You pay a yearly fee of $129 for them to delete you from data collection sites. There are about 30 different websites from which this service can delete your information. They check those sites every three months and delete any new information found. The one drawback to this service is that it doesn't work with data collection companies located outside the U.S.

Another popular company offering a similar service is ReputationDefender. This company is one of the most well-known in the business and was among the first companies to offer a service that deletes your information. The yearly fee for this service is $1,000. It's a lot of money, but with their Executive Privacy service, they delete you from the top 53 data collection websites.

They also complete five checks during the year to make sure your information doesn't reappear. So while there is a huge price difference, this service removes information from more websites. If you don't mind the expense, this is definitely a company I would look into.

When it comes to private websites, it's important to remember that they do not have to remove your information. If you've ever posted a foolish comment or written something you want removed, you have to contact the website owner directly and ask them to remove your information. If a website refuses to remove private information from their site — such as your Social Security number or bank account information — you can contact search engines sites (like Google) and they can remove the URL from their search engine.

For example, if you want to remove your Social Security number from a Google search, go to **www.Support.Google.com** and type "remove information from Google" in the search bar at the top. You will need to answer a series of questions about which website contains the information you want removed. Once you answer these questions, submit your request to Google and they should remove the information from their search engine within five days.

Lastly, once you've deleted all of your social media and shopping accounts and taken care of any personal information on private websites, delete your email address. Make sure this is the last thing you do, because you'll still need a valid email to complete many of the tasks above.

I realize this may sound extreme. But if you've ever been stalked or had anyone follow you on social media and then show up at your house, you may want to take some of these precautionary steps.

If you decide these actions are not necessary for you, at least keep this article in mind. And the next time you're out to dinner at some wonderful restaurant, you'll probably think twice before telling the world where you are.

FOUR WAYS TO PROTECT YOUR ONLINE PRIVACY

No one is safe from being hacked and having their secrets exposed — not even the government.

Beginning in March 2017, WikiLeaks released a cache of classified documents — code-named Vault 7 — on the hacking secrets of the Central Intelligence Agency (CIA) and the National Security Agency (NSA). The exposed tools and methods have been used to monitor and thwart major global attacks. And now anyone can access them.

Of course, most people's first thought is that this is the work of a hostile foreign government, but governments generally won't reveal their hacking successes or capabilities. When they discover a way to hack into another government, they'll keep it a secret so they can covertly continue to gather intelligence.

Hacker or Mole?

So the question remains: How did WikiLeaks get their hands on this sensitive information? Did a cyberterrorist hack into an NSA or CIA server? Or is there a mole within one of these agencies who is sharing information?

If it's a mole, the country or organization behind the operation would want to keep it a secret to protect their mole. Unless the mole has provided as much information as they can and their employer is ready to burn them and move on.

Or perhaps the mole isn't working for anyone. Maybe it's an Edward Snowden type who is doing this as some sort of crusade. Whoever it is — whether Russia, China or a rogue terrorist network — the important takeaway is that this will continue happening.

As long as there are humans on Earth, criminals will try to steal valuable information. This is why I want to share with you four crucial cybersecurity tips to prevent you from becoming a victim:

1. Be careful with emails. If you're like me, you spend a decent amount of time emailing each day. Since we use email so often, cybercriminals often use it to hack into your computer. This why it's always important to double-check the sender's email address to make sure it's from a real person or company.

   Be wary of any misspelled email address or addresses that contain a string of random numbers and letters. Also, never download an attachment or click on a link from an email unless you know the person who sent it and are 100% positive it's was sent by the actual person. Lastly, you could switch to using a more secure email service such as ProtonMail.

   ProtonMail: **www.protonmail.com**

2. Use two-factor authentication. People often get hacked because their passwords are easy to guess. By using two-factor authentication (also known as two-step verification), you can protect your online accounts from clever

criminals. In addition to a standard password, two-factor authentication uses a second piece of information to verify the user.

This secondary proof might be something only the account holder knows, like a PIN. Or it might involve sending a secret code to your smartphone or the use of biometrics. This way, even if someone figures out your password, they won't be able to access your accounts

3. Create strong passwords. I guarantee a lot of people use simple passwords — such as their child's name or date of birth — that are all too easy to figure out with a quick Google search. Creating a difficult password is one of the most critical things you can do to protect yourself online. Make sure you have a unique password for every online account. Each one should include capital letters, numbers and special characters

4. Be cautious with the cloud. I understand why people use cloud services — they're convenient for storage, backup and file recovery. But you should never upload confidential information to the cloud, because you can't always trust the cloud provider to keep your information secure. And in the event that a company like Dropbox is hacked, all your personal information would be up for grabs. That's far too risky for my blood.

Obviously, we know that hackers will continue to target unsuspecting users and weak networks in an attempt to collect confidential information. But if you follow the steps above, you're less likely to be a casualty of the next big cyberattack.

READ BEFORE DOWNLOADING

If you've ever been to the doctor, you know what it's like to be handed a sheaf of paperwork about health laws so you can sign a bunch of authorization forms.

And I'm sure you know what it's like to briefly skim those documents before scrawling your John Hancock at the bottom.

Well, I would imagine that you probably pay even less attention to the legal permissions you "Agree" to when you download an app to your phone. But you should be more careful. Here's why.

A popular photo-editing app called Meitu — currently available for Android and iPhone users — has been downloaded over a billion of times by users all over the world. In addition to its editing capabilities, this app collects data from your phone, including photos, calendars, contacts — even your geolocation.

It also collects the phone's IMEI number, a 15-digit serial number given to every mobile phone to verify the phone's country of origin, the manufacturer and model number. With this detailed information, a hacker could actually clone your phone and easily intercept your calls and texts.

And who knows what the company could be doing with all the data they're collecting and whether they're selling it to third parties.

And here's another possibility: Remember in 2015 when the U.S. Office of Personnel Management (OPM) was hacked by the Chinese? This app — or others like it — could be another way for Chinese hackers to steal information from Americans.

Anything is possible. It's certainly something to keep in mind the next time you download an app to your cellphone.

HOW TO CREATE HACK-PROOF PASSWORDS

The CIA doesn't play games with computer security. Ignoring cybersecurity protocol would put people's lives at risk. Which is why every agent knows the importance of having strong passwords — and why they change these passwords often.

Since my days at the Agency, I've continued to take my computer security just as seriously. I don't take any chances when it comes to my passwords. Unfortunately, not everyone can say the same.

Ironically, tech billionaire and Facebook CEO Mark Zuckerberg had his social media accounts hacked by a group of cybercriminals who guessed his passwords. Apparently, it began when the hackers gained access to the data of 117 million LinkedIn accounts — including Zuckerberg's.

Once they had this information, they used it to guess the passwords to his other social media accounts. At that time, Zuckerberg was a new father. Believe it or not, the hackers discovered that the password to most of his accounts was "dadada." You would think someone in the tech world would choose a password that's a little more difficult to guess, wouldn't you? Zuckerberg also made other rookie mistakes, including using the same password for different accounts.

Clever Is as Clever Does

With that being said, unique passwords can be hard to create — as well as remember. Honestly, how are you supposed to remember a different, complex password for each and every account you log into?

Well, first, allow me to quickly explain the importance of password entropy. Basically, without getting too technical on you, entropy is the measure of how unpredictable a password is. For example, the password "H}=HX5B[J)7Gdw5R" has a stronger entropy than the password "dadada." What it boils down to is this: A stronger password contains more — and varied — characters and will be much more challenging for a hacker or their computer software to guess.

A good password should always include upper- and lowercase letters, numbers and symbols. For the most secure passwords, I wouldn't create one with any less than 10 characters.

I realize that sounds daunting. But here's an easy way to remember your new password. Create a password based on a passphrase. To do this, you would make up a phrase (something meaningful to you and only you) like, "Bob jumped for glory and fell down." Then take that phrase and add in some punctuation, or swap the last B in bob for a 7 (because it's the seventh letter in the alphabet). Get as creative as you like — so long as you don't make it so complicated you can't remember it.

Password Dos and Don'ts

Once you've created your new, one-of-a-kind password, here are a few other points to consider. Specifically, these are things you should never do with your passwords.

Undoubtedly, hackers will come up with new ways to guess

your passwords in order to steal your personal information. Which is why it's critical to be aware of any mass cybersecurity breaches — like the recently disclosed Yahoo and Gmail hacks — and to change your password immediately if it might be at risk.

When creating new passwords, you can test them at **www.howsecureismypassword.net**. This website lets you type in a password and tells you how difficult it would be to guess. For instance, the password "Bojf9Y+&flLdwn!" would take a computer 380 quadrillion years to deduce.

Computers these days may be capable of sophisticated calculations, but you can still outsmart them with strong passwords. All it takes is a little imagination.

BEWARE OF SMISHING

According to the FBI, Americans lost $1.3 billion to cybercrime in 2016 alone.

This should not come as a surprise. Our lives are becoming more and more integrated with smart technology, and criminals are capitalizing on this, coming up with novel ways to steal your personal information.

Of course, cyberattacks are nothing new. Most people are already familiar with phishing scams, where a hacker sends an email in the hopes you click on an infected link or reply with your personal information.

Remember when Hillary Clinton's campaign chairman, John Podesta, was the victim of a phishing expedition? As a result, his Gmail account was hacked and a slew of emails related to Clinton's campaign were leaked.

Thanks in large part to stories like this, people are becoming increasingly aware of these types of email scams and exercising caution before opening or downloading a suspicious email.

A New Scam Emerges

However, criminals are always inventing new ploys to trick people into giving up their personal information — and what better way to accomplish this than preying on cellphones? After all, most people are connected to their phones at the hip. This has led to a new type of scam called "smishing" — a combination of 'SMS' and 'phishing'.

How does a smishing scam work?

Well, let's say you are sitting at home one evening and you receive a text that says, "$5,000 was just withdrawn from your bank account. If you didn't authorize this transaction, click here or call..." This would certainly get your attention and most likely prompt an immediate response.

But if you click on the link or call the phone number, the criminal at the other end will try to get more information from you. They may ask you to verify or update your account information or reveal other personal details. For some reason, people are more liable to trust a text message than an email, and criminals use this sense of security to their advantage.

The next time you receive a questionable or unusual text message, DO NOT RESPOND. Instead, take the following steps:

1. Read it carefully. People misread texts on a regular basis. Scammers know this and may use a link that looks authentic, but if you look closely you can easily spot a fake. For example, if the link is **www.ChaseBank123.com**, the "123" signals the link is likely not valid. But if you're not paying close attention, you may end up clicking on a hacker's link.

2. Ignore it. Some scammers will send text messages that say, "Reply with 'STOP' if you no longer want to receive these messages." The problem is a response lets the hacker

know that they have contacted a valid phone number and that someone will respond. Ignoring the message is best, because ANY response may lead to more texts and more attempts to gather personal details.

3. Call your bank. If you receive a text about withdrawals, or other questions related to your bank account, immediately call your bank at the number listed on your statement or the back of your bank card. NEVER call the number provided in the text message. Your bank will confirm whether the text is legitimate and if any money was actually taken out of your account.

4. Check your phone bill. Just as you should review your credit card statement each month, you also need to review your phone bill. Check to make sure there aren't any unauthorized charges. By checking your statement regularly, you can avoid being unwittingly enrolled in some type of subscription service by hackers.

The bottom line is hackers are constantly looking for new ways to steal your personal information, and — as technology advances — these criminals are devising new methods of committing cyberattacks.

One last thing: Credible companies (especially banks) won't ask for your personal information (or any sensitive information) in a text message. If you do receive a strange solicitation via text, take the precautions outlined above to verify it's a legitimate request before doing anything else.

HOW TO SHIELD YOUR KEYBOARD FROM HACKERS

Many years ago, when wireless keyboards were first introduced, large numbers of computer users followed the untethered trend into blissful, cordless ignorance.

Because what if I told you that for about $35, I could see everything you type on your wireless keyboard?

Most wireless keyboards work on an unencrypted radio frequency. The only wireless keyboards that are encrypted are specifically made for Bluetooth connections. So unless you have a Bluetooth-enabled keyboard, anyone who wants to could purchase a $35 radio device that will intercept your signal and share every keystroke you make.

This includes secure logins, passwords, banking information, personal emails — literally anything you type on your keyboard. No matter what type of security you have on the computer itself, it won't protect the information being intercepted from the keyboard.

Since these keyboards work on radio frequencies, the criminal would have to be within 250 feet of you to be able to pick up the frequency and intercept what you are typing. But if you work in a large office building, a hacker could easily set up shop within 250 feet of you. Or if a hacker walked into the local Starbucks where everyone is using computer in close proximity of one another? You can see how easy it would be for your information to be hacked.

To compound the problem, radio frequencies aren't traceable, which means if someone were intercepting your keystrokes, you wouldn't even know about it.

So what can you do to protect yourself?

Since this type of hack only affects keyboards that operate on an unencrypted radio frequency — this includes brands such as Hewlett-Packard and Toshiba — you should purchase a high-end keyboard that works on Bluetooth, such as one from Logitech or Kanex. Apple also makes Bluetooth-compatible wireless keyboards for their products.

As we continue to see new wireless technology devices, you need to keep in mind these devices may not be the most secure. Even though wireless keyboards have been around for several years now, most people have no idea how vulnerable they are.

Eventually, I imagine most companies will move away from using a radio frequency connection and toward the more secure, encrypted Bluetooth technology. Until then, I recommend a wired keyboard if you don't have a wireless one that uses Bluetooth.

In other words, don't cut the cord.

FIVE WAYS TO PROTECT YOUR PRIVACY ON VACATION

It's no secret that pickpockets prowl popular tourist spots. In fact, 33% of all travel insurance claims are for pickpocketing losses.

And with the increase in electronic pickpocketing (where criminals can electronically steal your information without even touching you), it's more critical than ever to be mindful of your mobile devices while on vacation.

Considering all the recent ransomware and phishing attacks, the security measures you take with your smartphone are incredibly important — even more so when you travel. Tourists often use their smartphones for taking pictures and finding landmarks, so thieves abroad have increased electronic targeting of these devices.

Here are five tips to prevent you from falling victim to an electronic thief:

1. Turn off your Wi-Fi and Bluetooth. Even if you aren't connected to a wireless network or a Bluetooth device, these applications allow access to your phone. Always

turn these functions off when you travel so your phone isn't constantly searching for a Wi-Fi signal with which to connect. This will prevent anyone from being able to track you electronically.

Why I Use the IronKey

When traveling, especially overseas, I always safeguard my information by using an encrypted USB drive.

On this drive, I'll have work documents, a copy of my passport, a copy of my driver's license, a copy of all my credit cards, a copy of my health insurance card, and my trip itinerary.

Obviously, I don't want this information to fall into the wrong hands, which is why I use the IronKey USB drive. It's about as big as a pack of bubble gum and was originally created for government intelligence agencies. Government employees, you see, were occasionally losing their USB drives, which had classified material on them. So the government put out a contract for a secure USB, which resulted in the IronKey

Ironkey USB drive: **https://www.amazon.com/IronKey-Workspace-Windows-Certified-Flash/dp/B00C6ICDQS/**

The beauty of it is that its encryption is made to military specifications (FIPS 140-2 Level 3 encryption). Also, the drive is very rugged and can handle extreme cold and heat, plus 16 Gs of force. What's more, the IronKey self-destructs after 10 failed password attempts, so don't forget your password!

2. Update your phone before leaving. Prior to leaving for your vacation, you should install the latest updates and remove anything you don't need from your phone. For example, if you have lots of pictures stored on your phone, I recommend downloading them to your computer or cloud storage. That way if someone gains access to your phone, they won't see all your pictures.

3. Don't make purchases from your phone. When traveling, never use your phone to make a purchase unless you

use an app that already has your credit card information stored. In other words, you should never type your credit card number into your phone while overseas because you never know if someone has hacked into your device and is stealing the information as you type. And you definitely shouldn't pull out a credit card and hold it up to punch in the number. This would make you an incredibly easy target.

4. Never use public Wi-Fi. Most public Wi-Fi networks overseas have no encryption, which makes it easy for a hacker to target you. In fact, they can even see what you are typing from your phone if they are physically within a short distance. If you have no choice but to use public Wi-Fi, I recommend downloading and using a VPN (virtual private network) such as TunnelBear.

5. Require a password on your device. This should be a given. In the event that your phone is stolen, you want to make it as difficult as possible for the thieves to access your smartphone (and therefore all your information). If you're an Apple user and your phone is stolen, you can use the "Find My iPhone" feature to locate your device. Similarly, if you have an Android, you can use the "Android Device Manager."

Whether you are going to a local hotspot or an exotic locale this summer, you should never let the fear of being a victim ruin your trip. That being said, there are thieves all over the world who will try to steal your personal information. By implementing these security measures, you can have a great vacation without worrying about your information being stolen.

Because if your family is anything like mine, your biggest worry should be keeping the kids from fighting and trying to avoid stopping every 20 minutes for a bathroom break.

CHAPTER 3:

HOME DEFENSE: HOW TO KEEP YOUR FAMILY SAFE

YOUR STEP-BY-STEP GUIDE TO SURVIVING A BREAK-IN

Recently, I was at a business meeting and happened to be sitting across the table from this woman who found out I was in the security business. The woman's hands were visibly shaking as she told me her house had just been robbed of over $100,000 in cash and jewelry.

Thankfully, no one was home at the time. The fear in her eyes was clearly visible as she asked me what she could do to make sure her home wasn't broken into again.

I certainly hope you, dear reader, never find yourself in a similar situation. But if you do, you'll want to follow the ABCs of home defense.

Make Yourself (Safe) at Home

First, of course, you'll want to take a few simple home security measures to help prevent a break-in in the first place. Invest in surveillance cameras and put them at every exterior entrance to your house. Also, don't go cheap on cameras — or really any item that is used to protect your family. The cameras I recommend are made by a company called Hikvision.

Next, get an alarm system and make sure everyone knows you have one. In other words, put an alarm sign in your front yard or alarm stickers on your doors or windows. You want to clearly advertise that you have an alarm system. That way, if a criminal is casing your neighborhood, they'll avoid your house and choose a house that bears no indication of having an alarm.

Also, invest in motion sensor lights. Be sure to get both traditional motion sensor lights that run on electricity and so-lar-powered motion sensor lights. After all, if the electricity goes out or a criminal cuts the wires, you still want all the exterior doors of your house illuminated.

Three Simple Steps to Prepare for a Home Invasion

1. Invest in surveillance cameras and put them at every exterior entrance to your home.

2. Get an alarm system and publicize it by putting signs or stickers on the outside of your house.

3. Install both electric and solar-powered motion sensor lights around your home.

Once you've taken these few simple steps to prepare your house, it's time to prepare your family for what happens if you're home when someone breaks in.

Follow This Advice to the Letter

The woman I mentioned above was fortunate in that her family wasn't home during the invasion, but there are thousands of Americans each year who aren't so lucky. However, if you re-member the ABCs of home defense that I'm about to share with you, you'll be in a good position to defend against any intruder.

A stands for Alert

If you hear someone trying to break into your home, you need to alert everyone who is in the house and tell them to go to the designated safe room (more on this in a moment). Of course, if you followed my advice and installed an alarm, chances are the blaring sirens will do this job for you.

B stands for Block

One designated family member needs to delay the intruder while the other family members move to the safe room. By "safe room," I don't mean some high-tech, expensive, bulletproof room. In reality, a safe room is the bedroom of the least able-bodied member of the family — the nursery or grandma's room.

If a home invasion occurs, you don't want to waste precious time moving the slowest person to the safe room. The safe room should have a cellphone to call the police. More importantly, you'll want to take a firearm that can be used to protect your family. In my house, I'd grab my gun, go to the top of the stairs and take a position there while my wife and kids get to safety. If the intruder chooses to rush up the stairs, I will not hesitate in using my firearm.

C stands for Call

Once your family members are in the safe room, they should immediately call 911. Be sure to give as much detailed information as possible, such as the number of intruders and if they have weapons. You also need to tell the dispatcher about the family member who is doing the blocking by saying something like, "My husband is at the top of our stairs. He is wearing a green T-shirt and he has a gun with him."

DEF Gee, What Next?

Once everyone else is in the safe room and someone has called 911, the blocking family member should retreat to the safe room if possible. Once everyone is in the room, lock the door, get behind some furniture and wait for the police to arrive. If the intruder is foolish enough to bust down the door to the safe room, you need to be ready to defend yourself (shoot them) as they enter the room.

One last thing: You always want to have an escape route from your safe room. If your safe room is on the second level of your home, buy an escape ladder. I suggest checking out the Kidde KL-2S Two-Story Fire Escape Ladder:

Kidde Fire Safety Equipment: **http://bit.ly/1RnwLCx**

Bottom line: If you protect the exterior of your home with cameras, lights and alarm signs, and you remember these ABCs if someone enters your home, you should be well prepared to survive and overcome a home invasion situation.

BUILD A PANIC ROOM WITHOUT SPENDING A FORTUNE

It was about 1:30 a.m. when the large crash awoke me.

I looked to my right at my wife, who immediately sat up too, and then I looked to the left to grab my flashlight and open up the gun safe on my nightstand.

The safe was open in less than three seconds, and I retrieved my Glock 19 loaded with 124-grain Speer Gold Dot rounds. I then made my way to the top of my staircase to ensure that nobody would come up the stairs past me as my wife ushered our kids to our "panic room."

As I stood at the top of the stairs with my gun pointed downward, I listened intently to hear who was in our house and what I needed to be prepared for.

The thing is, I didn't hear a peep.

I stood there for what seemed like an eternity, but I heard and saw no other signs of an intruder.

Finally, I began to slowly make my way down the stairs to clear my home. This isn't something I would necessarily recommend everyone do, but I'm fortunate to have been trained in how to clear buildings and homes.

Plus, at this point, I was pretty sure that nobody was in my home and that the large crash had to be something else.

After opening a number of closest doors, I was relieved to find the culprit of the noise that caused me to almost jump out of bed.

You're probably familiar with the large inflatable mattress called the AeroBed that seemed to be on every TV infomercial years ago. Well, we had an AeroBed on the top shelf of one of our closets, and it had fallen off, crashing down onto a bunch of kids toys. And since it weighs a ton, it caused the significant noise that woke my wife and me up.

Thankfully, it wasn't an intruder, but it was a great "dry run" to show that my wife and I were prepared for a home invasion and that we could react quickly to protect ourselves.

And yes, one of the most important elements of our home defense plan was that we utilized our panic room. Because the fact is, in the event of a home invasion, getting to your panic room is one of the key things that will protect you and your family from danger.

Identifying Your Panic Room

First, let me quickly dispel some myths that have been created by Hollywood to sell movie tickets. A panic room doesn't have to cost several hundred thousand dollars. It isn't only for multimillionaires and billionaires. And it definitely doesn't involve a bunch of fancy gizmos and sliding doors at the push of a button.

To create your own panic room, you don't have to open up your checkbook. You can just use one of the rooms already in your home. So this then is the first step: knowing where the room should be located.

A lot of people mistakenly think that the panic room should always be in the basement or the master bedroom. But in reality, the best panic room is whichever one is occupied by the weakest or slowest member of your family.

You Need a Strong Door

Once you've identified the room, it's time to start fortifying it. As I said, this doesn't mean spending six figures. It simply means getting a solid-core door, which means one made from wood or metal. Most people prefer a wood door because of the aesthetic factor, but the choice is yours.

The cheap, hollow-core bedroom doors most people have can be kicked in by an intruder in seconds. But a solid wood door will give you time to get ready to defend yourself. And to keep the intruder out, you should also install a quality deadbolt such as Schlage or Medeco on the inside of the room.

The Most Important Thing in Your Panic Room

Once you've got the door and deadbolt installed, then it's time to get to the most important factor of all when it comes to your panic room: what I refer to as the "crash box."

A crash box is a fancy name for a safe that is in your panic room and contains all the necessary supplies to fend off an intruder. A crash box is not a gigantic gun safe that is going to take you forever to open. Instead, it's typically a medium-sized safe, such as the SentrySafe model SFW123DSB or the First Alert model 2096DF.

SentrySafe: **http://amzn.to/2wGNyLt**
First Alert: **http://amzn.to/2gLl8Mx**

Once you have your crash box, then it's time to fill it with the items you need. These include a handgun and ammunition (I like Glock, Sig Sauer, and Springfield when it comes to guns, and Speer Gold Dot and Hornady for ammo), extra loaded magazines, a spare cellphone, a flashlight, medical items such as QuikClot and a CAT tourniquet, a fixed-blade knife, and whatever other items you choose to put in it.

QuikClot: **http://amzn.to/2f2chCf**

CAT Tourniquet: **http://amzn.to/2j3o08l**

If you ever do find yourself having to hunker down until police arrive, then you should be prepared to fend off attackers for a good amount of time.

The good news is unless you're a politician or celebrity who is more likely to face a coordinated attack, most likely a home invasion will involve some local thugs who are looking to get drug money for their next fix.

But once they see you're well-armed and prepared to stop them, they'll probably flee your house and go looking for an easier victim.

While none of us wishes to ever experience a home invasion, the people I know that have gone through it were grateful they were prepared. In other words, this weekend, take a few minutes to designate a panic room, begin looking at solid-core doors, and start writing down the supplies you're going to have inside your crash box.

FIVE HOME SECURITY MISTAKES TO AVOID

Imagine: You wake up in the morning and notice that your wallet is missing. Or let's say you pad down to the kitchen to make your morning pot of coffee and discover that someone has rifled through your belongings.

That's exactly what happened to a few people in Wisconsin last summer. Early one morning between 3:00–4:30 a.m., burglars entered three different homes in the Cottage Grove area while the homeowners were still asleep. Stolen items included wallets, purses, credit cards, laptops and other electronic devices.

Now, you're probably wondering how these greedy thieves gained access to so many homes so easily without getting caught. They weren't highly trained professionals, nor did they use any high-tech equipment. No — they simply walked in through an unlocked door.

In fact, studies have shown that the majority of burglars enter homes through an unlocked door or window. Which means something as simple as locking the exterior door could have prevented some of these burglaries, and the victims could have avoided a lot of hand-wringing.

Today, I want to review five common home security mistakes that make your home an easy target for a burglar looking for a crime of opportunity. Starting with...

1. Leaving doors and windows unlocked — Unless you live in Mayberry, I strongly recommend always locking your doors and windows. The reality is burglaries can happen anywhere. Even if you live in a small town where everyone knows each other, don't be complacent when it comes to home security. I have a relative who used to live in a small town of 1,000 residents, and they regularly left their doors unlocked — until one day someone entered their home and emptied their medicine cabinet. So trust me when I say a home invasion can happen anywhere.

2. Too much visibility inside — You should have curtains on all your windows and keep them closed at night and whenever you are gone. If a criminal can see into your home, they can pinpoint the location of any valuables inside and determine if anyone is home. This is especially important at night. When it's dark and the lights are on, it's incredibly easy to see inside from outside. So always make sure your windows are covered when you are at home and away.

3. No exterior lighting — I'm by no means an electrician, and I know installing new lights can be a bigger project than most people want to tackle. However, you can buy battery-operated or solar-powered lights that you can drill into the side of your home. Or, even easier, ones that you can simply peel and stick to the exterior of your home. Criminals use darkness to their advantage, so the more lighting you have around your home, the more risk the criminal takes of being seen. Since they aren't very expensive (you can buy quality lights for around $20),

I recommend putting them all around your house so there are no dark spots at all.

4. Hiding a spare key — When I was a kid, I would get locked out of the house sometimes because I forgot my key. Like a lot of people, my family hid a spare key in a fake rock that I would use to get in. Looking back on it now, this spare key rock appeared wildly out of place. It was a small rock that sat by itself and looked like it was made of plastic. Nowadays, many people still leave a spare key outside, but criminals know all the tricks. Consider other options if you keep a spare key under the doormat, in a fake rock or buried in a planter. These hiding places are not as inventive as you think they are.

5. Leaving things outside — My neighbor has a large ladder in his backyard leaning up against his shed. Every time I see this ladder, I think about how a burglar could use it to gain access to the second floor of his house. Criminals are often desperate and will use anything they can find to help them commit their crime. If you leave your shed unlocked or tools lying around your backyard, remember that not only can these items be stolen, but they can also be used to get inside your home.

A home security system complete with cameras is probably the best crime deterrent, but don't forget these common security lapses. Because no matter how great your home security is, a simple mistake like an unlocked door gives a criminal unfettered access to your home — and you'll quickly learn you don't live in Mayberry.

AN INVISIBLE SHIELD THAT KEEPS YOUR HOME SAFE

"This is where the bullets entered..."

My friend Dennis didn't waste any time. I'd only just entered his home — this was about a month ago — before he quickly ushered me into his master bedroom to show me the damage.

"Now that he'd suffered a terrifying home invasion, my friend was going to take his home security seriously."

Dennis and his wife had recently suffered a terrifying home invasion. Miraculously, they both got through it unscathed.

But it was a wake-up call for my friend. Now he was really going to take his home security seriously. And that was why I was there. I was helping him establish some precautionary measures, which included the setting up of a perimeter alarm.

Installing a perimeter alarm is one of the best things you can do to decrease the odds of being caught unaware like my friend was. Below, I will show you several different kinds of alarms, from a simple out-of-the-box option to DIY versions.

Their ordeal began one evening when they were sitting and watching a movie together. After the movie, Dennis' wife decided she was going to head to bed, while Dennis contemplated watching a second flick.

Suddenly, Dennis' wife rushed into the room. According to him, her face was as white as a ghost. She told him there was somebody in the house, and he immediately grabbed one of his guns.

Not wanting the intruder to get to his wife, Dennis left the room where they were watching the movie and made his way toward the bedroom.

All of a sudden, a person popped out of the bathroom in the master bedroom and fired three shots at Dennis. All three shots missed, and Dennis began firing in the direction of the intruder.

The intruder then fired again, and one of the shots missed Dennis' head by a mere six inches.

After a short firefight, Dennis heard the intruder yell to someone and then heard him flee out a bathroom window. Shortly thereafter, the police showed up (Dennis' wife had dialed 911).

Thankfully, neither Dennis nor his wife was physically harmed. The craziest part of all, though, is they actually slept in the house that night instead of getting a hotel!

A few weeks later, the police did end up catching the intruder and his accomplices, and since it was their third strike, they got life in prison.

The Infrared Perimeter Alarm

After this incident, my friend made sure that he always set his alarm (it was off that night), and he installed motion sensor lights around his home, too.

But one of the most important things of all that he did was to set up a perimeter alarm around his home. That way, if anyone even crossed onto his property, he would instantly be notified.

Three Essentials for Preventing a Home Invasion

1. Make sure there's an alarm sign in your front yard even if you don't have an alarm. In your backyard, you'll want to have alarm sign stickers on the back door and any sliding glass doors. You can get both alarm signs and stickers at amazon.com. These signs will make any intruder think twice.

2. Place a large dog bowl near your back door. Criminals are terrified of dogs. If they see the dog bowl, they'll move on to a dog-free neighbor's house.

3. Put solar motion sensor lights around all exterior doors of your home. Since these lights are solar powered, you won't have to worry about being vulnerable when the electricity goes out. The lights I use are made by a company called Swiftly Done.

Swiftly Done: **http://amzn.to/2eJLhuz**

The type of alarm he used is an infrared break beam system. The best way to explain it is to think of a laser beam pointing from one unit to the next, and if anything breaks that beam, an alarm is set off in his house.

These types of infrared systems can be set as much as 300 feet apart, meaning you can use them even if you have a very large yard. One such system is made by Dakota Alert, and these alarms work all year round, since they'll operate in minus 30-degree weather all of the way up to 120-degree weather.

Dakota Alert Alarm: **http://amzn.to/2x9QP9l**

If you read the sidebar on this page, you'll see that you can also get quite creative with DIY perimeter alarms. The infrared alarms will be the easiest to install and the most practical, but if the electricity goes out or there's some type of "grid down" scenario, then the low-tech alarms could become critical in keeping you and your family safe.

DIY Perimeter Alarms

While I certainly do recommend some type of infrared system such as the Dakota Alert system, there are plenty of low-tech perimeter alarms that you can easily use too.

Flash Bang Perimeter Alarm

For this alarm, you take fishing line and you run it around the perimeter of the place you want to secure, whether it is your home, a campsite, or an RV. The fishing line runs back to a small box that houses a shotgun shell blank with a nail right above it. If someone walks into the fishing line, the nail is released and it strikes the shotgun shell — which puts out a very loud warning signal that someone is in your area.

Air Horn Perimeter Alarm

Another low-tech perimeter alarm option I've used involves an air horn. First, you dig a hole and bury the air horn so that only about an inch of the top is exposed. Then, you find a large, semi-flat object such as a rock. Take a stick and prop up the rock so that it's above the air horn. Tie some fishing line to that stick and run it around your perimeter. If someone trips the line, then the stick is pulled and the rock comes crashing down on top of the air horn, setting it off. It's incredibly loud. You can hear it almost a mile away.

135dB Rip Cord Perimeter Alarm

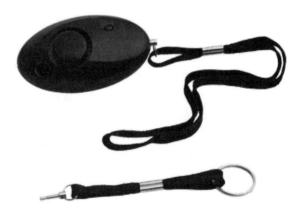

You can do something similar to the air horn version by using a hand-held personal security alarm like the Vigilant Alarm, below. Simply tie a piece of fishing string to the end of the alarm and then duct-tape the alarm to a wooden stake, which you'll hammer into the ground. Run the fishing line around your perimeter through other wooden stakes that have eyelets on them. If someone enters the area, the alarm pin is pulled and the loud noise will let you know someone is around.

Vigilant Personal Alarm: **http://amzn.to/2eEs0qw**

5 STEPS TO AN INVASION-PROOF HOME

Are you the "soft target" home invaders are searching for?

"Soft target" is simply a military term meaning "unprotected or easy to breach…"

Any given day, you can find a rash of home break-in stories.

Most people believe violence like this happens to someone else. It's human nature, really, to think that way. But when it happens to you or someone close to you, it's too late to do anything about it.

And the result can rip a family apart. It's heartbreaking.

It happens far more often than people think. Yet just a few shockingly simple and inexpensive steps can effectively protect you and your loved ones.

The truth is awareness and preparation are the key to staying out of dangerous situations… and 99% of Americans are oblivious to danger.

Preparing for these kinds of dangerous encounters is incredibly easy and more useful than you can probably imagine.

What I'm going to teach you today is going to transform your home from a "soft target" that silently and unknowingly invites criminals to your home… to a "hard target" that sends a clear message to thugs casing your neighborhood: "You better move on, punk."

Step #1: Identify Any "Tells" From Your Home That Are Easy for Invaders or Burglars to Spot

Homeowners don't usually think someone is casing their neighborhood and often leave strong clues that tell thieves and thugs, "This home is an easy target."

As one convicted burglar said: "If they're in a [wealthy neighborhood] and the yard is not manicured, I just think they're on vacation… and I will go to that house."

So what exactly are the "tells" that a criminal looks for? And how can you avoid them?

There are a few signs that make you and your home a target.

For starters, burglars look for full mailboxes. If you're going away, I suggest placing a temporary stop on any mail delivery while you're away. Because believe me… burglars really do notice that mail piled up in the mailbox or newspapers piled up on the driveway. It's a telltale sign that nobody's home and the coast is clear. You might even consider doing what I do — use only a UPS Store mailbox for all mail.

Bad weather could provide another "tell" that no one is home is. When it snows, a big signal that no one's home is virgin snow leading up to the house. So if it snows while you're out of town, you'll need to take precautions to protect your home. Simply have a neighbor create car and foot tracks into the house, to give the idea that you're there… even when you're not.

Have a dog? While this is a great way to deter any burglars, there is a way your own dog might accidentally reveal that you are not home in just a few seconds, without a criminal even entering your home.

In an empty house, rather than alerting an owner that a potential intruder is present, a dog might just stand by the door waiting for its owner to come home.

A barking dog will bring unwanted attention to a potential burglar, but don't rely on your dog to attack a criminal unless trained to.

Another "tell" that criminals will be looking for is an alarm system.

Not just any alarm system. A wireless alarm system. The response time is extremely quick, and any home invaders don't want to risk getting caught.

In fact, one career home invader from Allen, Texas, confessed that a wireless alarm system is particularly scary... if found, he said, "I'm not even going to attempt it."

There are a lot of alarm companies out there, and the top-name brands are all pretty good. But keep in mind those uncreative criminals are getting smarter these days and will often cut your phone lines. Therefore, make sure the company offers a wireless backup for your alarm system in case the phone lines get damaged during an attempted break-in (most of them do).

Step #2: Know Your Neighborhood

In a horrific home invasion triple murder in Connecticut back in 2007, one of the killers said he stalked two of the family members from a grocery store to their home, noting they had a "very nice house" and a "very nice car" that made their home stick out as a good target. He also believed the possibility that they had money in the house was "very decent."

There's nothing wrong with having a decent home and doing well for yourself. But there are certain ways people display their success that makes them targets.

Most homeowners never think about their home in the context of their neighborhood or other surroundings, but did you know that most criminals usually go for corner homes, since they tend to have fewer immediate neighbors?

This makes it easier for criminals to assess the surrounding area and occupancy, making corner houses an easier target for burglary.

Another factor for criminals when choosing a particular neighborhood is a certain kind of street sign.

Believe it or not, having a neighborhood watch sign is extremely effective. Criminals strenuously avoid neighborhoods that display these signs.

"A 2008 study conducted by the U.S. Justice Department revealed an average 16% reduction of crime in neighborhoods with active Neighborhood Watch programs," reports the Dornbos Sign and Safety blog.

Neighborhood Watch presents an intimidation factor for criminals, as the community works together to recognize criminal action and prevent it from occurring.

The key is to know what kind of weaknesses a criminal is going to look for, and the best way to make your home the least attractive one on the block.

Step #3: Invest in Security Cameras or Adequate Lighting

These days, it's so simple to make your home less appealing to a potential intruder.

Having an obvious security camera on a front or back door can be a quick deterrent to any thief, because no one wants to be recorded doing something illegal.

Alarm systems are affordable, and there are DIY alarm systems you can install yourself if you don't want to go with a major company. The same goes with camera systems. You can get a wireless camera system and install it yourself. The only real knowledge you need is how to use a screwdriver and how to log on to a company's website to set everything up.

Personally, I recommend Hikvision cameras for top-notch security that won't break the bank. You can get more information on their website, **www.hikvision.com**.

If you can't afford or don't want a security camera setup, there are work-arounds that can provide just as much deterrence.

A fake security camera is an inexpensive and easy way to "decoy" your house to make crooks move on to the next house.

Now you can deter robbery, theft and vandalism without the high cost of a real security camera.

Whether you have a real security camera or a fake one, make sure you turn it on. This is the biggest mistake homeowners who DO have a security camera make that ends up costing them.

While I definitely recommend everyone have an alarm system and video cameras, one of the most overlooked security measures is having motion-sensor lights around your home. Maybe this is because motion-sensor lights aren't a "super sexy" topic, but it's critical that you don't have dark areas around your house where a criminal can hide as they try to break into your house through a door or window.

Even though you've got a front porch light and a back porch light, there are likely still areas around your home that don't receive any light and are pitch-black. Most people focus their lights, locks and security systems on the front of their homes, but many home invasions occur somewhere else.

To discover where these "blind spots" are, take a walk around your house when the sun goes down today. Identify these areas and then purchase a motion sensor light or two. Since these lights have no wires, you can install them in unconventional places, such as on a tree, fence or shed. It doesn't have to be attached to your house to light up your yard.

You can go to Home Depot and most hardware stores and get motion-sensor lights. I prefer a motion-sensor light that simply runs on batteries and is about as easy to install as it gets. All you need is a Phillips-head screwdriver and the ability to screw in three screws. With those tools and just a few minutes, you can install these motion-sensor lights all around your home.

My choice is the Mr. Beams 300-lumen spotlight. If you go to Amazon.com and do a search for that phrase, it will be the first item that comes up on your screen.

As mentioned in the name of the product, this light puts out 300 lumens, which is bright enough to light up any lawn. The advertised coverage area of the light is 400 square feet, and I'd be willing to say it's a bit more.

The 300 lumens are powered by four D batteries, and the batteries seem to last forever. That's because whenever someone crosses in front of the light and sets off the motion sensor, the light stays on for only about 10 seconds, which prevents the batteries from getting drained too quickly.

The best part of this light, besides it doing exactly what it's supposed to, is the easy installation I mentioned earlier. You just install the four D batteries and then mount the light with the three screws to whatever location you wish.

By the way, these lights aren't too expensive. You can purchase three of them for $80, which means they cost only about $27 a piece. And depending on the size of your home and how many areas you need to cover, three of these lights may be all you need.

Step #4: Don't Be Too Trusting of Strangers at the Door

Before a burglar plans on breaking into a house, they will often knock first to see if anyone's home.

A recent Houston, Texas, home invasion began as a knock at the door. What appeared to be a UPS driver with a package, however, turned out to be an armed robber in disguise.

Criminals will often try to get you to open a door to them by pretending to be someone nonthreatening.

That could mean they impersonate a car crash victim, a neighbor, a police officer, a maintenance person, a mailman or anyone else you might open your door for.

Too often, people are trusting and get fooled. The results can be deadly.

So exactly how do you sniff out these liars and get them off your property before they can do any damage?

If there is a deliveryman at the door, one question you can ask him is where the distribution center is. There's no way a real driver doesn't know this.

Is there a person who says they've been in a car crash and needs assistance? There might be accomplices hiding somewhere. So before these thugs try to gain access to your home, make sure you scan the area for any accomplices hiding off to the side of the door.

Whatever the excuse, be very cautious if you answer the door.

Step #5: Remove Cheap Locks or Other Vulnerabilities

Home invaders know cheap security makes a break-in very easy.

In a recent home invasion in Atlanta, Georgia, two perps kicked the front door in with ease, pistol whipped the homeowner and stole $80 in cash.

Do you still have the same regular old locks your home came with?

Most locks are easily picked in as little as 30 seconds. They can also make a door easy to kick in. Which is why having reliable locks for the doors and windows in your home is a simple, vital step in home defense.

Let's start with the locks. One of the most common brands

of locks used in the U.S. is Kwikset. They're a go-to brand for contractors and builders, and there's a pretty good chance you use them in your own home.

If you do, go to the nearest Home Depot and buy new locks immediately.

Kwikset locks are poorly made and easily compromised. I myself can pick one easily, and so can most criminals.

Instead, I recommend buying Schlage or Medeco locks. You can get Schlage locks at Home Depot or any other major hardware store. Medeco locks are a little harder to find. I'd recommend searching for a local dealer using their website, **www.medeco.com**. Simply select "Dealer Locator" from their home page and type in your ZIP code to find out where you can purchase Medeco locks near you.

I also recommend having a reliable solid deadbolt from either Schlage or Medeco.

Getting a solid-core door is a good idea, too. One that's made out of sturdy, solid materials, like wood, steel or iron.

It's a sad fact that several types of doors can be kicked in with minimal effort. In fact, as I'm sure you're aware, most doors are hollow, and if you have a teenage son, you may know how easily these can be kicked through. Purchasing a high-quality solid-core door, particularly for your front door, is very important.

Many of us also have glass sliding doors in the rear of our homes. Hopefully, if someone breaks these doors to try to get in, you will hear the glass shatter and be prepared to meet the intruder. If you really want to ensure you'll hear them, I recommend putting a glass break detector on your glass doors. If someone jostles these doors at all, a loud alarm is set off. One example is the Doberman Security SE-0106-4PK Ultra-Slim Window Alarm, available on Amazon for only $29.99.

It's important that you reinforce the locks on these doors too. You can do so easily and cheaply by getting a wooden bar to put along the floor track. This costs about $2.00 at any home goods store. Just cut it half an inch shorter than the total track distance.

Now if an intruder wants to come in that way, they'll have to break the door. As I mentioned, the noise that creates will give you time to spring into action, especially if you use a glass break detector.

I'd also recommend locking and reinforcing your windows. Smaller wooden pieces similar to the bars for sliding doors can go in the bottom of window tracks or along the inside of the frames.

Criminals aren't usually the brightest bunch, which is why the majority of home invasions occur through the front or back door. To ensure that your door isn't easily kicked in and to give yourself extra time to get to safety, you may want to consider using a door barricade.

While it might sound like a big piece of equipment, a door barricade is actually quite small and you'll barely notice it. It's simply a metal plate that is secured to the floor directly in front of your door. This metal plate has a groove down the middle that allows you to insert a second metal plate, which goes perpendicular and blocks the door from opening. The door barricade that I like is called the Nightlock, available on Amazon. If you install one of these at home, it will be nearly impossible for someone to kick in your door.

Better Safe Than Sorry

As dangerous as America is becoming these days, you must take action to protect you and your family.

Most believe the police, their home security systems and their communities will keep them "safe"... and that taking even simple steps to prepare for violence is unnecessary.

That is a dangerous assumption that makes it easy for criminals to get what they want. Many victims of home invasion have realized this the hard way.

By utilizing the five essential strategies described above, you'll be able to sleep well every night knowing your family is protected.

HOW TO EFFECTIVELY CLEAR YOUR HOME OF A POTENTIAL INTRUDER

"Can you come home?" were the first words out of my wife's mouth when I answered the phone. Naturally, I asked why.

My wife said she had just pulled into our driveway and got a bad feeling that something wasn't right. She wanted me to come and clear the home to make sure nobody was in it.

My office is only a few miles away, so I was home in less than 10 minutes. I told my wife to wait in the car and to call 911 if she heard screams or gunshots. Even though the house looked normal to me, I walked all the way around it before entering to ensure none of the doors or windows was open and the alarm wasn't blaring.

If any doors or windows were ajar, I would have called the police immediately and not entered the home. Even though I'm well trained, I don't need to prove anything to anyone, and I prefer to avoid getting in a gunfight if I can help it.

Since everything appeared normal, I carefully unlocked my front door, turned off the alarm and proceeded to clear my home with my Sig Sauer P238 in hand.

I slowly headed up the stairs. You should always clear your

home from top to bottom, since most criminals go straight to the master bedroom, where they believe they'll find cash, jewelry, coins and other valuables.

I stayed close to the wall on one side of the hallway as I made my way to the bedroom. Staying close to the wall — instead of walking straight down the middle of the hallway — helps minimize your outline so you're a smaller target. In other words, if a criminal pops out of a doorway and fires a round straight down the hallway, there's a good chance he'll miss you if you're hugging the wall.

On the way to the bedroom, I passed our bathroom. Before I attempted to open the bathroom door to check inside, I pulled my gun close to my body so that my wrist was practically touching my rib cage. With the gun close to your body, you have more control in the event someone is hiding right inside the doorway and tries to grab your gun. Another reason to pull your gun close to your body is so you don't accidentally shoot your other hand when you open the door.

Stand to the right of the door as you reach for the doorknob. Don't stand in the doorway itself because if someone hears you and fires through the door, you don't want to get hit. Turn the doorknob, push the door open and step back to the right of the door.

If you don't see anything suspicious, slowly begin to "slice the pie." This is a technique used to clear corners and doorway entrances. Each area is cleared in small slices, hence the name. In my particular case, I was standing to the right of the bathroom door and couldn't see inside the entire bathroom. And I wasn't about to take a big step into the bathroom and fully expose myself.

I began taking baby steps in a semicircle from the right side of the door to the left. Each time you take a small step, slightly lean your body forward to look further into the bathroom. This way, if a criminal is lying in wait with a gun pointed at the door, you will expose as little of your body as possible, giving them the smallest possible target to hit.

Once you make your way to the other side of the door, it's time to enter the room. But don't just walk straight in. Instead, enter the room and quickly cross to the opposite corner. Since I was now standing to the left of the bathroom door, I quickly entered and went to the right side of the bathroom. As I did this, I looked over my left shoulder to make sure nobody was hiding on top of or underneath the sink. Then I checked the cabinets and the bathtub to ensure nobody was hiding there, either.

After my bathroom was clear, it was time to make my way to the master bedroom and my kids' bedrooms. I continued to hug one side of the wall, and I sliced the pie again before entering each of the other rooms. I looked under the beds, opened all of the closets and searched behind the dressers. Thankfully, I didn't find anyone and the top level of my house was now clear. But I still had two floors left.

On the main level, I continued to slice the pie each time I went around a corner. I looked behind the TV, in all of the kitchen cupboards large enough for a person and underneath our piano. Then I made my way to the basement. As I went downstairs, I looked over my shoulder to make sure nobody was sneaking up on me from behind. Then I cleared the basement rooms in the same manner I cleared the top two floors.

Once I cleared my entire home and confirmed nobody was in it, I told my wife and kids it was safe to come in. I was glad my wife called me to clear the house, because I'm a firm believer in always trusting your gut. Even though there was nobody in my house this time, I commend my wife's caution. Because your instincts are often right and you should follow them.

Remember, if you ever need to clear your own home, have patience and take as much time as you need. If there's any sign of entry, do not go into the house. Immediately call the police, because there's a good chance someone has broken in.

YOUR HOME SECURITY SYSTEM ISN'T AS SECURE AS YOU THINK

According to the FBI, a home burglary occurs every 13 seconds. These criminals tend to be desperate people looking to steal things they can turn into quick cash. The look for items such as jewelry, small electronics and credit cards that they can easily sell on the black market.

Sadly, there isn't much to stop these thieves from breaking in — only 17% of homes have a working home security system installed. And criminals are becoming more brazen and dangerous these days — choosing to rob even those houses with an alarm system.

In fact, many nationwide security companies are finding that their systems can be hacked with just a little bit of work. Big companies like ADT, Comcast and Vivint have had technology issues exposed.

Nowadays, most security systems are tied to the internet instead of using a telephone landline. An internet-based system allows you to add other technology features to your alarm setup. For example, you could add smart locks, light bulbs and a thermostat and control all these components from your smartphone.

Despite all of this fancy technology, criminals could still hack your system. And it's not very difficult to do. First, let's review how a basic home security system works.

Sound The Alarm

Most systems on the market today operate the same way, using sensors on the doors and windows that communicate with the home base system. If the signal from one of the sensors is broken, the alarm will sound.

The problem with this type of system is the radio signal the hardware uses to communicate can be easily disrupted. A criminal could simply order an inexpensive radio jammer from a company overseas and have it shipped to the U.S. Then all they'd have to do is find the frequency that your security company operates at and they could jam the signal. The alarm would never go off.

Using radio signals probably sounds outdated, but security companies haven't had a reason to change this technology, because it was never an issue… until now.

A False Sense of Security

To address this flaw, most of the major home security providers claim to have added anti-jamming software to their systems. But during testing, many hackers say the jamming technique still works. In fact, one company admitted that their anti-jamming software only alerted the homeowner to an issue with the security system and didn't actually set off the alarm.

Despite this, installing a home security system is still a good idea. There are also a few other things you can do to make your house less appealing to burglars:

- Place a large dog bowl near your back door. Criminals are terrified of dogs. If they see the dog bowl, they'll move on to a dog-free neighbor's house.

- Install motion sensor lights around your home. First, take a walk around your home at night and locate all of the "dark spots" so you know how many lights to buy and where you need to put them.

- Reinforce the locks on your doors and windows. Put a wooden bar along the floor track of your sliding glass door. Smaller wooden pieces can go in the bottom of window tracks or along the inside of window frames.

Remember, any home security system has its flaws. You should always have a backup plan to protect yourself if you're home when a break-in occurs. Mine happens to be a gun. Yours might be a gun, knife, baseball bat or something else. Whatever it is, don't rely solely on your home security system to protect you.

Secure Your Windows and Doors

Having reliable locks for the doors and windows in your home is a simple, vital step in home defense. Let's start with the locks. One of the most common brands of locks used in the U.S. is Kwikset. They're a go-to brand for contractors and builders, and there's a pretty good chance you use them in your own home. If you do, go to the nearest Home Depot and buy new locks immediately. Kwikset locks are poorly made and easily compromised. I myself can pick one easily, and so can most criminals.

Instead, I recommend buying Schlage or Medeco locks. You can get Schlage locks at Home Depot or any other major hardware store. Medeco locks are a little harder to find. I'd recommend searching for a local dealer using their website, **www.medeco.com**. Simply select "Dealer Locator" from their home page and type in your ZIP code to find out where you can purchase Medeco locks near you.

I also recommend having a reliable, solid deadbolt from either Schlage or Medeco. Getting a solid-core door is a good idea, too. One that's made out of sturdy, solid materials, like wood, steel, or iron. It's a sad fact that several types of doors can be kicked in with minimal effort. In fact, as I'm sure you're aware, most doors are hollow, and if you have a teenage son, you know how easily these can be kicked through.

Purchasing a high-quality solid-core door, particularly for your front door, is very important. Many of us also have glass sliding doors in the rear of our homes. Hopefully, if someone breaks these doors to try to get in, you will hear the glass shatter and be prepared to meet the intruder. If you really want to ensure you'll hear them, I recommend putting a glass break detector on your glass doors. If someone jostles these doors at all, a loud alarm is set off.

One example is the Doberman Security SE-0106-4PK Ultra-Slim Window Alarm, available on Amazon for only $29.99. It's important that you reinforce the locks on these doors too. You can do so easily and cheaply by getting a wooden bar to put along the floor track. This costs about $2.00 at any home goods store. Just cut it half an inch shorter than the total track distance. Now if an intruder wants to come in that way, they'll have to break the door.

As I mentioned, the noise that creates will give you time to spring into action, especially if you use a glass break detector. I'd also recommend locking and reinforcing your windows. Smaller wooden pieces similar to the bars for sliding doors can go in the bottom of window tracks or along the inside of the frames.

Being Prepared on Every Level of Your Home

There's one sound that makes even hardened criminals run in the other direction during an attempted home invasion:

gunshots. I have at least one gun stored on every level of my home. Because I have small children, every one of these guns is in a rapid access safe, made by GunVault or Stack-On or Console Vault. I've set it up this way so that if someone breaks into my home, I don't have to worry about running all of the way upstairs (and possibly past the intruder) to retrieve a firearm to defend myself.

But guns aren't the only preparedness item that I have on every level of my home. I also have a flashlight on every level so that they're easily accessible from anywhere in my home if the lights go out. When it comes to flashlights, I have plenty of tactical flashlights that I carry with me always. Tactical flashlights are very small, with a high-powered beam, which makes them easy to use and reliable. My tactical flashlights are made by SureFire and Nextorch.

However, in addition to my tactical flashlights, I also have larger (nontactical) lights, which have batteries that will last for dozens of hours. On the low price point of things is the 6V Eveready flashlight that can be bought at hardware stores for about $7. This is the large yellow flashlight that you've probably seen a million times. The beauty of this flashlight is that it lasts 100 hours before you need to get a new battery, and a new battery is only about $8.00. If you're looking for a cheap, no-frills flashlight, this is it.

Recently, I got another larger flashlight that will also last 100 hours. The light is the O2 Beam by Nebo. It's a brand-new flashlight that has five different settings, ranging from 85 lumens with a 100-hour battery life to 420 lumens with a 20-hour life. It also has strobe and beacon settings. I've been very impressed with this flashlight so far because not only does it have five settings, but you can adjust the light beam to go from being wide to a concentrated spotlight.

Surprisingly, this flashlight isn't too expensive, only $80, which is a good deal for this type of flashlight. In addition to flashlights and guns, I also have food storage on every level of my home, in case we experience any type of flooding. I get all of my food storage from the LDS Cannery, run by the Mormon church. Don't worry — you don't have to be Mormon to qualify. Visit them at providentliving.lds.org to learn how to order canned goods.

The bottom line is crazy events seem to occur every week in this country that remind us about the importance of being prepared. So it's important to be prepared for any situation by gathering the correct supplies and making sure that they are easily accessible from anywhere in your home.

Buy These Batteries

Have you ever taken a count of how many items you use every day that rely on batteries? Electric toothbrushes, children's toys, remote controls, flashlights… in the technological age that we live in, batteries are a necessity. And because we rely on these devices and we want to be prepared when the electricity goes out (even if it's just for a few hours), it's important to have quality batteries.

Sure, you can go to Wal-Mart and buy regular Energizer or Duracell batteries, but if you use your flashlights as often as I do, and if you use an electric toothbrush or any other item frequently, you may want to consider rechargeable batteries.

Now, rechargeable batteries are nothing new, but like every other product, you don't want to buy poor-quality rechargeable batteries that let you down when it counts. This is why I recommend you check out the Panasonic Eneloop rechargeable batteries. These are the ones that I personally use. These batteries come pre-charged from the factory, which is an added bonus — you can immediately put them to use. They can be recharged up to 2,100 times, which is not only convenient but will save you a ton of money over the years. Another good thing about these batteries is that they actually maintain their charge when not in use.

I have never left these batteries charged for years on end, but according to the company, they can maintain up to 70% of their charge after five years. What's more, they can work in freezing temperatures all the way down to minus 4 degrees F without losing their charge. The fact is these are tough batteries that will last. Even if they're not as glamorous as a gun or a knife, having high-quality batteries could come in handy much more often.

If you decide you want to get these batteries, you can buy them on Amazon.com by simply searching for "Panasonic Eneloop batteries." Where to Hide Your Guns As with all of your valuables, it's important to make your guns hard to find. Never store guns and valuables in your master bedroom (with the exception of your home defense gun, which should sit on your nightstand in a rapid access safe).

The master bedroom is the first place burglars will look, as most burglars want to be in and out of your house in eight minutes. You want to keep your guns in a place like an attic. This often requires a ladder to get to. In your attic, you want to store the guns in a box marked "old clothes" or "child's toys."

If you have a large gun safe, consider getting a dummy gun safe too. I know one guy who has his large dummy safe and then behind it, in a wall, is his real safe full of guns. Other good ideas are the safes that look like an electrical box or a vent. A friend of mine owns a company called Console Vault. One of their products is called the Red Herring Secret Safe. It looks exactly like an electrical panel built into your wall but it is covered with "high voltage" warnings and nobody in their right mind would ever touch it.

Other places to consider are in your kitchen behind your pots and pans or in a fireplace (that you don't use) behind a stack of wood. Wherever you decide to hide your guns, I do recommend having them locked up in some type of gun safe, even if it's just a small safe such as the SnapSafe Lockbox or the GunVault NV200.

Stop Oversharing

A Texas couple returned home from vacation to realize they'd been burglarized to the tune of over $200,000. The burglars had broken into a safe and stolen 45 guns, ammunition, gold coins, and jewelry. According to police, it appeared to be a well planned job that took several hours, and the thieves likely knew that the couple was out of town.

Obviously, this is a terrible event for the couple, who lost family heirlooms and lots of money. But let's be honest here — it could have been prevented.

First, it's imperative to have an alarm system, especially if you have over $200,000 worth of goods in your house. These days, alarm systems are so inexpensive there's no excuse not to have one.

Second, be careful of who you tell when you're going out of town. Make sure a trusted neighbor knows so that they can keep an eye out for anything suspicious. But DON'T post on Facebook. Anyone with ill intentions can easily see that post and get a bad idea. It's an easy trap that too many people fall for. If you must post pictures and brag about your trip, save it until after you return.

Family Emergency Plan

One question that I'm often asked is what you should do when a crisis actually hits. If you're at work when a terrorist attack or a terrible natural disaster occurs, what should you do to get to your family? When these things happen, it causes mass chaos. That's why it's vital to have a family emergency plan in place, which all of the members of your family are aware of.

The first thing you want to do is go get the youngest and weakest members of the family. For me, this means going to school and getting my kids, starting with the youngest child. Also, if you are unable to get in touch with one another, it's important for both you and your spouse to go to get the kids.

In a crisis event, you hope for the best but always assume the worst. So I have to assume my wife is dead and that I need to go pick up the kids. My wife has to assume that I am dead and that she'll have to go pick up the kids. Whoever gets to the first child leaves a note for their spouse. This is critical to do. In the bag in my car, I have some Rite in the Rain paper and an Inkzall marker. This marker can write on all types of wet and oily surfaces.

I also have Gorilla tape to tape the note to the preschool door or in some other easy-to-see place. On this note, write something such as "Sandy, I got to the school first and picked up Lucy. I am headed to get Tom. Love, Jason. 10-13-15, 9:05 a.m." (Always put the date and time so your spouse knows when you got there.)

Once you have gotten your kids, then you head home or to the designated place you're supposed to meet the rest of your family (have two of them). Obviously, if your home or first designated meeting place is no longer standing or safe to enter, then you'll go to the secondary meeting place, which can be anything from a church house to random parking lot or park. And if the secondary meeting place isn't safe, you'll go to a third place.

This is an incredibly simple plan that I recommend you talk with your spouse about tonight. In a true disaster, the chaos is going to be extreme, and you'll be grateful you know exactly what to do and the places to meet your loved ones. Plus, don't forget the paper that you can write on in the rain, the Inkzall marker, and the Gorilla tape.

You should also have a well-developed family emergency

plan within your own home. Just as in the plan I just described, you're going to want to get to the weakest or youngest members of your family first. Once you've established they are safe, clear your home, room by room, to look for intruders.

WHITE HOUSE-WORTHY HOME SECURITY TIPS

When it comes to the security of government facilities — like the CIA headquarters in Langley, Virginia, or the White House in Washington, D.C. — the government typically employs a layered defense system, where the security level increases as you pass through each "ring" or layer.

This security concept is referred to as concentric circles of protection or concentric rings of security. Whatever you call it, one of the best examples of this type of layered protection is the way the government secures the airspace around Washington, D.C.

Unauthorized Aircraft Detected

In 2005, two pilots breached D.C. airspace and experienced this security protocol firsthand. Pilots Troy Martin and Jim Sheaffer left Pennsylvania en route to North Carolina on May 11, 2005. At some point, they veered off course and entered the Air Defense Identification Zone near D.C.

The men kept flying and proceeded to enter a second, more

restricted area: the 15-mile radius of the Flight Restricted Zone. In response to their actions, a Department of Homeland Security helicopter intercepted the Cessna Martin and Sheaffer were flying.

The helicopter attempted to make radio contact with the pilots but was unable to reach them. When the helicopter flew away, the men believed they had left the restricted airspace. But a few minutes later, two F-16 jets appeared, and the two pilots quickly realized the gravity of the situation.

One of the F-16s deployed red flares to get the attention of the disoriented pilots. They had flown within three miles of the White House, causing it to be evacuated along with the U.S. Capitol.

Finally, radio contact was made with the pilots, and they were advised to head toward Frederick, Maryland, where they could land at a small airport.

Even though one of the pilots of the F-16s confirmed they were able to verify the Cessna was not a threat and they never intended to fire upon the aircraft, I guarantee those two lost pilots had the scare of a lifetime.

As I mentioned, this is a perfect example of concentric rings of security. As the Cessna crossed each ring or circle, the security response increased. And if Homeland Security had determined that the plane posed a serious threat, further action would have been taken.

DIY at Home

Even if you don't live at 1600 Pennsylvania Ave., you can still apply this idea to your home. In its simplest form, the concentric circles of protection break down in three different layers:

The first layer of security is the perimeter of your property. Make sure to include EVERY direction by which a criminal could approach your home. Protections may include a fence, motion sensor lights, security cameras or even an alarm system yard sign. The point of these security measures is to deter criminals from considering your home as a target.

The second layer of security is designed to prevent entry into your home. Here are some questions to consider: Are the bushes or shrubs around your home cut back, or can a criminal easily hide in your yard? Are ALL of your doors and windows regularly locked? Have you installed Medeco or Schlage locks? Have you thought about using a door barricade, like Nightlock? All of these measures will hopefully keep criminals from ever setting foot in your home.

Nightlock: **www.nightlock.com**

The last circle or line of defense is the security measures inside your home. This should include an alarm system that alerts you when a window or door is breached. For me, this also includes my Sig Sauer P226 and extra magazines in a rapid-access safe on my nightstand. Another aspect of this circle of protection is the safe room your family has chosen as a meeting point. Inside this room should be another home defense weapon and a cellphone to call 911.

When you evaluate your home defense plan, consider implementing the concentric ring approach. Then assess each layer to see where your home may be vulnerable. Start at the first circle and work your way inward.

If you're able to successfully apply this information, your home will be as secure as the White House — minus the F-16s.

THE #1 ITEM FOR HOME DEFENSE... AND IT COSTS JUST $13

By Cade Courtley | *Former Navy SEAL Sniper*

Legal Disclaimer: Bear spray is intended for use against bears — any use of bear spray other than its intended use may be deemed unlawful and lead to prosecution. The information given in this article is an opinion and not a recommendation or advice. Use bear spray at your own risk and in accordance with State and Federal laws/regulations.

Several years ago, my girlfriend and I were driving home from a movie in my Ford Raptor. For some reason, the car in front of me was stopped at an intersection — even though the light was green.

As I came to a stop, I quickly realized why the vehicle in front of me wasn't moving...

A rough-looking guy in dirty black jeans and an open black jacket was walking across the intersection. He was bare-chested with his arms outwardly stretched, practically "inviting" a vehicle to hit him. It was clear from my vantage point that this individual was not in his right mind.

As he continued slowly across the intersection, I blasted my horn. That's when he switched directions and began advancing directly toward my truck. He was 25 feet away.

As I was taught in the SEAL teams, I did an immediate threat assessment: HANDS — empty. No visible weapons. This limited my options should I need to respond to this situation.

As he continued to advance toward my truck, I quickly reviewed my options:

1. Glock 22C (.40 cal) handgun in my door panel. Deadly force = NOT AUTHORIZED.

2. Drive over him. Deadly force = NOT AUTHORIZED.

3. Get out of my truck. This would be considered confrontational/accelerating the conflict. Deadly force = NOT AUTHORIZED.

Suddenly, he started running toward the passenger side of my truck, where my girlfriend was seated with her window down. When he got within six feet of the window, I told my girlfriend to hold her breath and pushed her head into her lap.

That's when I sprayed the assailant with a three-second burst of bear spray. Nonlethal = AUTHORIZED.

He was immediately incapacitated. The threat was neutralized and we proceeded home. This all occurred in just eight seconds.

Approximately two hours later, two officers from the Boulder Police Department arrived at my door and charged ME with third-degree assault.

I was BEYOND angry. I had never been arrested in my life.

Welcome to the People's Republic of Boulder.

In the months that followed, I would have to spend over $8,000 on lawyer fees only to have the charges dropped by the district attorney the day before my trial. I would later learn that the individual who approached my truck had been arrested 18 times in the previous two years on charges that included assaulting a police officer.

Now, given the identical situation reoccurring — I would still react in the very same way. I'd rather be judged by 12 than carried by six.

Your Home Defense Tool

Bear spray, Wikipedia says, "is a type of pepper spray or capsaicin deterrent that is used to deter aggressive bears, typically in wilderness environments."

I used to do a lot of trail running in the area, which is why I happened to be carrying a can of Counter Assault Bear Deterrent with me.

Now, let me once again emphasize that bear spray is only intended for use on bears. Use bear spray at your own risk and in accordance with state and federal laws/regulations.

However, if you feel that your life or the life of someone else is a risk — you should do everything and anything to protect yourself and others.

Memorize this statement:

"I FELT MY LIFE WAS IN DANGER AND I DID WHAT I HAD TO DO TO PROTECT MYSELF."

Given my situation that required a response, I did what I felt I had to do.

What to Carry

Frontiersman Bear Spray is a great brand that allows for maximum strength and maximum range. On sale, you can find this for as little as $13.

While Frontiersman is a great option, I happen to carry Counter Assault deterrent. It's a little more expensive at $45, but I've found it to be a very effective nonlethal option.

Frontiersman: **https://www.sabrered.com/bear-spray**
Counter Assault: **https://www.rei.com/product/623173/
counter-assault-bear-deterrent-spray-81-fl-oz**

I can tell you from personal experience that bear spray is incredibly effective as a non-lethal form of self-defense. Keep in mind, however, bear spray is a form of pepper spray. And while it's legal to possess pepper spray in all states, some states do have restrictions including: the capacity of the cartridge, potency of the spray, selling to minors, selling to felons and special labeling requirements. Massachusetts and New York even require a license to sell tear gas, Mace, or devices that emit a substance designed to incapacitate.

In Canada, bear spray is considered as a prohibited weapon if it is used against a person instead of a bear. Buying bear spray with the intent of use on a person is illegal. It's illegal to carry a product designed for personal protection against a human attack. You can buy bear spray for using on bears, BUT you can also be charged with having a concealed weapon if you are carrying it in a place that you are unlikely to see bears. If you use bear spray against a person, you can face additional charges if it's not considered a legitimate self-defense situation.

Bear spray should only be used as a means of protection in life-threatening situations. And please make sure that you're aware of the rules and regulations regarding the use of bear spray on people before you actually use it. Take it from me, the police won't take it lightly... but it may mean the difference between life and death.

If you're ever in a bind, this $13 spray might be your No. 1 ticket for home defense.

A SEAL'S GUIDE TO HOME DEFENSE

By Cade Courtley | *Former Navy SEAL Sniper*

Most of us can't afford a Level 1 security system with immediate armed response and all the high-tech bells and whistles you could ever need. But here are four steps anyone can take to deter a would-be intruder:

1. Install an external Wi-Fi security camera. There are several very reasonably priced external cameras available — many for under $200. A security camera has two functions. First, they allow you to monitor the exterior of your house with a live feed through your phone or TV. Second, if a criminal sees a camera at a point of entry — they will likely move on to a home without one.

2. Secure ALL points of entry. If you can fit your head through it — secure it! This includes all ducts, crawl spaces and especially basements. Plywood or several layers of high-tensile-strength mesh wire will do the trick.

3. Fortify your windows and doors. For doors, I'm a big fan of using two Grade 1 deadbolts. The second lock should be keyless, meaning it can only be locked from

the inside, not accessed from the outside. To secure your windows, buy a few dowels (at least 1" diameter) from the hardware store. If the window opens from the bottom, cut the dowel ½" shorter than the height of the window and place it in the top half of the window. This will stop anyone from opening the window without removing the dowel on the inside. If your windows slide open sideways, cut the dowel ½" shorter than the width of the window and simply lay it in the track. Be sure to secure any sliding glass doors this way as well.

4. Make your own alarm system. Add a magnetic alarm unit to every door and window in your house. I'm a fan of the ones made by Swann — you can buy 10 for just under $30. These little devices sound with a screaming 110-decibel siren when the two pieces of the unit are separated. If that doesn't scare away your intruder altogether, it should at least give you a few extra seconds to respond.

Remember, criminals will follow the path of least resistance. When confronted with even the slightest challenge, they'll simply move on to the next house.

DIY SAFE ROOM

Designate a safe retreat to accommodate any number of emergencies:

1. Select an interior room or large closet with no windows or skylight.

2. Install a solid-core or steel door with weld-on hinges. Hang it so it opens outward.

3. Replace the wooden doorjamb with a steel one, or reinforce the door trim with steel angle iron to prevent the door from being kicked open.

4. Install a keyless Grade 1 deadbolt.

5. Furnish your safe room with the following: defensive weapon, fully charged cellphone (preferably a secondary that stays in this room), first aid kit, flashlight, water and fire extinguisher.

This Is Not a Drill

Unfortunately, no amount of preemptive safety measures will keep a tenacious trespasser from gaining entry into your home. Which means you should know how to respond once a breach has occurred — with zero hesitation.

Once a criminal is inside, the No. 1 goal for you and your family is to avoid the intruder. To that end, here are some helpful SEAL-inspired tips to consider:

- If you don't have an alarm system to alert the household to the presence of an invader, establish a code word or words that everyone knows mean trouble to initiate a predetermined escape plan — i.e., leave the house and rendezvous at an agreed-upon meeting point or head to the safe room.

- Draw a sketch of the interior of your home and mark alternate points of exit that could be accessed while avoiding the area the intruders have breached. Be sure to have more than one exit strategy, including alternate escape routes for the front, rear and second floor.

- Rehearse, rehearse, rehearse. In special ops, we rehearse dozens of times before going on a mission. It's one of the most important factors of success. The plan becomes second nature, and if something does go wrong, you are better able to adjust. If you have kids, don't turn these practice drills into a scary situation, but be sure to rehearse with the lights off, so they get used to maneuvering in the dark.

- Speaking of kids, teach your children how and when to dial 911. And if they get separated from you, they should know which neighbor to go to and what to say.

Make Your Home a Fortress for Under $100

You can spend hundreds of dollars each month on a professionally installed home security system with cameras, automated lights, door locks and 24-hour monitoring. However, this may not be realistic for many people. The good news is there are several simple steps you can take to make criminals think twice about breaking into your home.

You can purchase the following for under $100. These items will make your home much less attractive to a criminal casing your neighborhood for an easy target, and chances are they'll end up choosing someone else's house to break into instead of yours:

- Fake security cameras — For as little as $10, you can get a fake security camera with a blinking red light and wiring that looks authentic. Simply install one of these on the exterior of your home and put in batteries to make the light blink. I had a client in Salt Lake City do this, and a criminal broke into his neighbor's house instead of his. The best part was the police wanted the video from my client's cameras to catch the criminal, and my client had to tell the cops they were fake

- Dog bowl and "beware of dog" signs — It's no secret that criminals hate dealing with dogs, because they can be loud and unpredictable. That being said, for $5, you can buy a large dog bowl to place by your door. Plus, for around $10, you can add a "beware of dog" sign to your door or fence. With these two signs that a dog is present, criminals will likely go to a neighboring house that doesn't have the appearance of a dog

- Doorstopper alarm — For around $15, you can get a pair of doorstopper alarms to place at your exterior doors. In short, these devices emit a loud sound when they are tripped by the door opening. If someone does attempt to break in, these alarms would stun them for a moment and wake you up in time to thwart the intruder

- Motion sensor lights — Criminals like to hide in bushes and sneak around to case a house, so I recommend installing motion sensor lights. If a thief enters your yard and your property is flooded with light, it draws unwanted attention. You can even purchase battery-operated or solar-powered lights so you don't have to wire in new fixtures. And you don't even need to break the bank — you can get quality lights for $30 or less

- Install window stops — Window stops allow a window to open only about six inches, which isn't enough space for any criminal to squeeze through. All first-floor windows should have these stops installed to prevent easy access. Opening a window is one of the simplest ways to break into a house, but most criminals won't want to break a window because the noise will blow their cover. You can purchase window stops for under $15

- Alarm signs — Go on eBay or Amazon and for $10, you can buy signs for an alarm company. Put one in your front and backyard to make burglars think your home is professionally monitored by an alarm service. Just make sure you buy signs that look legit, such as those by ADT or Brinks, and not ones by ACME alarm company that look totally fake.

CHAPTER 4:

PERSONAL DEFENSE: TACTICS FOR TAKING DOWN ANY ATTACKER

WHY "SELF DEFENSE" IS A SHAM

When you think of "self-defense" or "self-protection," what do you see?

I see nothing.

OK, maybe that's a little too harsh, too fast.

If I try really hard to cut through the ambiguous fog of those phrases, I can almost see someone getting attacked, desperately trying to get away, maybe getting backed into a corner. Flailing like a terrified animal.

At worst I see someone curled up in a ball on the ground.

That's what "self-defense" means to me. And that's why I won't teach, practice or do it.

I'm only ever interested in hurting people.

The term "self-defense" has no operational value. It does not paint of picture of me doing anything of consequence. It suggests passivity, being acted upon by someone else, moving second and hoping for the best. It does not mean getting anything done.

This really hit home while I was doing some reading on combat handgun use. I grew tired of the constant, politically correct phraseology of "self-defense," "self-protection" and "home de-fense." One actually has to dig deep to find any reference to killing people with bullets. And here I always assumed that's what guns were for: a tool to enable a person to kill another without undue effort or training.

Of course, that's the elephant in the middle of the room that we dance around by using sanitized code words. Why can't we just call it like it is?

Because every use of violence is a crime.

If someone breaks into your home in the middle of the night and comes after you and your family — threatening or outright harming you or others — and you shoot/stab/beat him to death, you have committed, at the very least, manslaughter.

It is then up to the district attorney to look at the circum-stances surrounding the case and decide whether it was OK for you to commit that crime. This is where the legal definition of self-defense comes in.

Unless you're studying for the bar, the term is meaningless. Slapping "self-defense" on physical training for combat or for firearms use is just society's way of really, really hoping you'll wait your turn and go second like polite, civilized folk do...

... and not go around terrorizing or hunting people.

Just to be clear: In purely legal terms, I will only use my training when my life or the lives of others are in danger, just as I would find it necessary to shoot somebody only under identical circumstances.

While this is the very definition of legal self-defense, I would not use that term to describe my practice. When I go to the range or the countryside I practice marksmanship because that's how you kill someone with a gun. When I hit the mats I practice hurting (and yes, killing) people with fists, boots, sticks and knives.

"Self-defense" and its wishy-washy, go-second connota-tions do not figure into the physical execution. While it may describe the situation under which such behavior may be deemed acceptable by the legal system, it is a poor descriptor of the act itself: Hurting people.

"Self-defense" is a marketing term, because it's what we've all been told is acceptable. Nobody searches for "how to use violence" because it's assumed that only the "bad guys" use violence — the rest of us are stuck with self-defense.

It is far more effective for training to peel all the padding off the hard corners and make the accepted generalities specific. Instead of a hopeful "for serious self-defense, go for the eyes," we get specific on the mechanical process of gouging an eyeball out of a skull. How to get it done, how to get it right, the resulting injury and associated disability and how to practice to make that injury the most likely outcome.

While I would advocate that you only use the information we train in serious life-or-death situations (textbook self-defense scenarios) you should find the term itself to be insufficient to describe your actual training and practice. I don't teach people self-defense. I teach them how to hurt people.

And therein lies our issue of contention: Violence — hurting people — is precisely what the winners are famous for doing. I want to practice winning in violent conflict, not training for second place.

Second place, as we all know, is first loser, and in life-or-death violence, the losers are usually dead.

Don't Be Fooled by Survival Semantics

Self-defense means many things:

It is the moral imperative we use to draw a line between predatory and "civilized" use of force: "I will only fire in self-defense."

It is the legal rule we use to judge whether or not that use of force is a crime: "The defendant claims to have acted in self-defense."

It's a catchall term used to describe physical training for such activities: "I'm taking a self-defense class."

It can also refer to the unarmed techniques learned there: "If someone comes after me, I'll use self-defense on him."

It means many things — and this vague imprecision is exactly why it is useless for our needs in training to do violence by hand.

The moral imperative and the legal rule are fine for what they do — one informs the decision process before the fact and the other helps society figure out how it feels about it after the fact. It is the carrying over of the term to describe physical training and technique that is harmful.

As was pointed out in the comments to the previous post, words mean things. A single word can connote entire constellations of meaning, in varying shades and intensities.

When it comes to training for physical action, we must choose the words we use to describe that action very carefully: The more direct and concrete, the better. We need the words to conjure up a clear vision of that action that has you acting decisively.

"Self-defense," as a descriptor for hand-to-hand combat, is unfortunately vague. It fails because it says nothing about the other guy or you doing anything to him. It mentions you and protecting you. And that's it. "Self-defense" does not describe any direct action.

The popular narrative looks no further than the attacker/defender dichotomy. If you're training for self-defense and doing self-defense, you're automatically accepting the role of the defender. In criminal violence, attackers are usually the "bad guys" and defenders the "good guys." No sane, social person wants to be a bad guy — we all want to be the good guy. We want to have a good reason for doing what we must and be in the right after the fact. So we've picked sides. We venerate the doughty defender and vilify the animal attacker.

And in doing so, we put our blinders on.

Most videos of criminal violence involve an attacker savaging a victim. Since we can't identify with the attacker, we see ourselves as the guy on the ground getting stomped, stabbed, shot, whatever's happening to him at the moment. We then desperately try to come up with a plan to prevent those things from happening, all the while ignoring what the bad guy's doing.

This is training for second place.

And all because we picked a role with the language we chose to describe our actions.

It is far more useful to replace the attacker/defender dichotomy with the idea of winners and losers. In every successful use of violence, there will be at least one winner and one loser. Instead of identifying with the loser and looking to them for answers, we need to figure out what the winner is doing. Why did he win? How can I do what he did? What mistakes did he make? How can I improve on his process?

Of course, we have to step outside what is socially acceptable to see it from this perspective. No one wants to venerate the bad guys or take on the mantle of the evildoer. But when you stop painting black hats and white hats on the people in the situation and look purely at the mechanics of success in violence, it becomes clear that it is easier to win than to fulfill the various needs of self-defense.

Words dictate how we think, and how we think directly dictates how we move.

Don't "defend yourself" — hurt the man.

Don't train for "self-defense" — practice using violence as a survival tool.

Leave self-defense where it's best suited, in the realm of ideas, where it bookends the act of violence as the moral imperative to not use force needlessly and for legal consideration after the fact.

That's why I don't do, practice or teach "self-defense." I've spent my career figuring out why the winners win in violence and how to teach anyone who'll listen how to do what they do.

In hand-to-hand violence, defense gets you killed. Hurting people gets you home.

The difference starts with mere words.

ARE YOU A PREDATOR OR ARE YOU PREY?

By Damian Ross | *Self Defense Co.*

Self-defense size-ups happen in the first few milliseconds you're in someone else's space.

They see you as a possible target of opportunity, and they need to make a quick decision — a COST/BENEFIT analysis — on whether you are going to be worth it.

In other words, will they be able to impose their will on you without being injured, captured or identified?

When walking in rough neighborhoods, people who don't know any better will tell you to AVOID EYE CONTACT, keep your head down and just keep moving.

This is not good advice.

At our core, we're animals, and in the animal kingdom there are PREDATORS and PREY.

If you act like either one, you will be TREATED as such.

When criminals and bullies pick targets, they're looking for PREY — not a title fight.

Take this story I just received from one of my elite members, Lee:

"I was walking out of a Walmart when a male in his 20s

hocked up some phlegm and spit right across my path. He was standing next to the wall, and my inclination was to swing my right arm around and plaster his head against the wall before he could escalate the situation.

"Needless to say, I didn't, but I did make eye contact and maintain my distance while walking past, and he went back against the wall.

"I do believe he got the message.

"I have come to discover that the will to act is the currency of respect in some circles. It sends a message that it's not a real good idea to mess with me.

"However, on a bad day, this could have degenerated into an ass-kicking contest really quickly.

"So I'm glad I have something stronger to control these animals."

The spit was the punk's way of testing Lee to see if he was going to be a problem.

This is how most crimes of violence begin. Criminals try to get away with a little and then take a little more and so on. Make no mistake: Once they have you on the tracks, it's only a matter of time until it gets out of control.

Imagine if Lee had looked down and tried to avoid dealing with this punk altogether. There's a good chance this kid would have decided to follow him to his car, ask him for some spare change and then continue to see what he could get from Lee.

The good news is WE WILL NEVER KNOW, because Lee acted like a PREDATOR, not PREY.

Are You Predator or Prey?

Predators...

- Make strong EYE CONTACT

- Walk with their head up, scanning the environment
- Are looking to HUNT and DEFEND
- Move with purpose.

Prey...

- Avoid eye contact
- Constantly look for ways to escape
- Are looking to GRAZE, SCAVENGE and ESCAPE
- Move with panic.

Remember, wherever you go, you're being SIZED UP and TESTED. How you're perceived is entirely up to you.

Now, this doesn't mean you should overtly CHALLENGE the local thugs on the corner, but casual eye contact for less than a second is enough. And when you move your eyes off them, KEEP YOUR EYES AT THE SAME LEVEL. Look past them and slowly scan the area, left to right and right to left. PLEASE — DON'T GET INTO A STARING CONTEST.

Always keep your head up and chest out, and move with purpose and intent.

It also helps (a lot) if you have a plan of action mapped out like Lee did.

Having a plan will:

- Instill purpose in your movement
- Emote confidence
- Calm your nerves and channel that adrenaline rush
- Give you something to focus on
- Stop you from panicking.

Remember — be predator, NOT prey.

TRIDENT: A SIMPLE SELF-DEFENSE TECHNIQUE THAT ANYONE CAN MASTER

"Give me your wallet or I'll kill you."

These words would be enough to make most of us freeze up and panic.

But imagine hearing them uttered late at night in one of the most dangerous cities in the world… while you're on a mission that's vital to the security of the United States.

That's the situation one of my fellow ex-CIA officers (let's call him "Robert") found himself in several years ago when he was overseas in a country I'm unable to disclose.

When the suspicious man first approached him, Robert thought the man was part of a foreign intelligence service and that he was about to be "rolled up," meaning he was about to be put in jail for getting caught as a spy. However, once the guy made that threat, Robert quickly realized he was dealing with a street criminal.

He could have done a number of things, including giving the criminal his wallet, hoping the thug would go away. But that's not always the best choice. Especially in this particular part of the world, where, even if you comply and give the criminal your wallet, they'll often still kill you just for the fun of it.

So instead of complying, Robert did what is known as the "Trident" — and it saved his life.

The best part of the Trident is that you don't need years of martial arts experience to learn it. It's a simple self-defense technique anyone can master.

Self-Defense Basics

Intelligence officers don't have 30 years to get trained in martial arts. Instead, when you attend your top-secret training, you learn the critical self-defense moves needed to keep you safe no matter where in the world you may travel.

You learn moves that are not only devastatingly effective, but also incredibly simple, so that in a stressful situation they can be quickly deployed.

And while I imagine you (hopefully) won't be traveling to the world's most dangerous countries, you and I both know that anything can happen here in America, even when we're doing something as mundane as shopping at the grocery store.

Before we get started, it's important to remember that if someone pulls a knife on you or threatens to harm you, you always want to immediately escape if you can. Or, if you carry a gun like I do, you want to draw your gun to defend yourself.

However, if you're in a confined area, without a firearm, and you think that you have no choice but to fight back, then you want to overwhelm them with force. In other words, you should perform the Trident with everything you've got.

The goal is to inflict damage on your attacker as quickly as possible, thereby creating a window for you to flee to safety and call the police.

Trident: Three Combo Attack

As the name suggests, this technique can be broken down into three separate moves.

Step One: The first move is to strike the head area, specifically the eyes. Put simply, reach one of your hands out and claw and poke the eyes, to disorient your attacker.

Step Two: As soon as you strike the eyes with one of your hands, immediately punch the throat with your other hand. I know this may sound harsh, but we're assuming someone is trying to kill you. A punch to the throat is incredibly effective and will likely have your attacker recoiling forward in pain.

Step Three: The third and final move is a swift knee to the groin. This will send almost anyone to the ground, thereby giving you a chance to escape to safety.

Remember, all three of these moves are quickly done one after another, going from the eyes to the throat to the groin. When you do them lightning fast — and with power — your attacker will be caught off guard, giving you a chance to escape with your life.

Visualize yourself carrying out this technique. Then, if you ever find yourself in a potentially deadly situation, you'll know exactly what to do.

SIX SIGNS YOUR SELF-DEFENSE INSTRUCTOR SUCKS

By Damian Ross | *Self Defense Co.*

Your instructor could be a world champ, Navy SEAL or black-ops killing machine… but that doesn't mean they can teach a good class or be a good coach. We've put together the TOP six signs you might not be getting what you bargained for in your training. Starting with…

1. No course curriculum

Not having a curriculum is like embarking on an around-the-world journey without a map and compass. It's nearly impossible to teach and even more impossible to learn without a road map to tell you where you're going. You should know exactly what is expected of you for each rank and certification.

A curriculum does two things:

First, it keeps the validity of your training intact. This ensures that you're learning the correct skills and there's continuity in the system. Without it, your style will fall victim to being modified by every instructor who teaches it. Like the child's game of telephone, it will be changed by everyone who touches it.

Second, it holds your instructor accountable. Learning is a two-way street because you take the time and pay money for a product and you should receive that product. As an instructor, I am always reviewing lesson plans because the majority of the time, I discover an important point I would have left out of the lesson.

2. No lesson plan

The worst thing an instructor or coach can do is "wing it." Showing up to a class and not having a plan to take full advantage of the time is disrespectful to your students and your system. Every class should be well-thought-out with a progressive learning structure.

Your instructor should also have a monthly lesson plan so you know exactly what's being covered in each class. This will help you work toward your rank faster because instead of showing up and hoping you're going to learn what you need, you will be able to plan to attend those classes.

3. No out-of-class reinforcement

The University of South Florida Teaching College conducted a study and discovered that after a class or a seminar, without any outside reinforcement, students only retained 10% of what they learned. And after a few weeks, 90% of that was forgotten.

In a typical martial arts system, the only time you're learning is IN CLASS. This means the only time you learn is in front of the instructor. Furthermore, beginners are discouraged to practice on their own for fear of doing it wrong.

This is true, however, if you are given access to self-defense videos, books and other multimedia; like in any other education program, you will be able to practice on your own. This will accelerate your learning exponentially. To be honest, in this day and age, not having tools like video to practice what you learned in class is unacceptable.

4. Excessive conditioning

A sign of a lazy instructor is excessive conditioning. Anyone can make you run wind sprints or do a bunch of calisthenics — it takes ZERO thought. A good instructor will provide the same type of conditioning training through drills based on developing your skill.

Burst drills in the system for example (30-second rounds of beating the crap out of your target as hard as you can) will give you the same cardio benefit as burpees but with the added benefit of developing real fighting skill.

At the end of the day, it's not complicated. It just needs to be set up and administered.

5. Excessive sparring

This is similar to excessive conditioning. It doesn't take any imagination or effort to have a class where everyone is rolling around and the instructor corrects random mistakes he happens to catch.

The problem with sparring too much is that people get lazy and form bad habits. Because there will come a point where both you and your partner will slack off. It's only natural when you're working with friends. Instead, controlled, short-term drills and frequent rotation of partners work A LOT BETTER.

In reality, your typical class session for a sport martial art should only be about 10–15% live sparring.

6. Low energy level and lack of engagement.

When you're teaching, YOU NEVER HAVE A BAD DAY. It's not about you, it's about the people who are paying you to prepare them. It doesn't matter what happened in your life for those few moments you're on the floor teaching — you'd better be on your A-game. If not, pick another career.

Being an instructor doesn't mean you're the best fighter in the room or whatever BS you want to believe. If you're an instructor, you're an educator. You're providing a service, and when it comes to the Self Defense Co., it's a service that will save a life. Find out more at **http://bit.ly/2eZBVaM.**

SEND YOUR CHILD BACK TO SCHOOL WITH THE SUPPLIES TO SURVIVE

It's back-to-school season and parents everywhere are nervously sending their children off to college. More and more these days, we see universities and college campuses make the news for deadly parties, mass shootings and rallies turned violent. How can a parent possibly prepare their child for the array of dangers they may encounter?

Even though most colleges and universities are required by law to report crime statistics to the federal government, not all of them do. Not only that, but these stats typically aren't accurate, because some crimes are handled entirely by campus police who fail to contact local law enforcement. And unfortunately, a lot of crimes that occur on campuses go unreported by the victims.

So while it's difficult to say what the statistical risks are when kids go off to college, there is no question they are more vulnerable when they're living on their own.

With that in mind, here are five safety and survival items I recommend sending with your kids or grandkids back to school:

Doorstopper alarm — Just like it sounds, this is simply a doorstopper with a built-in alarm that emits an incredibly loud sound when someone opens the door. Whenever your child is alone in their dorm room or apartment, they should put this behind the door to alert them in case someone tries to enter without their knowledge.

Stun-gun flashlight — I know a lot of people like to carry mace or pepper spray, but I recommend packing a stun-gun flashlight instead. A flashlight is something everyone should have on them anyway — the stun gun is an added bonus. I know of a young woman who was being followed in a parking lot one night. She turned around and hit the stun feature on her flashlight and the loud zapping noise was enough to make the creeper flee.

Diversion safe — It's always a good idea to store money and important documents (like a passport) in a safe. This is especially crucial if your child is living in a dorm with people they don't know. You can purchase all kinds of diversion safes that range from a fake shaving cream can to a decoy can of soup. Just be sure to pick one that won't look out of place.

Bug-out bag — Your kids should be prepared for any emergency or natural disaster that may occur. This is why I recommend sending with them a fully stocked bug-out bag that includes a first-aid kit, three days' worth of food and water, extra clothes and a paper map of the area surrounding their school, among other survival items. This is another place I suggest stashing some emergency cash in case your child needs money for a bus ticket or gas to get somewhere safe after bugging out.

Bulletproof panel — Unfortunately, we have seen many instances of mass shootings on college campuses, which is why I recommend adding a bulletproof panel to the backpack or school bag your child carries. I suggest buying a 10x15" panel that is rated Level 3A, which can stop up to a .44 Magnum.

My kids are still very young, so my wife and I don't have to worry about sending them off to college anytime soon. But when we do, we'll be sending all this (and probably more) with them.

SEAL SELF-DEFENSE FOR SENIORS

By Cade Courtley | *Former Navy SEAL Sniper*

Let's face it — fighting is a young person's game. Strength, agility, reaction time and an offensive mentality are all paramount to the success of a physical altercation — or a ride to the hospital.

Which is probably why you don't see this very often:

But that doesn't mean that someone in their twilight years won't ever find themselves in a situation that requires some form of self-defense.

Unfortunately, it makes perfect sense. Older folks are more vulnerable targets because they can no longer rely on the physical prowess that youth affords. Which is why they must be able to employ effective techniques.

Now, I'm a huge fan of learning self-defense skills in such disciplines as Muay Thai and Brazilian jiu-jitsu — and training weekly, if not daily — but this is simply not a practical undertaking for our aging population.

So let's keep it simple.

Three Surefire Clues You're About to Be Attacked

1. A person is giving you way too much eye contact. A criminal does this because they've "locked onto you" as a target. When normal people are on the streets and they make eye contact, they quickly break it and don't stare people down.

2. A person is matching your pace. Normally, if you're walking on the sidewalk with a stranger, you would both try to avoid walking side by side by speeding up or slowing down, since it's awkward to keep pace with one another. But a criminal who's targeting you will match your pacing so they can rob or attack you at the moment they choose.

3. A stranger comes up to you out of the blue and asks you a strange question. They do this to distract you so they can snatch your wallet, punch you out, or worse. Always maintain good space between you and strangers, and remember that it's better to be rude and alive than polite and dead.

Be a Fall Guy

First, you need to understand that a deliberate, controlled fall is much safer and less injurious than the impact from being thrown to the ground. If you're assaulted, quickly and calmly lower your body to the ground, curl up in a ball, cover you head and scream as loud as you can. If you have a whistle — even better. Use it.

Now, this goes against everything I believe regarding physical conflicts. But if you're able to control your descent to the ground and take a defensive posture that protects the most vital areas of your body, you will have a much better chance of surviving the attack.

If you happen to be one of many elderly folks who carry a cane — I have an alternative to curling up in a ball. It's an aggressive maneuver — but personally, I'd rather die on my feet than on the ground.

Here it is in four simple steps:

STEP 1: Take a broad stance — greater than shoulder width. Your foundation is key.

STEP 2: Focus all of your energy and swing your cane at the outer side of the knee closest to your cane-carrying hand. If done correctly and with enough force, your attacker will drop to half their height.

STEP 3: This step is critical. Don't waste the momentum you created from the first blow. Strike again with even more force to your assailant's neck/temple region. They should be around waist height after your knee strike, which will make this blow much easier to land.

STEP 4: Immediately exit the area and find anyone and everyone who can offer you support and/or security.

Whether you curl up in a ball or lash out with your cane, the point is to stay alive. So if you find that you're no longer as up for a fight as you once were, remember my advice and you'll be a survivor, not a statistic.

STAY SAFE WHILE EXERCISING IN THE GREAT OUTDOORS

Recently, there have been some horrific murders of joggers. Many of these murders occurred in broad daylight, dispelling the myth that these attacks only happen in the dark.

Here are some quick tips to share with your friends and family. Keep them in mind when you go trail running or jogging in your own neighborhood:

1. Never, ever run while wearing headphones. You can't hear your surroundings and you won't know if someone is approaching you from behind. Unfortunately, several of the recent victims were found with their headphones.

2. Join a running club. This way, you'll have a partner or two when you run. There is safety in numbers, and criminals will seldom attack a group.

3. Make eye contact with passersby. If you think someone is following you, look them in the eye and let them know you see them. What's more, don't be afraid to say something. The worst thing you can do is to put your head down, look afraid and avoid eye contact. The criminal

will continue to follow you if he thinks you are an easy victim.

4. Carry self-defense tools. Whether it's a gun, pepper spray or a tactical pen. One benefit of both pepper spray and the tactical pen is that you can run with them in your hand, so you won't waste time accessing them. I know several women who run with their tactical pens, and it gives them a huge boost of confidence.

5. Be brutal. If you are attacked, you have to be ruthless. Gouge your attacker's eyes, kick them in the groin and punch their throat. If you don't fight with everything you've got, you might not make it out alive.

6. Change it up. If you see someone suspicious and think they're watching you, you should vary your route. That person might see you run by the same lake at the same time each day, and they could be planning to abduct you. At the first sign that something doesn't look or feel right on your usual route, try a different one.

7. Stay in relatively public places. Don't go jogging in the woods alone or run down a gravel road that only gets one car a day.

While exercising is important, it's also crucial to remain aware of your surroundings so you can stay safe. Following this simple advice will help minimize potential dangers and ensure you return home to your loved ones.

COULD A FLASHLIGHT REALLY SAVE YOUR LIFE?

The club was packed as one of my agents escorted Jay Z into the corner of a dark VIP room. As soon as word spread that Jay was there, people immediately began trying to sneak into the room any way they could. One gentleman in particular was quite bold. He walked right up to the agent guarding the entrance and said he was there to have a drink with Jay.

The agent informed him it was a private party and he needed to go back to the club area. This gentleman looked my agent up and down and said, "What you gonna do? I ain't no shorty!"

He repeated over and over, "I ain't no shorty." Each shout grew louder in volume and intensity.

The gentleman began to advance with a chest bump in what seemed to be an attempt to close the distance between himself and Jay. Another agent witnessed what was going on, got Jay on his feet, and moved him toward the private exit that had previously been designated for egress.

The agent dealing with the angry man pulled his tactical flashlight from its holster and shined it in the gentleman's face. With a loud, direct shout, he said, "Hey, that's enough. Let me see your driver's license."

The intensity of the light from the tactical flashlight did the trick: The angry man stopped for just a moment, his face went blank, and the agent was able to step away to leave through the open door. As he exited and the door closed, the agent looked back to see the angry man still trying to regain his focus.

I realize you're probably not a bodyguard to the stars, but this is a great reminder that a tactical flashlight is an excellent tool to blind and stop someone in their tracks, giving you time to flee to safety. If you find yourself walking alone, particularly at night, I recommend keeping one on you at all times. Plus, if you need to, you can use the flashlight as a self-defense tool to strike an attacker. They're made out of top-grade, heavy materials and will help to deter an attack.

Fortunately for you and me, there are numerous companies that make quality tactical flashlights these days. I recommend checking out brands such as SureFire, Streamlight, and Fenix. More specifically, the SureFire G2X, Streamlight 88040 ProTac HL, and the Fenix PD35 TAC.

SureFire: **http://amzn.to/2eFW0m3**
Streamlight: **http://amzn.to/2wGfn8t**
Fenix: **http://amzn.to/2xOsx1C**

I guarantee a tactical flashlight will come in handy far more often than you think, and it's a smart investment for boosting your personal safety.

IS THAT A TOSS WALLET IN YOUR POCKET?

A toss wallet is a decoy wallet containing a few cards and around $60 in cash made up of ones, fives, tens, etc.

Why carry a toss wallet?

In the intelligence business, you often find yourself in less-than-desirable areas where it's not the local authorities you have to worry about but your average, run-of-the-mill street criminals. If some ne'er-do-well tries to rob you with a gun or knife pointed at your chest, you can use your toss wallet to distract the thief long enough to safely escape — without giving up your belongings.

How do you use a toss wallet?

There are two ways you can use a toss wallet.

1. If you're in an open space, take out your fake wallet and throw it at the criminal's face. This will likely stun them, giving you time to flee to safety.

2. If you happen to be in a confined space and there's nowhere to run, you'll have to take a different approach with the toss wallet. You still chuck it at the criminal's face, but then immediately charge, punching them in the throat, gouging their eyes or kneeing them in the groin. Once the criminal has been neutralized, quickly make your exit.

What else can you do with a toss wallet?

If you want to take this concept one step further, you can make sure the criminal gets caught. Here's what one fellow I know does: He calls his credit card company and says his credit card has been stolen (even though it hasn't). The credit card company flags the card in case anyone tries to use it. Then he puts his "stolen" credit card in his toss wallet. If a criminal ends up with the wallet and tries to use the card, they'll likely get in trouble. I'm not necessarily suggesting you go this far, but it's worth considering.

Either way, using a toss wallet is a really simple trick. One that could save you the complicated hassle of replacing credit cards and IDs if you're robbed of your real wallet.

BRING A KNIFE TO A GUN FIGHT: THE BIGGER, THE BETTER

On a quiet summer night in Clearwater, Florida, Mr. and Mrs. Steve and Heather Aiosa awoke at 2:10 a.m. to find an intruder standing in the doorway of their bedroom.

The intruder, later identified as Robert James Alcalde, began ransacking the bedroom while the frightened couple called 911.

Then Steve Aiosa retrieved his .22 rifle from underneath the bed and went outside to load it. But the rifle malfunctioned and wouldn't fire. At this point, Heather Aiosa ran from the home to join her husband, the intruder following closely behind.

There Will Be Blood

The criminal tackled Mrs. Aiosa, and a struggle ensued. Mr. Aiosa ran into the house to grab his machete, also from underneath the bed, and rushed back outside. The intruder was still on the ground fighting with Mrs. Aiosa. Mr. Aiosa hacked his legs repeatedly with the machete, causing large, gaping wounds. Per Pinellas County Sheriff Bob Gualtieri, "It was a very, very bloody scene."

When the police arrived, homeowner and intruder were fighting over the rifle, so the responding officers stunned the suspect with a Taser. Mr. Alcalde was transported to the hospital, but due to the severity of the wounds on his legs, he was pronounced dead upon arrival.

As extreme as it sounds, Mr. Aiosa did the right thing. He used the necessary means to protect himself, his wife and his property. Who knows what the intruder would have done had Mr. Aiosa not struck him with the machete?

Obviously, this is a great lesson in preparation. Mr. Aiosa retrieved his gun, which malfunctioned, but thankfully, he had another weapon readily available. I'm a firm believer that a gun is the best tool for self-defense, but for this very reason it's always wise to have a backup weapon. I strongly urge you to consider what other tools you could keep on hand that might save your life. Perhaps a baseball bat, a golf club, a knife or, yes, even a machete.

No Reloading Needed

Now, I'm sure that when most people think about a machete, they picture someone clearing a path through the jungle, slicing away at the undergrowth. It's true that in many tropical countries, the machete is used as an agricultural tool to clear brush, chop sugar cane, split wood and butcher animals for food. But the machete also makes a deadly improvised fighting tool. In fact, today the machete is still widely used in many parts of the world, both for agricultural purposes as well as for fighting.

Clearly, the machete has many uses, but is it realistic or necessary for you to own one? Obviously, it's not practical to carry one on you for daily self-defense, but should you keep one in your car or your home as a backup weapon? If you were in a situation such as the Aiosa couple, what would you use as a second weapon? Would a knife, for example, be a better option?

Maybe not. The biggest advantage of a machete is that it allows you to attack from farther away. For a knife to be effective, you have be very close to the threat, but a machete can cause damage from a greater distance.

Not only that, a machete's size, makes it very intimidating. An attacker would probably think twice if they saw you wielding such a large blade. A machete would also be a better weapon to defend against wild animals. And finally, it can still be used for agricultural and other nonviolent uses.

Chop Shopping

If you're interested in adding a machete to your gear, make sure you purchase a quality tool that will last. Check out the Kershaw Camp 18 Machete, which sells for around $65 on Amazon or the Ka-Bar Combat Kukri, which is about $75. There are many different sizes and shapes when it comes to machetes. Shop around to find the best option for your needs.

And just like I recommend always keeping your home-defense gun loaded, always keep your machete sharp. You never know when you may need this versatile blade to defend hearth and home.

SEAL TACTICS FOR AN ACTIVE SHOOTER SCENARIO

By Cade Courtley | *Former Navy SEAL Sniper*

In an active shooter scenario, the FIRST THING you must do is remove yourself from the immediate vicinity of the source of the gunfire, which is referred to as the "kill zone" or the "X," and do so without hesitation.

Simply put, you must do whatever it takes to get clear of the "kill zone" if you expect to have any chance of survival or retaliation. If you survive the first 10 seconds of this type of ambush, you have a much better chance of making it out alive.

Fight, Flight or Freeze

When a shooting occurs in a public place, the natural and initial response is to flee, but you need to do it with forethought. There is little time to think, but you must make your flight a calculated one so you don't turn yourself into a more visible and attractive running target.

By scrambling in panic, you could end up going nowhere worthwhile or even moving closer to the line of fire. Your flight must be for the purpose of getting clear of danger — off the "X" — and not flagging your position.

In many shootings, it's bystanders who freeze who are added to the casualty toll. Do not freeze or burrow in — react and move immediately. Hitting the floor and lying flat is usually the first thing people do instinctively, but don't just cover your head and hope for the best.

Maintain Cover

You must begin moving immediately while staying low. If you are able to dive for one of the objects you previously identified as cover, make that move while the shooter is aiming somewhere else. Get to your cover while staying as low as possible, and do it with maximum purpose.

Continue to move away from the shooter, going from cover to cover. Visualize the path you will take — this will help you set your mind to achieving small goals or little victories, as each move takes you farther from the "X."

For example, you see a potted plant 15 feet away. Your goal is to make it to that point, and thus you gain one more little victory in your overall escape plan. Once you make it to that secure cover, follow your path to get to the next one.

At first, get to covers by making small bounds. As you gain distance from the shooter, you can increase the distance you travel between covers. Start by low-crawling, but note that the farther you are away from the shooter, the faster you can move, until even sprinting if the situation warrants it.

But remember — assault rifles have a maximum effective range of 600 meters (or six football fields), and sniper rifles can hit targets even further, so if you can hear gunfire, you can be shot. You must continue to move with maximum purpose and calculated caution.

Danger Crossings

Even when places have numerous objects that afford cover or concealment, your escape route will often have open spaces, like hallways, that must be crossed. These junctions, while you are still in the line of fire, are called "danger crossings."

If you come upon a dangerous crossing, take a moment to discern a pattern in the shooting and try to move when there is a pause in the gunfire. This will generally happen when the shooter is reloading.

Even after you have cleared the kill zone, there is still a good chance of being shot. Maintain a lower profile (slightly hunched over, with your weight over the balls of your feet). Continue to move from cover to cover. Utilize shadows or "dead space" areas that are obstructed from view.

Be sure to stay at least a foot off the walls. When a bullet ricochets off a wall, it tends to travel along the wall approximately 6 inches. If your body is against the wall, you will get hit.

Exiting the Area

Once you have successfully cleared the kill zone, you need to quickly decide the best way to gain even greater distance from the shooter or ultimately exit the building.

Remember where you saw the main exits. Fire exit doors in malls and many other public buildings are required by law to be at the rear of the building or at the back of each store.

Continue to move, but take no chances, because the shooter could be following you. Put as many obstacles as you can between you and danger, by closing doors as you go or tumbling merchandise to the ground, making it harder for the shooter to trail you if that is his or her intention.

If, and only if, you feel you are at a location of relative, short-term safety, gather yourself. When you are in a defensive position that is well hidden and away from the site of the shooting, take a moment to calm yourself, but keep your mind alert.

Moving as a Group

If you find yourself among a group of other survivors, it's your job to assign responsibilities. This will help focus individuals who are still in a serious panic mode.

Maintain group cohesion by displaying a sense of purpose and by offering a reasonable game plan. Remind people: "We're in this together, and we're going to get out of this together."

Think of your group as a small unit, which can benefit by using standard, small-unit tactics and techniques employed by the military. Usually, but depending upon the scenario, it's better to move in single file, with a couple of feet or an arm's length of separation between each person.

Assign each person on the line to scout out areas that you plan to travel to during your evacuation. By using all eyes, the group can maintain 360 degrees of awareness. The leader, or the one in point position, is responsible for the front 180 degrees — or from 9 o'clock to 3 o'clock, with 12 o'clock always being the direction of travel.

The second person covers the left, the third covers the right and so on. The last person on the line scopes out the rear to alert the group of any indication that the shooter is following them.

If you are in the rear, don't walk backward; you will undoubtedly trip and fall. Instead, every three or four steps, stop momentarily and turn back. Then continue moving forward. This person is responsible for the 180 degrees (or 3 o'clock to 9 o'clock) field of the rear view.

Once you are in a defensive position that is well hidden and away from the site of the shooting, you can take a moment to calm yourself — but keep your mind alert. Now is the time for the next phase of survival.

Stop and Assess

You'll naturally think, What the hell just happened? Don't sit there and ponder this. Visualize your trigger and focus. The calmer you are, the better equipped you'll be to outthink your assailant.

To devise a trigger, you must dig deep, identify the single-most-important thing in the world to you and make a mental portrait of this image. Whatever it is, your trigger is how you ignite the will to survive. Use this memory file as the ultimate motivation to get you through life-and-death situations.

If able, call 911. Give police as much HUMINT (human intelligence) as possible, including:

- Who you are, what's happening and where

- How many shooters there are and their physical description

- What types of weapons are being used, and what special gear, such as body armor, you observed

- The shooter's skill level, ethnicity, language or accent — and anything else that may be helpful to first responders.

Next, check yourself for wounds. If you have made it this far, you are probably not critically injured. Present breathing and a heartbeat rule out serious injuries, but many times, in great stress, people will be injured and not know it.

Do a quick head-to-toe self-assessment, paying particular attention to bleeding and potential fractures. If you are with others and someone is injured, you may need to figure out a way to transport that person. Also, take a moment to remove excess or brightly colored clothing and any accessories you don't need (coat, purse or shiny jewelry).

Another part of this assessment step is to take an inventory of the resources at hand that could help you further. Is there anything that can break a window, for example, or something to act as a transportable shield? Is there a vending machine or a water cooler nearby to get some nourishment? You have just been through strenuous physical activity and significantly more effort may be required until you are safe.

Make a Plan

Success in warfare often comes down to the side that knows their battlefield better. If a mall or school turns into a battlefield, knowledge of the environment will be a great advantage.

If you are in a familiar environment, such as an office building where you work, where your previous situational awareness provides knowledge of the exits, this is the time to figure out where you are.

If you are in an unfamiliar place, like a mall, and your smartphone still works, get a map from the website, or use evacuation placards or signs posted on walls to get your bearings.

Make a decision as to the next course of action. There isn't time to second-guess yourself or for debate. Pick the best plan for evacuation and then follow it.

In an active shooter scenario, here are your three options:

1. Head to the nearest exit.
2. Run to the highest level and attempt rescue from the roof.
3. Set an ambush, recover a weapon and shoot your way out.

Even if the police are on their way, don't wait for help. You might be dead before the cavalry gets there. In making your decision to evacuate, choose the most discreet way out and the one most likely to limit your chances of meeting the shooter again. Your goal now is evacuation. However, remember that the safest evacuation route may not be the most direct. The best exit may not be the closest one.

Fight for Your Life

Sometimes, the only way out is to fight. There will be times when your only course of action might be limited to taking on the shooter. If that's the case, it's best to try to capitalize on the shooter's lack of discipline or training and attempt to set an ambush.

The best ambush is one in which your target ends up in the exact location you want them in. Essentially, walking right into your trap. Put yourself in a hidden position that the shooter must pass by. This is known as the "strike zone." Obviously, surprise is the key to a successful ambush. Additionally, you will increase the odds of your success with a weapon.

An ambush with using multiple people is the ideal form of ambush because you are able to strike from multiple positions simultaneously. Just remember that with multiple people, the odds of hurting one of your own increase. Make sure that you direct those in your party to remain at pre-established set points in the ambush to avoid casualties from "friendly fire."

If the ambush is successful and the shooter is dead — good, the mad dog is done. If the shooter is alive, make sure to bind and gag them. Never assume this is the only shooter or that the incident is now over.

Instead, be sure to:

1. Stop and listen: Do you hear any more gunfire?

2. Does the shooter you took down have a radio? If they do, they must have accomplices.

3. Attempt to get information on the number and their location from the assailant using any effective form of

coercion. Yes, I mean torture. This person was trying to kill you and other innocent people — I would use whatever means necessary to know whether or not they are acting alone.

4. Immediately inform the police of your status and pass on any useful information.

Again never assume an active shooter situation is over until law enforcement declares it.

Hands in the Air

If your efforts are successful and you've made it out alive, you surely don't want police to think you are one of the assailants. As in the military, law enforcement are taught to look at the hands of anyone first. If your hands are free of weapons, then you aren't considered a shooting threat.

When you are about to exit and think there is a high probability of encountering law enforcement, you must empty your hands. Put all weapons on the ground and away from you. Place hands high in the air and yell out, "Friendlies — we are unarmed." Keep repeating this, and do so loudly.

At this point, do exactly as you are instructed. There will be time for police to realize you are a survivor once they have you in a non-threatening position.

COMMUNICATE COVERTLY IN AN EMERGENCY

By Thomas Lavin | *Founding Partner, Global Protection and Intelligence*

A day in the life of Halle Berry is a great example of how to use nonverbal cues to communicate in an emergency. Ah, to be a celebrity.

She was traveling, being presented with an award at a film festival, doing media interviews and scheduled for a nightclub appearance — all in one day. As a protection agent, the situation was in constant flux, and we were there to protect her in every way possible.

Nonverbal codes helped Halle let us know if she felt stressed out or in danger. One concern expressed by Halle's publicist was that she had an extremely tight schedule. If we didn't stick to it, several of her obligations would have to be cut short on time.

According to her publicist, Halle was "so nice that she wouldn't say no to anyone who requested to talk to her, take a photo or sign an autograph." So I offered to be the bad guy. I have no problem intervening in situations when needed.

Even though I was also helping to manage Halle's itinerary,

my primary objective was to protect her. Nonverbal communication served to accomplish both tasks.

A Show of Hands

If Halle felt uncomfortable, she would make a fist with her thumb extended and scratch her eyebrow. This was my cue to make this person in front of her go away — immediately. If we were running out of time, Halle's publicist would fold a piece of paper with the agenda on it in half. This was my cue to interrupt and remove Halley from the event.

This is not uncommon. Protection agents, spies and undercover operatives regularly use nonverbal communication during covert operations and protection details.

Every client has slightly different requests and preferences, but all of them want to feel safe and crave some degree of comfort as they go about their day. Celebrity clients are often placed in awkward social situations, and as their protector and facilitator, I'm significantly more effective if I can communicate with them nonverbally.

The reciprocal is also true. If the client can use body language to communicate with me — especially in potentially threatening environments — I am much more successful in completing my mission objectives safely and fluidly.

A Bird(ie) in the Hand

Take golfer Lee Trevino. One event I worked for him had so many attendees expecting to meet and greet him, but Lee didn't have time to interact with every single guest. In true golf fashion, we arranged a code playing off of the golf warning "FORE."

If Lee got stuck talking to someone for too long, he simply put his arm straight down with four fingers. That was our heads-up to move the guest along.

Nonverbal codes even work with clients who don't interact with us directly. On several occasions, I've worked with Sir Richard Branson of the Virgin companies. He doesn't particularly like to have "security guys" around him. So we adapted and arranged his security in layers.

A female agent stays close, looking like an assistant, and other agents are deployed close by. The female agent needs only to signal silently to the other agents if there is a need for intervention.

You might think these are just fun, inside stories about celebrity life. But you can apply this nonverbal signaling approach to situations in your life as well.

Your Life Is in Your Hands

If you're in a situation and don't feel safe, you can use it to communicate calmly and quietly to your family members. Or if you find yourself in a dangerous situation and you're not at liberty to speak openly about your concerns.

Your child can also use it to tell you that he or she doesn't feel safe or is in danger. Or you can alert your significant other if you're annoyed at a party and just want to get away from the people in the room.

This technique will significantly increase your ability to stay safe in a variety of circumstances. I strongly recommend that you work out code words and nonverbal emergency signals in advance with your family.

Whether it's a hand sign, a body gesture, a certain stance or a noticeable facial expression — you can escape danger without saying a word.

[**Jason's note:** Tom and I run our corporate company called Global Protection and Intelligence (GPI). For more information about GPI, please visit **www.GPIagents.com**, or you can reach Tom at **tlavin@gpiagents.com**.]

A STEP-BY-STEP GUIDE TO CULTIVATING A SEAL MINDSET

By Cade Courtley | *Former Navy SEAL Sniper*

Hell Week — the defining event of BUD/S training — consists of 5½ days of cold, wet, intensely difficult operational training on fewer than four hours of sleep a night. I've witnessed men bigger, stronger and faster than I quit during one of the many hypothermic nights of Hell Week.

Why the harsh conditions? Well, this is SEAL training in its simplest form:

1. Break the individual down.
2. Build them back up, achieving a physically and mentally tougher trainee.
3. Repeat, repeat, repeat.

Even though I've seen many a soldier throw in the towel when the going gets tough, I truly believe anyone can overcome even the most brutal circumstances.

When you're born, you instantly figure out how to breathe on your own — or you die. The first time you skin your knee, you quickly realize that a boo-boo isn't going to kill you. And as you get older, life only gets harder — broken bones, broken hearts — you have to learn how to deal with it all. The instinct to survive is in all of us.

But how do you take that foundation of perseverance and forge it into a mentality that enables you to endure the worst event you could ever imagine — a nationwide blackout... a complete societal breakdown... a devastating natural disaster... or perhaps something even more catastrophic?

Well, here it is: My four-step guide to developing a SEAL mindset so you can competently and confidently handle anything life throws your way:

STEP 1: Expand Your Comfort Zone

Consider your current comfort zone — your day-to-day routine and the things that make you feel content, secure and in control. Most of your daily rituals leave you completely unprepared to deal with even the smallest disruption or discomfort — and they certainly render you incapable of handling a sudden emergency or life-threatening challenge.

Don't believe me? Try spending a day without your cellphone.

You need to push the boundaries of your comfort zone regularly. Here are some easy examples. Try climbing the stairs instead of taking the elevator or adding an additional mile to your morning run. Or this might mean one less beer, forgoing dessert or waiting an hour more before eating dinner. These daily victories will build up and ultimately expand your comfort zone.

When I was younger, I felt bulletproof — but it's hard to stay hard. So I blast the water on cold for the last minute of my shower as a friendly little reminder not to get complacent.

STEP 2: Make a Fear List

Fear can be healthy. Everyone has it. Fear can make you alert and keep you alive, as long as you never let it take control.

I believe your brain is your strongest asset — but it only works if you work it. Start by making a list of five things that make you nervous or scared. It could be heights, fighting, small spaces or open water. Then starting confronting the fears on your list one by one.

Let's take public speaking, for example. I've seen some of the toughest guys in the world turn into gummy bears when required to speak in front of a group of people. If this is also a fear of yours, create a five-minute presentation on something you are familiar with. Rehearse it several times until ultimately you are ready to organize a group of people — be it your co-workers or an assemblage at a public event — and give your presentation.

There! You've just confronted and conquered an item on your fear list! Move on to the next one and see how quickly you can remove other fear-induced limits.

SEAL training aims to push people to their very limits in order to build a level of confidence so that when we are "in the sh*t," we don't let our fear get the best of us.

STEP 3: Create a Trigger

One of the most important things you need to do to create a SEAL mindset is to devise a trigger. In order to do this, you must dig deep and identify the single-most-important thing in the world to you. Make a mental portrait of this image.

This is the thing that makes you want to live, no matter what. For some, the trigger will be the image of their children, a spouse or elderly parent. Whatever it is, your trigger is how you ignite the will to survive. Use this memory file as the ultimate motivation to get you through anything life throws at you.

To maintain the effectiveness of your trigger, you should save it for only the direst situations. But when it comes to life or death, PULL THAT TRIGGER!

STEP 4: Violence of Action

In the SEALs, the phrase "violence of action" refers to the application of complete and unrestricted use of speed, strength, surprise and aggression to achieve total domination against an enemy in an adversarial situation.

Humans have three acute stress responses when confronted with a potentially life-threatening situation: fight, flight or freeze. The best response will always depend on the situation.

To freeze in a life-or-death moment is rarely a desirable reaction. If you are in public and hear gunshots or explosions, freezing will almost certainly mean serious injury or death.

If the situation merits fighting, you better be ready to go all out. Remember: violence of action — complete and unrestricted.

You may not have years of special ops experience — but if you follow the four steps above, you'll be mentally prepared to come out on top in a life-threatening situation.

Never give up — BE A SURVIVOR, NOT A STATISTIC!

CHAPTER 5:

FIREARMS COMBAT: TACTICS FOR LETHAL RESPONSE

THE ULTIMATE GUIDE TO HOME DEFENSE GUNS

"It's currently 11 p.m. here in Vegas on Saturday. Julie and I usually go to bed around 10. We were sound asleep when I heard four (it's crazy that I can tell you exactly how many) gunshots in front of our home.

"I immediately jumped out of bed and retrieved my handgun from the safe. I ran and grabbed both girls and passed them to Julie and set up a chokepoint at the top of my stairs. I proceeded to clear my house, working my way to the front door. As I carefully looked out the window, I could see cars and people scrambling everywhere outside. Julie was on the phone with 911.

"The people who live directly across the street were having a birthday party. Apparently, there was a drive-by shooting targeting their home. There were four shell casings in the middle of the road directly in front of my home. Our street was blocked off, with two helicopters above.

"It is amazing how quickly you react from your training. I was out of bed and had my gun safe open before Julie even realized what had happened. I have no doubt that if there'd been someone breaking into my home, I would have stopped them at the stairs."

A close friend of mine, who happens to be a former law enforcement officer, sent me this heart-pounding email after hearing the sound of gunshots in front of his home.

My friend did everything correct that night. If an intruder had entered his home, his quick action would have likely saved his family.

But this would not have been possible had he not owned a firearm.

If you don't yet own a gun — and think it's high time to get one for home defense purposes — where do you start? After all, there are dozens to choose from. Which is the best one?

Here are three steps to take before making a purchase.

Step One: Choosing the Gun for You

The first step is to decide whether you want a handgun, rifle, or shotgun. Depending on your circumstances, one will be more practical than another.

For instance, my home defense gun is a handgun, a Sig Sauer P226. My friend in the story above also uses a handgun, a Glock 19. I'd recommend either model if you're looking for a handgun.

The reason I use a handgun is because I have three kids under the age of 4 and I want to make sure my gun is secure on my nightstand in a rapid-access safe. Although they do make safes for shotguns and rifles, I haven't found one I

My very own Sig Sauer P226, which I rely on for home defense.

like that would allow me the quick access that my handgun safe does.

I also believe it's easier to clear a home using a handgun.

Say, for example, you awake one night to hear someone breaking into your home. You may be forced to confront the intruder, in which case a handgun is ideal.

With a handgun, you don't have to worry as much about knocking into walls and drawing attention to yourself or turning the corner and having the intruder grab the end of your gun — all of which are more likely with a long gun like a rifle or shotgun.

"There is no 'right' gun. You need to take the time to figure out the perfect gun for you."

But if in this situation you only had to protect you and your spouse, you would want to stay put in your bedroom. In which case, you may prefer a shotgun or rifle over a handgun.

[Fight or Flight? A quick aside... If you and your spouse are alone in the house and hear a break in, it's generally best to hunker down there, secure the door, call 911, and wait for the police to arrive.

However, if you have children or an elderly parent in the house, you shouldn't leave them unprotected. In that case, you'd want to leave your bedroom and clear the home, to ensure that the intruder doesn't get to them before you do.]

My favorite shotgun is the Remington 870. It's a pump-action shotgun, the kind you've probably seen in the movies dozens of times. It's built like a tank and is very easy to operate.

If I were using this gun for home defense, the shells I would use would be 00 (double-aught) buckshot. A shell of double-aught buckshot sends nine lead balls downrange, which is something you would not want to be on the wrong end of!

If you do opt for a shotgun, please disregard the horrible myth that all you have to do is "rack the shotgun" to send the intruder fleeing. Yes, the noise is scary and intimidating, but you cannot let your guard down on account of the sound — you have to be prepared to use the gun to defend yourself.

If you're not a fan of handguns or shotguns, then a rifle may be right for you.

The major benefit of a rifle is that it holds a lot of ammunition. So unless you live in a state that isn't gun friendly, you can have a 30-round magazine ready to go. Criminals tend to travel in packs, so if you had to fend off three or four intruders, a rifle would be ideal.

The rifle I like best is the AR-15. You can put plenty of accessories on it, such as lights and lasers, so you can easily see any threats in the dark. If you're going to get one, though, definitely buy from a quality manufacturer, such as Colt or Rock River Arms.

The bottom line is, when it comes to choosing a gun for home defense, there is no "right" gun.

You need to take the time to figure out the perfect home defense gun for you… which leads me to step two.

Step Two: Give It a Test Run

Step two is a fun one: You need to go to your local shooting range to try out whichever gun you're thinking about buying.

I don't care what your spouse, friend, or guy behind the gun counter says, you should never, ever buy a gun for home defense until you've put several rounds through it.

After all, this is the gun that could save your life one day, so you need to feel comfortable holding and shooting it — and the only way to be sure of that is to get out there and test it.

Step Three: Practice Makes Perfect

OK, so you've tested and purchased your new gun. Now comes the final, critical step: You need to train with it by taking a live-fire course and practicing a dry run in your home.

To attend a live-fire training course, you can go to a national firearms school such as Gunsite Academy (with locations in Arizona, Indiana, Tennessee, Virginia, and Washington) or Front Sight (located outside of Las Vegas). You can also do a quick Internet search to find a local firearms trainer. There is one in almost every city in the country. Depending on what gun you purchased, you'll be able to take a handgun, rifle, or shotgun course to learn (or further increase your) firearm skills.

Gunsight Academy: **www.gunsite.com**
Front Sight: **https://www.frontsight.com/**

To practice a dry run, make sure your gun is empty and triple-check that there's no ammunition in it.

Then secure the gun however you plan to keep it (in a safe, in your closet, etc.) Next, walk through the motions. Lie in your bed and pretend you hear someone trying to kick in your front door.

Immediately hop out of bed and arm yourself, timing how quickly you were able to get your gun.

You need to be able to access it in less than 10 seconds, so if it takes you longer, you'll need to pick a new place to store it.

By taking the steps above, you'll ensure that if the day ever comes when you hear someone smashing in your door, you'll be fully prepared to defend yourself.

THE ONE GUN MISSING FROM YOUR COLLECTION

Today, I'm going to tell you why I think your gun collection is incomplete.

This is assuming you already have a good pistol and (possibly) an AR-15.

Look, the AR-15 is a GREAT rifle, and it will get the job done for 99.9% of what you need. You can use it for everything from home defense at close-quarters battle (CQB) distances all the way to making accurate, effective hits at 500 yards or even more, depending on your skill.

That's why I think it's the perfect first or second gun to own. With a midsize fighting pistol like a Glock 19 or Smith & Wesson M&P (suitable for concealed carry) and an AR-15, you have almost all your bases covered.

Almost.

The fact of the matter is that beyond 500 yards, while you CAN make effective hits with the AR-15, the 5.56 cartridge starts to run out of steam.

If you want something bigger than the standard AR-15 in 5.56, then I believe there's no better caliber than the .308/7.62x51 mm NATO.

Why I Think the .308 Is One of the Best All-Around Rifle Round Choices

The fact is that the .308/7.62x51 mm NATO is a great full-power rifle round. Here's just a few reasons why...

1. It has excellent terminal ballistics. To quote leading ballistics expert Dr. Gary Roberts (emphasis mine):

   While snipers like to talk of head shots, there are an inordinate number of torso hits in the law enforcement forensic literature. As posted above, ASA indicates 47% of sniper shots were to the head (104/219), while 53% were to the body (115/219). As a result, law enforcement sniper bullets need to exhibit terminal performance which can consistently induce rapid incapacitation with shots to the torso, as well as the head. If you use a 5.56 mm, what happens if you have to shoot through a window or into a vehicle? How about if the bad guy has something over his chest — perhaps AK mags? The 5.56 mm is suddenly not looking so good.

2. It's an accurate rifle caliber. Here's a bit of history that was new to me, from SniperCountry.com, comparing the .308's inherent accuracy with the .30-06 (emphasis mine):

   Let's go back to when the .30-06 and .308 were the only cartridges allowed in NRA match rifle competitions. In comparing accuracy between the .308 and .30-06, folks who used each quickly agreed on one thing: .308s were two–three times more accurate than the .30-06.

   Most top high-power shooters feel the main reason the .308 is much more accurate than the .30-06 is its shorter, fatter case promotes more uniform and gentle push on the bullet due to a higher loading density (less air space) and a more easily uniformly ignitable powder charge.

3. It is a very, VERY popular cartridge. The best thing, to me, about the .308 is that it is a super-popular caliber.

Look, I worry about things like gun grabbers in government making it hard to get ammunition... "grid down" situations in which it may be hard to get ammo... or the government scaring millions of Americans so that ammunition becomes super expensive.

So I don't want a "special snowflake" caliber.

"I don't want a 'special snowflake' caliber. I like to stick to a few calibers and stack them deep so I know I have plenty of stores of ammunition."

I'm not even that much of a gun or caliber collector. I like to stick to a few calibers and stack them deep so I know I have plenty ammunition stored for practice and for if (God forbid!) I find myself in a crisis situation.

That's why I like the NATO standard calibers. They're VERY plentiful because they're used by armies and governments all over the world. The 9 mm, 5.56 and 7.62x51 mm are all NATO rounds.

Combine that with an ample stash of 7.62x39 (if you have an AK-pattern rifle) and you've got the same ammunition stores of all the world's armies. In short, there's almost ALWAYS going to be ammunition somewhere for you to use.

Sure, I might be paranoid or whatever... but it's something to think about.

Also, because it's so popular, there is plenty of commercial support. That means tons of different loads, bullets, weights, grains, etc., are available for you to use.

Lastly, because it's so popular, it's a GREAT choice for hunting and will take down practically any medium or big game in North America. 'Nuff said on that, as the .308 is a proven hunting round.

So if a .308 will do 80–90% of whatever any other "full power" rifle round will do, why not go with the most plentiful, popular, easy-to-find and commercially supported ammunition there is?

Semi-Auto AR-Style .308 or a Bolt-Action .308?

Specifically, I don't think there's any better .308 — especially in semi-auto form — than the AR-style .308 rifle.

I'll even go as far as to say that I believe the advent of reliable, accurate, ergonomic AR-style .308 semi-auto rifles make the bolt-action sniper rifle somewhat obsolete. At least in .308.

Why?

"The .308 is a GREAT choice for hunting and will take down practically any medium or big game in North America."

Because a semi-auto .308 is so much more versatile than a bolt-action .308 if we're talking about self-defense or grid-down, SHTF type situations…

Even if all you had was ONE AR-308 rifle, then that one rifle could be put into use just like an AR-15 (at close-quarter battle distances, midrange, large volume of suppressive fire, etc.) and used for long-range "sniping"-type roles too.

It's that versatile.

And it seems like many of the U.S. snipers over in "the sandbox" are moving in this direction too.

This Is the "Golden Age" of AR-308s

The truth is that for a long time, compared with the AR-15, the AR-10/AR-308 market was known for producing not-very-reliable rifles.

But in the last few years, that has really changed.

Now more and more manufacturers are coming out with .308 caliber rifles, and they're becoming more popular by the day.

Should You Get an AR-308?

Only you know if you may need one, but I think it's a good choice if you want to round out your collection.

Again, I think an AR-15 in .223 and a midsize concealed-carry-appropriate handgun like a Glock 19 are the perfect "first guns," but an AR-308 may be the perfect "next gun" if you want to do some midrange to long-range shooting and move up to a heavier caliber for things like hunting.

THE BEST ACCESSORIES FOR YOUR FIREARM

If you've ever gone to a gun store and purchased a firearm or just picked up a gun magazine, you have undoubtedly been inundated with the many, many gun accessories you can add to your firearm.

The reality is there are some people who spend more on gun accessories than they do on the gun itself. Which begs the question are any of these accessories really necessary?

The short answer is yes — as long as you purchase the right accessories.

Accessories for your gun are worth every penny if you buy ones that actually make a difference in performance. Don't waste your money on an add-on that has no functional purpose.

With that in mind, here are the most important gun accessories I recommend for your firearm:

Tactical Light: This is the No. 1 gun accessory I recommend. If you wake up in the middle of the night from the sound of someone in your house, you'll need a light to investigate. Most people will just grab a flashlight in this scenario, which is fine.

But if you decide to go this route, I encourage you to practice shooting while holding your flashlight so you get used to having only one hand on the gun instead of two. You can also buy a tactical light/laser combo that will help you aim in the dark, but like anything gun related, these gadgets can be expensive, and they're not something you want to go cheap on

Holsters: Whenever you purchase a new gun, you should buy a holster at the same time. Owning multiple holsters is beneficial for a few reasons. First, you need to make sure you always have a holster that works with the clothes you're wearing. For example, the holster I wear with my jeans wouldn't work with the shorts I wear on my morning run.

Second, you need to have a holster that best fits your lifestyle. What I mean is if you're always going to carry concealed, you might want an inside-the-waistband holster. However, if you live on a large piece of property and regularly patrol it, you may find that an outside-the-waistband holster is more comfortable and convenient

Sling: When it comes to long guns, I believe a sling is a must-have accessory. A sling makes it easier to carry your gun while hunting or patrolling. Plus, a sling often makes it easier to transition from a long gun to a pistol in an emergency. Don't forget, if you buy a sling, you will have to purchase swivels to attach the sling to your gun, but this accessory is well worth the price

Extra Magazines: I recommend everyone have — at the absolute minimum — three magazines for each gun they own. The fact is if you are in a bug-out situation, you should have all three mags loaded and ready to go. Even if you just keep your guns at home, you should keep your extra mags ready. If, heaven forbid, multiple intruders break into your home, you'll be glad you're prepared. In addition to having extra magazines, remember to practice reloading them so you won't miss a beat in an emergency

Gun Cleaning Kit: A basic gun cleaning kit isn't expensive, and while it's certainly not the sexiest gun accessory, it's one that's often overlooked. Keeping your gun clean and well oiled is critical to ensure it functions properly when you need it. Now, I know people who say they've shot thousands of rounds with a Glock without having to clean it. While that may be true, the fact is grime and dirt will build up eventually, so always remember to clean your gun regularly.

Some people spend thousands of dollars to add all kind of bells and whistles to their firearms, but I'm a big believer in the idea that a quality self-defense gun doesn't need a lot of fancy add-ons.

One final note: No matter what, please don't do a trigger job on your self-defense gun. You don't want to find yourself facing a prosecutor trying to explain why your gun has a two-pound trigger.

FIVE KEY FACTORS OF THE PERFECT POCKET PISTOL

By Larry Ellis | *Hunting & Firearms Expert*

According to the latest study by the Crime Prevention Research Center, "Last year, the number of [concealed carry] permit holders grew by a record 1.83 million. This is more than the previous record increase of 1.73 million, set just the year before."

Clearly, every year more and more Americans are purchasing firearms for concealed carry, which is why pocket firearms are becoming increasingly popular.

The truth is pocket guns are great — they're comfortable to carry, and you can conceal them in all types of clothing, which makes them easy to access. In fact, one of my favorite guns for everyday carry is my Sig Sauer P238, which I keep loaded with Speer Gold Dot ammo.

Since pocket guns are becoming so popular, here are five factors to consider when selecting the right pocket pistol for you:

Sights: Some pocket guns don't come with sights, but I highly recommend buying one that does. You also might want to consider purchasing a laser sight for your pocket gun. Remember, it's pointless to carry a firearm if you can never hit your target.

Recoil: There is a common misconception that a smaller gun will have less recoil than a larger gun. The truth is exactly the opposite — smaller guns usually have more recoil than larger guns of the same caliber. This is why you should test a pocket gun at the range before you buy it. The Sig P238 I carry, for instance, has significantly less recoil than the original Ruger LCP.

Speed: One of the biggest advantages of a pocket pistol is that you can draw it quickly. It's perfectly natural to walk down the street with your hand in your pocket; if something happens, you will be ready to defend yourself. That being said, think about any external parts that could snag on your clothes. Some pocket pistols feature an internal hammer, like the Smith & Wesson 642.

Holster: If you carry a pocket gun, you should use a holster that changes the outline of the gun. Some people would be very alarmed if they saw the distinct outline of a gun in your pocket. Plus, you don't want to always want people to know you're carrying. Make sure the holster you choose stays in your pocket when you draw (you don't want it to come out with the gun). My favorite pocket holsters are the plastic holsters made of Kydex.

Ammo: There are a lot of different options when it comes to ammo, but I recommend carrying self-defense rounds in your pocket gun. As I mentioned, I prefer Speer Gold Dot rounds. Another great round for your pocket gun is Hornady Critical Defense ammunition.

If you decide a pocket pistol is the way to go, keep these factors in mind and you'll have no problem choosing the perfect gun for you.

FIVE MISTAKES TO AVOID WHEN SELECTING A HUNTING FIREARM

Before you consider purchasing a firearm for hunting, it's important that you do some homework and build your knowledge base. It is highly recommended that you attend a hunting education or safety course so you can learn the basics and how to get started. Novice hunters are encouraged to learn from an experienced hunter through an apprentice licensing program. After you've got a good grasp of the fundamentals, you can proceed with purchasing your own firearm for hunting.

If this is your very first firearm purchase, however, there are several buying considerations to take into account. Selecting a reliable, quality firearm requires a little background knowledge so you can make the right investment. Amateur hunters tend to make mistakes that can end not only in poor shopping decisions, but also in potential safety issues. This article aims to present the five most common mistakes people make when selecting a firearm for hunting.

"Amateur hunters tend to make mistakes that can end in potential safety issues."

1. Caliber

By far, one of the most frequent mistakes that beginners make when getting their first firearm is choosing the wrong caliber for hunting. Even though there is not an ideal caliber for hunting in general, or for a specific animal, there is a range that you should take into consideration.

This means that you need to know the difference between a .17 HMR and a 577 Nitro Express, as well as when and how to use them. An infographic created by Hunter Ed is a quick, easy reference that shows you how to choose the right caliber depending on the animals you will hunt:

- Varmint hunting: .22 Mag, .22 Long or .17 HMR are all suitable for hunting small animals
- Deer Hunting: You can look into .22-250, .223 or .243 Win for hunting deer
- Big Game: For hunting bears or elk, choose .338, .300 Win Mag or 7mm Rem Mag.

2. Ammunition

Another significant factor you need to remember when selecting a firearm for hunting is your choice of ammunition. First of all, not all ammunition works for all types of firearms, so you need to ask what ammunition is suitable for the gun you want to buy.

Choosing the proper type of ammunition involves critical safety aspects. If you select the wrong kind, you'll waste money on ammunition you can't use, and you'll be putting yourself and the people around you in danger. Always double-check with the company you plan on buying your firearm from to see if the ammunition you get on the side is compatible with your choice of gun.

3. Scope

Most beginner hunters get excited when buying their first rifle and tend to forget about this essential component: the scope. You could spend a considerable amount on your rifle but not get the right scope and ruin your hunting experience from the beginning.

Optics are just as important as the firearm you choose and a basic part of the firearm selection process that many tend to overlook. The best way to avoid this mistake is to organize your budget in advance with both the firearm and the scope in mind.

4. Investment

Speaking of budget, this leads us to another common mistake when buying hunting firearms. Those who lack hunting experience might end up purchasing a firearm that is way over their budget. This results in not having enough money left over to spend on accessories (like the scope as we discussed above) or for carrying out the practice afterward.

After all, hunting licenses and permits also cost money. You should always weigh your options and check out various sources before buying your hunting firearm from a store. If you decide to purchase your hunting firearm online, it is recommended that you search for a particular model through at least three sources to see where you can get the best deal.

5. Complexity

Last but not least, complexity tends to be a trending mistake among amateur hunters. This mistake can go one of two ways: A hunter might purchase a firearm that's too complex for his or her level of training and knowledge at that time, or they might get a gun that's too basic and won't meet their needs. Be aware of your skill level as a hunter and choose the complexity of your firearm accordingly.

To avoid these five crucial mistakes, I strongly encourage you once again to spend time with an experienced hunter learning the ins and outs of the sport. Visit several gun ranges to try out different weapons, and don't be afraid to shop around. You'll enjoy a better hunting experience with a quality firearm, so take the time to choose wisely.

10 THINGS TO LOOK FOR IN A QUALITY FIREARMS INSTRUCTOR

I realize most people don't have access to the same training that I did when I was in the CIA. But there are plenty of exceptional instructors throughout the U.S. that anyone can train with.

I'd say 98% of these instructors are good, honest folks who know what they're doing. However, since the training from these instructors can literally mean the difference between life and death, you need to avoid the 2% who could put your life in jeopardy because they don't know what the heck they're doing.

To help you weed out the careless, inexperienced or down-right dangerous demonstrators out there, here are 10 questions to ask when you're looking for a quality firearms instructor:

1. What's their employment background? What did the instructor do for a living — or what do they currently do? Are they a former cop, ex-FBI, ex-Secret Service agent, ex-CIA or former military? The training connected with this type of background is far superior to that of the average person, and they'll also be able to share real-life experiences with you. In other words, you want someone who doesn't just

spout theory, but knows what they're talking about from firsthand experience.

2. What's their training background? The groups I mentioned above have trained with some of the best instructors in the world at state-of-the-art facilities. However, even if a particular instructor has years of experience in the military or a government agency, they should still have plenty of extracurricular firearms training.

A true instructor never stops learning, and there are private firearms schools all over the country that anyone can attend. If I were you, I would avoid any instructor who doesn't train often and can't rattle off the schools and trainings they've attended.

3. Are they NRA certified? This is crucial because then you know they at least went through the NRA instructor class and have been taught proper instruction and safety techniques. This ensures you don't sign up to learn from someone who doesn't know the first thing about firearms.

4. Do they guarantee their training? This is a topic I'm sure will make more than one instructor a little squeamish. Too bad! If they truly believe they are offering the best training to their students, there is absolutely no reason why they shouldn't offer a 100% money-back guarantee. Why would you want to train with someone who doesn't stand behind their product?

5. Are they friendly, open-minded and non-militaristic? Do you know this type of instructor? The one who says, "This is my way and there's no other way to do it"? Or the instructor who finds it necessary to intimidate people to stroke his own ego? If you haven't, just visit your local gun shop — I've met many of these types working there.

When looking for an instructor, you want someone who is humble and willing to learn from others, as well as share their own wisdom.

6. Do they emphasize safety? A firearms instructor should make safety paramount. If the instructor doesn't cover the four basic safety rules or makes light of safety in ANY manner, walk the other way. There's a video floating around of an instructor who had a cameraman down range next to the targets,taking pictures of his students as they were shooting. I won't waste your time discussing the stupidity of this. I don't care if the instructor is a former sniper or Rambo himself: If they violate safety protocol, they should be avoided.

7. Speaking of Rambo… You want an instructor who lives in real world and trains his students for the practical scenarios they may encounter. An overdramatic instructor who tells students they shouldn't leave their house without wearing bulletproof vests, carrying 12 different guns on them and having a bazooka in the trunk should also be avoided. You laugh, but I'm sure you've seen some of these hyperbolic trainers.

8. Do they listen to you and genuinely care about you? When you ask an instructor about the first gun you should purchase, do they listen to you and to the reasons you want to buy a gun? Or do they pontificate about their preferred model? "Everybody should own a Glock, just buy a Glock and you'll be fine." Firearms needs vary greatly from person to person. Look for an instructor that understands this.

9. Do they walk the walk? I admit, this trait is difficult to get a feel for. But it's important to know whether an instructor believes in their training. If you ran into them,

would they be carrying a concealed firearm? Or do they just teach classes, yet never carry themselves? Obviously, I'd like to learn from someone who lives by what they teach.

10. Can they teach? Pretty obvious, right? I know a number of excellent marksmen with incredible self-defense knowledge who are terrible teachers. You need someone who is articulate and able to explain why we do the things we do. If an instructor loses patience with someone for asking a few innocent questions, they probably shouldn't be teaching.

As I mentioned, most instructors should fit this bill, but this handy list of questions will help you avoid the 2% who don't. Plus, it will give you good laugh when you inevitably encounter some knucklehead instructor who thinks they're training ninjas instead of the average American who just wants to protect themselves in everyday America.

REVOLVER VS. SEMI-AUTOMATIC

I'm often asked which type of handgun is better, a revolver or a semi-automatic? Well, the truth is there are pros and cons to both — it all depends on which one you're more comfortable using. So allow me to break down the facts to help you decide which type firearm fits your needs best.

Revolver Raves

First, let's go over some of the reasons people prefer revolvers for self-defense:

1. They're easy to fire. A typical revolver has a cylinder that rotates with each fired shot. There is no need to feed the next round, and each round is separate, so there is no way for the rounds to jam or double-feed. Anyone who shoots often has at some point experienced an ammunition malfunction or feeding issue with a semi-auto. While it's not something that happens all the time, it does happen. And if you don't know how to fix it, you could be in trouble

2. A revolver is simple to reload. It's easy to reload a revolver, because all you have to do is push the cylinder out and remove the expended cartridges. Then reload each chamber with fresh ammo and push the cylinder back into place. It's not exactly a quick process, but it's very basic. Reloading a semi-automatic weapon can be difficult for some people, because first, you have to pull back the slide to chamber a round. Someone who is elderly or has weak hands may not be able to manipulate the slide very well, which is another reason to consider a revolver

3. They require less maintenance. I'm a big believer in keeping your guns clean and properly oiled. Even if you don't shoot often, it's important to make sure you oil your semi-auto to keep the contact points lubricated. While this is especially important for a semi-auto, it's less important for a revolver. Now, don't get me wrong, I'm not saying you never need to clean or oil a revolver, but you don't need to do it as often as with a semi-automatic.

When semi-autos first arrived on the scene, most people agreed that revolvers were more reliable and dismissed them. But over the years, handgun manufacturers have improved the durability and functionality of semi-automatic weapons.

Semi-Auto Advantages

Now here are the top three reasons to consider a semi-auto:

1. They have a higher capacity. Most revolvers have a five- or six-shot capacity. However, semi-autos have a much wider range of magazine capacity — usually anywhere from 7–19 rounds depending on the firearm. Obviously, if I was in a gunfight, I would rather have more rounds. In fact, when police departments around the country began switching to semi-autos, one of the biggest reasons was so officers had more rounds in the event of a shootout

2. They're quicker to reload. There are people who will tell you that they can reload a revolver faster than you can reload a semi-auto. And someone who has practiced reloading a revolver can probably do it pretty quickly. However, the average person will likely always be faster at reloading a semi-automatic than a revolver

3. They have better accuracy. The majority of people will be more accurate shooting a semi-automatic than a revolver because of the more modern design. Most semi-autos have less recoil and muzzle jump than revolvers. Also, semi-autos tend to have a smoother trigger pull than revolvers, and when you combine these factors, they usually allow for better accuracy.

When it comes down to which type of handgun is better, it really depends on personal preference. If you suffer from arthritis and can't pull the slide back on a semi-auto, then you might want to consider a revolver. However, if you carry concealed often, you probably want a semi-auto that can hold more rounds.

To figure out which side of the fence you're on, I recommend going to your local gun range. Rent a few different guns of each type and see what works best for you.

BE SAFE AND CONFIDENT AT THE RANGE WITH THESE 10 TIPS

Clayton Brumby of Sarasota, Florida, is a gun owner and father of seven. He has always enjoyed target shooting and keeps multiple guns in his home for self-defense. At an appropriate age, he has taught each of his children gun safety and regularly takes them to the shooting range.

On July 3, 2016, Clayton and three of his sons went to the local Sarasota gun range. Clayton was shooting his new .22 semi-auto pistol in the end lane. He and his boys were having a great time.

Then Clayton fired a round and the shell casing bounced off the wall and fell down the back of his shirt. He reached back to get the hot casing out of his shirt, pointing the gun behind him. While his gun was pointed in this direction, Clayton accidentally fired a round. In gun lingo, this is called an accidental discharge, or "AD" for short.

Clayton thought the round went into the ceiling, until one of his sons yelled, "Dad, Stephen's been shot!" Immediately, Clayton looked at his 14-year-old son Stephen and realized he had shot his son while trying to fish the piece of hot brass out of his shirt.

A Parent's Worst Nightmare

Tragically, Stephen passed away that afternoon at Sarasota Memorial Hospital. The bullet had pierced Stephen's jugular vein, causing irreparable damage. Doctors were able to keep Stephen alive only until his mother arrived at the hospital to give her son a kiss goodbye. Sadly, Clayton will have to live the rest of his life with the pain of knowing he made a mistake that took his son's life. I'm sure there is not a minute that goes by in which Clayton doesn't think about his son. As a parent myself, I can't even begin to imagine his grief.

There is no question that this was a horrific accident. Clayton simply wasn't thinking when he reacted to the hot casing the way he did. Unfortunately, hot casings are common when handling firearms and something every shooter needs to know how to deal with.

Be Safe, Not Sorry

Since safety is the No. 1 priority at any gun range, here are some rules and etiquette tips that will help keep you and your fellow shooters safe at your next — or first — range visit. Pay attention to the first four tips, which are critical safety rules that everyone needs to follow:

1. Always treat every gun as if it is loaded.

2. Never point a gun at anything you are not willing to destroy.

3. Always keep your finger off the trigger until you're on target and ready to shoot.

4. Always be sure of your target and what is behind it.

5. When you put your gun down, it should be empty, with the slide locked back and the gun pointed down range.

6. Never pick up someone else's gun unless you ask their permission first.

7. If you have any questions, ask the range safety officer. Don't bother another shooter. You don't want to distract another shooter who may be firing.

8. When transporting your firearms, make sure they are secure. Which means always carry your guns to and from the range in a bag or case, never in your hand.

9. Don't hover over, coach or correct other shooters unless they ask you for help (which they shouldn't). In other words, don't be "that guy" who thinks he's a commando and tries to give everyone advice when nobody wants it.

10. Always clean up after yourself at the range. Most importantly, pick up all your shell casings and never leave empty ammo boxes or trash lying around.

As I mentioned, safety is the biggest concern. By being familiar with the rules specific to your local range and keeping these basic etiquette tips in mind, you'll be able to have an enjoyable time without any awful accidents.

CHAPTER 6:

DISASTER PREPAREDNESS: HOW TO SURVIVE ANY CRISIS

HOW TO ENDURE A BLACKOUT

People living on the East Coast will no doubt remember the severe snowstorms of 2010 that many dubbed "Snowmageddon."

Because of these storms, for the first time in history, the federal government shut down for four straight days.

However, I never got a day off and still headed into work each day, as did most of my colleagues at the CIA. Even though there were several feet of snow on the ground and many people had lost power at home, the agency continued to run as usual.

This is possible because the agency has a thorough Continuity of Operations (COOP) plan. In other words, the agency is prepared to continue with business as usual despite snowstorms or any other type of event that may cause a blackout in the area.

While you and I certainly don't have the budget of the CIA, that doesn't mean you can't operate as normal when a storm knocks out the power.

The truth is the chances of experiencing a blackout at home are rather high. In winter, all it takes is an ice-covered tree falling on a power line to knock the power out for a few hours or, if you're unlucky, even a few days.

But on the more severe end of things, a blackout could last weeks if a terrorist attack were to damage a major portion of the power grid.

Either way, whether it's a few hours or a few weeks, here's how to ensure you survive (and stay as comfortable as possible). Below, I'd like to share with you my family's COOP for our own home in case we have a blackout.

We'll cover my most reliable and efficient light sources, food storage planning, how to keep warm in an extended winter outage, and a few bonus topics.

Lighting Basics

A simple thing you can do is to have flashlights placed strategically throughout your house. My family has one on every level of our home, in our glove boxes, and on our nightstands. A neat flashlight that I like is called the Blocklite, which is a small light you pop on top of a 9V battery.

Blocklite: **http://amzn.to/2xOxzen**

These lights are plenty bright for getting around the house, you can carry them in your pocket, and they're inexpensive, so if you lose one, it's not a big deal.

In addition to the Blocklite, I do have several tactical flashlights from companies such as SureFire and Fenix around my home. However, these tactical flashlights are only for self-defense purposes, because they eat batteries, so I'm not using them to wander around my home in the dark doing normal tasks. I'm using them in the event of a home invasion, which is why these also sit on my nightstand every night.

SureFire: **http://bit.ly/2f2tKL9**
Fenix: **www.fenix-store.com**

Since you don't only want to rely on flashlights for light, I also use a Coleman propane lantern. I use this lantern for outdoor tasks, and I'm a huge fan of propane-run devices, which I'll expand on in a moment.

"At a minimum, I would have a 30-day supply of food and a one week supply of water."

Of course, there are other ways to provide light, such as candles, but if you have multiple flashlights, batteries, and propane lanterns, you'll be in good shape.

Extreme Long Life Batteries

Once you've picked up several flashlights, don't forget to stock up on batteries. While you can get batteries almost anywhere. I prefer the Panasonic Eneloop rechargeable batteries.

Panasonic Eneloop: **http://amzn.to/2xOxVSf**

These batteries come pre-charged from the factory so you can immediately put them to use. Also, they can be recharged up to 2,100 times, which is a huge money saver, since you're not constantly buying new batteries for all of your flashlights and other gear.

Keeping Warm & Well Fed

If a blackout occurs in the summer, keeping warm obviously won't be a problem, but if it occurs this weekend, you've got to be able to provide heat to your home.

One of my favorite ways to do this is the Mr. Heater Buddy portable propane heaters. I talked about these heaters in last month's issue of the Laissez Faire Letter (which you can read here. In that article, you'll also be able to read about one of my favorite sleeping bags for keeping warm.)

In a blackout, you're also going to want to continue to eat well to stay healthy and keep up your strength. This is why I recommend food and water storage. I personally have a one-year supply of food and a 30-day supply of water in my home.

I realize not everyone can or wants to store this much food, so at a minimum, I would have a 30-day supply of food and a one week supply of water.

My food storage comes from the LDS Cannery (from the Mormon church), and any person of any religion can order from the LDS Cannery. It's the cheapest place to get food storage, and there might be a cannery near you to pick up the food. If not, you can just order it online. As far as my water storage, I use the seven-gallon Aqua-Tainer jugs that can be stacked on top of one another.

LDS Cannery: **www.providentliving.lds.org**

For cooking my food, I rely on propane stoves, more specifically, the Coleman one-burner stove. If you're looking for a stove with more burners, check out the Stansport two-burner propane stove, which I also own. Keep in mind, unlike the propane heater I mentioned earlier, these stoves are not designed to be used indoors.

Coleman stove: **http://amzn.to/2xOtFCA**
Stansport: **http://amzn.to/2vL7nUO**

The Need for Power

So far, I've mentioned several smaller items to help you survive a blackout, but now let's get to something bigger — a generator.

The generator I own does not run on gas or diesel but is a propane generator. Gas or diesel will provide more "juice," but I don't need to run every appliance in my house at the same time. I simply want to keep the fridge going and be able to use a few small appliances.

But don't get me wrong, the propane generator I own is still plenty powerful and is nothing to scoff at.

"If everything else is down, a landline is the best way to call 911 or anyone else you need to contact.

The reason I got a propane generator is because you can

essentially store propane indefinitely and it won't go bad.

If you've ever tried to store gasoline for a long period of time, then you know what a pain in the butt it can be. Plus, most of us don't want gallons and gallons of gasoline sitting in our garages or backyards. (The smell isn't exactly appealing.)

With propane, though, you don't have to worry about the smell, and you can easily store the propane tanks in your garage or in a shed in the backyard. What's more, you can easily purchase the regular 20-pound tanks that are sold at Home Depot and Wal-Mart, or you can purchase a 100-pound tank for even more storage.

The propane generator that I own is the Sportsman 7,000-watt propane gas-electric-start portable generator.

This generator is rather inexpensive and cost me about $700 at Home Depot. You can buy more expensive generators for $3,000 or more, but this one has everything I want and I didn't feel the need to have the unit attached to my house. This generator has always worked well for me, and I don't have any complaints.

Sportsman Portable Generator: **https://thd.co/2eFlPTq**

Easy Backup Emergency Power Supply

Here's my personal backup power system for smaller devices such as cell-phones and tablets. This system only requires three items, and you can have it up and running in less than 60 seconds.

The first item you need is a car battery. While you could go to your local auto store and get a regular car battery, I recommend and use an absorbed glass mat (AGM) battery. These batteries last about 10 years, are more reliable, have no chance of leaking fluid, and are used by NASCAR. The brand of AGM battery I use is Optima, and they're available on Amazon.

Optima AGM Battery: **http://amzn.to/2xa0OLR**

Once you've got your battery, you'll need an inverter. I use a 400-watt inverter made by a company called Bestek. My inverter has two standard outlets and four USB ports, so you have plenty of space to plug items into.

Bestek Inverter: **http://amzn.to/2gLybO4**

When the lights go out, all you do is hook up the inverter to the car battery terminals and you can start plugging devices into the inverter, so you'll be all set to go.

The final item you'll need is a battery charger to recharge your battery when the lights come back on. I use a 10-amp battery charger by Schumacher, and it's available on Amazon.

Schumacher 10-amp Recharger: **http://amzn.to/2gLybO4**

When Cell Phones Die

Besides ways to power devices, you've also got to make sure you have ways to communicate with family members during a blackout. Depending on the cause of the blackout, there's no guarantee cellphones will work.

This is where the old reliable landline comes into play. The fact is if everything else is down, a landline is the best way to call 911 or anyone else you need to contact.

Another backup communication option is a satellite phone. Both my wife and I have satellite phones in the back of our cars because they'll still function when cellphone towers won't. The satellite phone I use is the Inmarsat Isat-Phone Pro.

Inmarsat IsatPhone Pro: **http://amzn.to/2gGB9zs**

Creating a Survival Group

Building a survival team is crucial. It is much more difficult to survive alone than with a small group of people who have different skill sets to bring to the table.

No man is an island, as they say, so it's important to find a trusted and capable survival group of like-minded people who keep things on "the down-low."

Basically, people have a better chance of getting through dangerous situations together. I realize that the movies make it seem "sexy" to be a lone wolf. But in real life, you'll be much more successful if you're willing to work with others.

It would also be wise to learn how to read people, as you need to be careful whom you're telling about your prepping and especially whom you trust to have access to your plans, your supplies and your family.

First thing you need to do is vet members and make sure they have compatible personalities and similar goals. Learn about your neighbors, and get to know people. Start looking for what kind of people you might need in certain situations and figure out how to meet them and work together. Look for unique skills that would make a person a great member of a survival team. Military veterans, medical professionals, mechanics and farmers, to name a few, have skills that could be an asset to you and your survival group.

Next comes the hard part. Learning to work together as a team. You need to find out exactly where everyone excels, so that when the time comes you are fully prepared to operate as a team.

Drilling With Your Family and Survival Group

When it comes to survival gear, people often forget to familiarize themselves with the ins and outs of all their gear so they know how to use it in an emergency. Learn how your gear works and be sure to test it periodically. This may seem basic, but remember, during a stressful situation, you won't have time to figure out your equipment. Believe me, if you knew all the prep work that spies do before going on an operation, it would make your head spin. After all, if an operation fails, people may die. The same could be said in an emergency, so it's important to know your gear.

A good way to bring the whole group up to speed is to take your gear camping. Once, my family lived off of survival food — you know, the kind that comes in pouches — for an entire week to make sure we liked it and our kids would eat it. The food wasn't too bad, the kids ate (almost) everything and now we all know what we're in for. Figure out what everyone packed and then decide if it is a necessity for next time.

Make each outing tougher and longer than the last. And don't let the weather stop you — plan some outings in the cold or snow. A grid-down exercise will show you where your strengths and weaknesses really lie. Tim MacWelch from Outdoor Life recommends you:

Kill the main breaker for your home's electricity, and then get to work — cooking, cleaning, performing sanitation and hygiene tasks, providing alternative heat and even figuring out how to keep the kids entertained. It should also be a high priority to keep your home from getting damaged, especially in sub-freezing weather. Drain all the water pipes, or keep a small amount of heat going to prevent freezing.

The tougher the situations get, the tougher your team gets.

You should also make sure you have a Plan B or C. Just because you prepped on the idea that things will go a certain way, things don't always happen like you planned. Murphy's law: "Anything that CAN go wrong WILL go wrong."

A WARNING FROM THE OTHER SIDE OF THE WORLD

By JAVELIN | *Ex-CIA Operative*

Pulling into a deserted harbor will give anyone goosebumps. I was training a new spy in Kobe, Japan, and the target we were after was a crime boss known simply as SCORPION.

We needed a secluded location where we could talk freely and build a relationship with SCORPION. As you might imagine, it is extremely difficult to get a crime boss alone. My trainee and I lucked out in setting up this meeting on his boat.

I could sense my new partner wasn't the biggest fan of the ocean, but the advantages of this location outweighed the risks. The meeting was going as planned until the lights went out in the city. The only source of light for miles came from the running lights on the boats bobbing in the harbor around us.

My thoughts quickly went to my family. Through my work, I had managed to build up a serious list of enemies. Enemies that are skilled at hiding in shadows. And now the entire world was shadows.

Act Natural

My protégé had a look of pure panic on her face. I could sense her fear. We had to get out of there before she blew our cover. Just my luck. I was stuck on a boat in complete darkness with a crime boss and a nervous spy. Just another day at the office.

We wrapped up the meeting and managed to make it back to the pier, where we parted ways with SCORPION. Getting home to my family was my top priority. But my car was 30 miles away.

To top it off, I had to get rid of the two men following us.

Even with the blackout, SCORPION had surveillance ready to follow us once we stepped off the boat. As intelligence officers, we're trained to disappear, but we couldn't disappear too quickly. The men following us would be watching our every move to gauge if we were spies or just regular folks.

We needed to make sure that SCORPION's men thought we were just a couple of regular Joes, which is why we took our time that night and avoided making any suspicious moves.

If you've ever been to Japan, you're probably familiar with the massive number of people on the sidewalks. Now imagine those crowds in total darkness, made larger without the use of the subway lines. We didn't have to walk far to casually lose SCORPION's men.

When I got home that night, I was more grateful than ever to see my wife and kids. A few hours later, the power came back on and everyone went back to business as usual. But I'll never forget that day and how dangerous it can be when the lights go out. Which is why I believe a blackout is something everyone should prepare for.

Lights Out in the Big City

In December 2016, Russian hackers temporarily disabled Ukraine's power grid, cutting off electricity to one-fifth of the capital city. Some experts believe that this attack was meant as a diversion. Others believe it was a direct attack against the

Ukrainian government. I think it's both. Launching an attack on the power grid is as much a statement of power as a distraction.

But there's another angle people fail to recognize: A system in disarray can give away a lot of information.

Think about it. All attempts to bring back power give information on restoration techniques. Let's say Russia is planning a larger attack. This smaller attack has revealed Ukraine's recovery protocol, so hackers can plan more attacks to increase the duration of the next blackout.

We also face cybersecurity threats from Russia.

Now the U.S. is not nearly as vulnerable as Ukraine. And thankfully, we've greatly improved our power grid since the Northeast blackout of 2003. Our system has undergone numerous hardening projects, and extra power grids have been put in place in case others fail. There are also monitoring satellites that serve as an early-warning system.

The Bottom Line

That day in Japan, my family stayed safe because we had sat down together and made emergency plans for almost every scenario we could imagine. I was happy to see that my children knew what to do when the lights went out. And now I get to watch my children teach the same principles to my young grandchildren. I recommend preparing your family in a similar way.

You should also have a flashlight, weapons, water, food, a radio, money and a full tank of gas in your car. Most power failures are localized. Depending on the situation, you should be prepared to leave the affected area.

Our network systems — which include the power grid — are under constant threat of attack. I certainly hope that our security efforts keep us protected, but my family and I are prepared if our defenses fail.

You don't have much control over a blackout. But you do have control over how you handle it. Prepare now and stay safe.

HOW NOT TO DROWN

We lived in fluid for our first nine months, so swimming should be instinctual — but for many people, it's not. The human body (for most of us) is naturally buoyant. We are designed to float.

That said, there is a large percentage of the population who can't swim. And an even larger percentage will be hopeless in churning seas and the surf zone.

Trust me when I tell you when you have 30-foot waves crashing above you that the safest place is UNDER the water. I have avoided death many times by simply swimming down and grabbing sand with my hands to anchor myself until the break in sets (the time between the waves) and taking that time gap to swim to shore.

If you can hold your breath for 30 seconds, you will find that under the waves is the safest place to be. It's utter calmness. If you can't, here are some other things you can try.

DIY Flotation Device

According to the Navy Swimming and Water Survival Instructor's Manual, you should "carefully weigh the pros and cons of removing clothing, as clothing can protect against hypothermia and offers protection from marine life, fuel oil and sunlight."

If you find yourself in the water without a life vest, here's how you can improvise:

According to the Navy manual, you should take your pants off and "tie the two legs together using a square or overhand knot," and then zip and button the waist closures.

Holding the pant legs vertically about two inches beneath the surface of the water, take a deep breath and exhale into the submerged waistband. The air will rise and be trapped in the leg knots. Place your neck in the crotch of the pants. Congratulations — you now have a makeshift life vest.

A few things to keep in mind: Make sure you keep the waistband below the surface of the water to keep air from escaping. Also, as the manual explains, "The trousers should be kept wet by splashing water on them periodically. If the trousers are allowed to dry out, they may leak."

Face-Down Survival Float

As also stated in the Navy Swimming and Water Survival Instructor's Manual, the back float (often preferred by bad or non-swimmers who have not learned proper breath control) "is effective only in calm water, and can be hazardous in rough seas."

So the best way to stay afloat in choppy seas is the face-down float. Here's how to execute this maneuver by the book just like a trained Navy SEAL:

1. Place your face in the water with your chin to your chest and the back of your head just above the surface of the water. "The upper back and shoulders are underwater, horizontal to the surface, and the arms are at the surface with elbows bent and hands separated slightly." Allow your legs to dangle beneath you. "These actions balance the floater around the chest, the center of buoyancy."

2. To take a breath, "pivot at the neck, lifting your chin off your chest until your mouth clears the surface... As your mouth clears the surface, the swimmer exhales quickly and forcefully through the mouth and nose." Then inhale deeply. Once you've inhaled a full breath of air, lower your head back to the resting position with your chin on your chest.

3. When you lift your head to breathe, keep your arms parallel to the surface and press your hands outward (palms facing out) to a point near the width of your shoulders. This motion is called sculling and will help you keep your head above water while you take in a new breath.

You can also use your legs for additional support — the best method is a modified frog kick: Kick while your head is above water. "Only one or two short, quick kicks are required to support the head while breathing."

The most important aspect of this maneuver is that it will help you conserve energy while you wait for help to arrive. Also, remember to stay calm and keep your breathing consistent so you don't hyperventilate or aspirate.

Make sure you check the local conditions before heading into the water on your next vacation so you can avoid this issue altogether. But if you do find yourself in suddenly violent waters, you'll know what to do to make it out alive.

THE SECRET TO AVOIDING PSYCHOLOGICAL DEFEAT IN A LIFE-AND-DEATH SITUATION

By The Survival Ready Blog Team

Your mission in a survival situation is to stay alive. You are going to experience an assortment of thoughts and emotions. These feelings can work for you, or they can work to your downfall. Fear, anxiety, anger, frustration, guilt, depression and loneliness are all possible reactions to the many stresses common to survival.

These reactions — when controlled in a healthy way — help to increase your likelihood of surviving. They prompt the would-be survivor to pay more attention, to fight back when scared, to take actions that ensure sustenance and security, to keep faith and to strive against large odds.

When the survivor cannot control these reactions in a healthy way, they can bring that person to a standstill. Instead of rallying their internal resources, the survivor listens to their internal fears. This survivor experiences psychological defeat long before they physically succumb.

Remember, survival is natural to everyone; being unexpectedly thrust into the life-and-death struggle of survival is not.

Don't be afraid of your "natural reactions to this unnatural situation." Prepare yourself to rule over these reactions so they serve your ultimate interest — staying alive.

This preparation ensures that your reactions in a survival setting are productive, not destructive.

The challenge of survival has produced countless examples of heroism, courage and self-sacrifice. These are the qualities it can bring out in you if you have prepared yourself. Below are a few tips to help psychologically prepare yourself for survival.

Know Yourself

Through training, family and friends take the time to discover who you are on the inside. Reinforce your stronger qualities and develop the areas that you know are necessary to survive.

Anticipate Fears

Don't pretend that you will have no fears. Begin thinking about what would frighten you the most if forced to survive alone. Train in those areas of concern to you. The goal is not to eliminate the fear but to build confidence in your ability to function despite your fears.

Be Realistic

Don't be afraid to make an honest appraisal of situations. See circumstances as they are, not as you want them to be. Keep your hopes and expectations within the estimate of the situation.

When you go into a survival setting with unrealistic expectations, you may be laying the groundwork for bitter disappointment. Follow the adage, "Hope for the best, prepare for the worst." It is much easier to adjust to pleasant surprises about one's unexpected good fortunes than to be upset by one's unexpected harsh circumstances.

Adopt a Positive Attitude

Learn to see the potential good in everything. Looking for the good not only boosts morale, but it's also excellent for exercising your imagination and creativity.

Remind Yourself What Is at Stake

Remember, failure to prepare yourself psychologically to cope with survival leads to reactions such as depression, carelessness, inattention, loss of confidence, poor decision making and mentally giving up before the body gives in. At stake is your life and the lives of others who are depending on you to do your share.

Train

Through self-defense training and life experiences, begin today to prepare yourself to cope with the rigors of survival. Demonstrating your skills in training will give you the confidence to call upon them should the need arise. Remember, the more realistic the training, the less overwhelming an actual survival setting will be.

Learn to Manage Stress

People under stress have a potential to panic if they are not well-trained or psychologically prepared to face the circumstances — whatever they may be. While we often cannot control the survival circumstances in which we find ourselves, it is within our ability to control our response to those circumstances.

Learning stress management techniques can enhance significantly your capability to remain calm and focused as you work to keep yourself and others alive. A few good techniques to develop include relaxation skills, time management skills, assertiveness skills and cognitive restructuring skills (the ability to control how you view a situation).

By cultivating these skills and attending some survival training and self-defense classes, you can develop the survival attitude. The last thing you want is to find yourself in a life-and-death situation and be overwhelmed by the rush of emotions.

Remember, the will to survive can also be considered to be the refusal to give up.

Never, ever give up.

AN ESSENTIAL TOOL TO HELP YOU SEE THE LIGHT OF DAY

By Cade Courtley | *Former Navy SEAL*

3:00 a.m. — Location: Undisclosed

I'm seated on the deck of an MH-60 Black Hawk. My legs are hanging out the starboard door. I lean forward into the night, my weight supported by my anchored harness. The warm prop wash hits my face as we continue to slowly orbit the compound 500 feet below.

I'm intently scanning the city of green through my night vision goggles (NVGs). I train my rifle with infrared (IR) laser site, providing sniper cover as my team clears the structures beneath me.

If you own the night — you own the operation.

Early warfare seldom engaged at night. The lack of adequate vision increased confusion, hampered communication and seriously increased the possibility of fratricide (friendly fire). Only the most highly trained soldiers with a well-rehearsed plan could take to the battlefield at night with any chance of success.

But this began to change with the invention of night vision.

Originally designed and used by the Germans in World War II, it wasn't until Vietnam that night vision truly proved itself in combat. Today, night vision is standard issue for most of our fighting forces.

How It Works

Basically, night vision devices use image enhancement technology to collect all available light — including IR, which can't be seen by the naked eye — and amplify it so that you can easily see what's going on in the dark.

Night vision technology has made enormous advancements since the German Generation 0 optic. Modern night vision devices are significantly smaller, lighter, waterproof, more durable and have a far longer battery life. The latest MIL-SPEC (military standard) Generation 4 night vision goggles boast beyond an 80,000 times amplification rate, resulting in an incredibly crisp image with a 120-degree field of view. And if you have $65,000, you can own a pair.

So why is it green?

Green presents a night vision device wearer with the most accurate and user-friendly picture possible. What's more, because the eye is most sensitive to light wavelengths near 555 nanometers — that is, green — the display can be a little dimmer, which conserves battery power.

Game Changer

During one of the military operations in Mogadishu, Somalia, colloquially known as Black Hawk Down, the use of night vision goggles changed everything. The amazing pilots of the Army's elite helicopter squadron (TF-160 SOAR) — Night Stalkers and their Little Birds (MH-6) — were able to conduct nonstop gun runs in support of troops that found themselves pinned down and out numbered. This gave dozens of American troops the opportunity to get out alive.

But you don't have to be a member of an elite Tier 1 special ops unit to know that having the advantage in the night could mean all the difference. Night vision could be extremely valuable:

- When hunting or camping
- In the event of a power disruption during a natural disasters
- During a home invasion
- When you don't want to give up your position by using a flashlight
- Or if you a hear a strange noise in your backyard at night.

Choosing the Right Night Vision for You

OK, so you've decided to invest in a night vision device. Here are some things to consider when narrowing down your list:

1. Gain — This refers to the ability to enhance images even as it gets darker. Typically, night vision falters as the amount of ambient light dwindles and the viewing distance increases.

2. Range — To capture objects that are far afield, night vision goggles need a magnification factor greater than 1x. A long and powerful lens is required to achieve this. But unfortunately, long lenses perform poorly in low light.

3. Image Quality — The best night vision images are those that remain sharp at the center and at the edges. To avoid blurring and distortion, the goggles must produce high-definition images with a high resolution.

4. Mounting Gear — Do you want or need the ability to head mount your night vision so you can be hands-free?

5. Budget — As with most things in life, the more you are willing to spend, the better product you will get. But if you keep these other factors in mind, you'll be able to find a device that fits your needs without breaking the bank.

Here are several options available for civilian use that I recommend.

- The ATN PVS7-3 is identical to the AN/PVS-7 — the night vision goggles issued to the U.S. Army. It can be used as a handheld, head-mounted or helmet-mounted device. **$3300**.

- The Armasight Vega is an affordable and capable head-mounted Gen 1+ night vision device. It weighs 0.54 pounds and comes with flip-up headgear. **$300**.

- The 6x 50MM Bushnell Equinox Z is the top model in Bushnell's stellar Z Night Vision line. This night vision monocular weighs 1.7 pounds and runs on four AA batteries. **$475**.

- The ATN Viper X-1 is a small Gen 1 night vision device for outdoor enthusiasts. This monocular not only is lightweight and compact, but also comes with a headgear kit. **$275**.

Only you can decide if night vision would be a useful addition to your survival gear. And now that you know a little bit more about what to look for in a quality device, if you do pick up a pair, you can own the night like a SEAL.

5 TIPS FOR SURVIVING WHEN LOST

Imagine you and a friend are enjoying a beautiful hike. Then it begins to snow and your hiking partner disappears.

Well, that's exactly what happened to 33-year-old Pavlina Pizova and her partner Ondrej Petr. Pavlina and Ondrej were hiking in the New Zealand wilderness when clouds overtook the area and heavy snow began to fall, making it difficult to see where they were going.

Ondrej slipped down an icy slope and became trapped between some rocks. Pavlina carefully made her way toward Petr before she realized he had died during the fall. She ended up spending the night out in the freezing conditions next to his body.

The next day, Pavlina trudged through waist-deep snow to a hut she knew was nearby to rest and get some supplies. She ate food other hikers had left behind and then attempted to hike her way back to safety. But avalanches nearby made it impossible for her to get very far, so she decided to stay put in the hut.

Lost and Found

Pavlina survived in that hut for 30 days. She was finally rescued after her family became concerned that they hadn't heard from her. Unfortunately, Pavlina and Ondrej didn't tell anyone where they were going and they didn't have a GPS locator, which prolonged the search.

Getting lost in the wilderness can be a terrifying experience — even without suffering the death of someone you care about — and I know Labor Day weekend is a popular time for hiking and other outdoor activities. So today, I want to share some tips on what to do in case you ever find yourself stranded in the middle of nowhere.

1. **Stay put.** Hopefully, you left behind detailed plans of where you planned to go on your trip. If you did, stop moving and make a camp with the supplies you have on hand. The fact is you could walk for days and never find help. You could end up wandering in circles, wasting precious energy and supplies. Besides, a search-and-rescue team will most likely start from your car and work their way from there in a specific pattern, which is why you should stay put if it's safe to do so.

2. **Look for water.** Water will quickly become one of your biggest concerns if you become lost in the wilderness. Ration the water you do have and be on the lookout for new water sources. Remember that water flows downhill, so go low. Also look for plants or other growth that are signs of water in the area. And don't forget to use your ears and listen for the sound of water — you might be close to a water source and not even know it. When you find water, it's critical that you have the means to filter it. The SurvFilter has saved my life more than once in the wilderness — I highly recommend picking up one of these survival water filters for yourself.

Survfilter: **http://bit.ly/2gC9GPD**

3. **Signal for help.** Provided you are well-prepared, you should have the tools and the ability to make a fire. This is one of the best ways to signal rescuers. The international signal for help is based on the number three. If possible, start three campfires in a triangle pattern to let people know where you are. Depending on the terrain, try to start the fires on a high ridge so they can be seen more easily.

4. **Build a shelter.** If you brought a tent, a tarp or other camping gear, set it up before it gets dark. If you don't have any gear on hand, make a shelter out of whatever is available. Frankly, if you get lost in the wilderness, you need to be prepared to spend a few nights in the elements, which means having a shelter is critical. I can assure you from personal experience that sleeping outdoors without any shelter is miserable and it will make your situation a whole lot worse.

5. **Leave clues.** Let's say you make camp but you have to hike downhill to retrieve water. You definitely want to let search parties know where you're headed in case they find your camp while you are gone. This can be as simple as leaving a note with the direction you left to find water. In addition, you need to ensure searchers in the air can find you, so you should also make a large arrow out of rocks or branches pointing in the direction you traveled.

The key to safety is being prepared so you can deal with any unexpected issues that arise. But if you do ever find yourself lost and unprepared, remember these five tips to keep safe until help arrives.

HOW TO BUILD A SURVIVAL SHELTER ANYWHERE

For Mike Vilhauer, knowing how to build a shelter in the wilderness is the reason he survived for five days in the rugged Sierra Nevada mountains.

It began as an ordinary fishing trip, but the day took an unexpected turn as night fell and Mike realized he was lost. Knowing he was going to have to spend the night in the mountains, Mike decided to make a shelter using pine needles and willow tree branches to keep warm. The next day, Mike tried to hike his way back to safety, but no such luck. He was forced to stop and erect another shelter the second night.

Mike survived for five full days by drinking water from streams and building shelters to stay warm at night. Even though he didn't get much sleep or food during the ordeal, search and rescue crews eventually found him and he made it home safe and sound.

The lesson here is that Mike absolutely did the right thing to stay alive. If he hadn't had the wherewithal to build shelters for warmth, the story likely would have had a different outcome.

For this reason, I'm going to teach you how to build simple, effective shelters in three different types of environments — in case you ever find yourself stranded in the elements.

In the Woods

A lean-to is one of the simplest shelters to set up in a forest. The first thing you'll need to do is find a large tree or boulder. Then take tree limbs (approximately 6–7 feet long) and put one end on the ground, leaning the other end against the large tree or boulder you've staked out.

Next, take smaller branches, leaves, pine needles, bark or anything else you can find and place them on top of the leaning limbs. You'll need enough to cover all the limbs that are leaning to protect yourself from the elements.

You should also use leaves, bark or pine needles to cover the ground inside the lean-to. If you sleep directly on the ground, you will lose body heat.

In the Snow

If you are stranded in the snow, one of the quickest ways to build a shelter is by making a snow cave. When digging a snow cave, the most important factor is choosing a safe location.

Ideally, you need to find an area with large snowdrifts, such as a mountainside. Avoid building a shelter up against a tree because there are usually air pockets in the snow around trees, which means the snow won't be deep enough.

Once you've picked out a good spot, start by digging an entrance into the cave and then dig up to create a dome shape. In other words, the entrance should be lower than the rest of the snow cave. This will help keep warmth inside since you will need to leave the entrance open for air movement.

In the Desert

Desert conditions are typically the most challenging environments in which to build a shelter. The key is to give yourself protection from the elements — most importantly, the sun.

One of the best shelter options in the desert is a pit shelter, which is essentially just a large hole that you can fit your whole body into. But don't waste your energy digging one that's too large, because you want to keep your body close to the walls of the pit for insulation.

For the finishing touch, place a tarp, poncho, clothing or anything else you have over the top of your pit. The more layers you can add, the better off you will be.

The Bottom Line

I'm sure you've heard of the "rules of three" when it comes to survival. Basically, you can survive three minutes without air, three hours without shelter, three days without water and three weeks without food.

In a survival situation, provided that you are still breathing, shelter should be your next priority because hypothermia and heat stroke can kill you pretty quickly. Once you've got a shelter to protect yourself from the elements, you can tackle finding food and water and — like Mike — you'll eventually make it home alive.

THREE SURVIVAL TIPS FOR SENIOR CITIZENS AND THOSE WITH LIMITED MOBILITY

By Jeff Anderson | *Modern Combat & Survival*

I hear it ALL the time…

Bugging out may be the way to go for "young bucks," Jeff… but I'm older and I don't really have any choice but to ride out a disaster in my home.

Sure, I get it.

I mean a lot of survivalists assume that everyone will just be able to throw half their house on their back and head off into the urban wasteland to escape the chaos, right?

But what if you really ARE older… can't stand or walk for long periods… use a walker or wheelchair… or just simply can't see yourself scaling walls, carrying a giant bug-out bag and dodging armored vehicles like Jack Bauer?

Or what if YOU can… but you also have to plan for an elderly parent or neighbor you watch out for? Well, here are three survival tips for older people and those with limited mobility:

1. Be Realistic With Your Survival Plan

Are you and your loved ones unable to move over long distances?

If so, shelter-in-place may be your only option if mobility is a real problem.

This forces you to really put a lot more focus into fortifying your home against not only storms... but also the aftermath of them.

Stock up heavily on food and water... have plywood, a hammer and nails stashed in your garage to board up against high winds and rain... and jack up your home security (including keeping your guns and ammo dry and at the ready against possible looting).

But be warned... even with a solid shelter-in-place plan, you may be FORCED to pick up and go if you're in the path of a disaster — in this case...

2. Be the First to Go

When you have no other choice but to get out of Dodge, you absolutely MUST be in that first wave of evacuees.

Your best means of transportation will always be your vehicle.

However... when the SHTF, everyone around you will have the same idea.

In no time flat, highways, bridges, tunnels, even train routes will bottleneck and become impassable.

Younger, more agile people can get out of their cars and find their way to safety easier... but if you — or someone you're with — has a harder time being mobile, this makes it all the more critical you're ahead of the pack.

Make no mistake... the first to move have the advantage when bugging out and you need to be able to evacuate your family in five minutes or less when it's go time!

And there's one key secret to doing that...

3. Yes, You STILL Need a Bug-Out Bag!

I know a lot of older people who think they don't need a bug-out bag for their survival supplies.

Wrong, wrong, WRONG!

Here's what they just don't get...

While you may not see yourself strapping on a backpack and walking through the forest, that's not really what a bug-out bag is for anyway.

It's simply a way for you to pre-assemble all your essential supplies with you — in an easy-to-carry method — in order to remain self-reliant if you're forced to evacuate your home.

That's it.

If you're forced from your home, you're still going to need clothes, food, clean water, any prescription medications, etc. — and you can bet that you're not going to get those things right away (especially when emergency services are focused on rescues rather than caregiving).

And look...

If part of your plan is to have someone come and get you (like a responsible son or daughter or grandchild), then you simply MUST be ready to go when they pull up in the driveway.

Remember... every single second counts and if YOU are the one holding everyone up because you're trying to think about what to bring and throwing it all in a suitcase, you put EVERYONE'S life in danger by not being prepared.

Don't be one of the clueless "older" people who fail to plan for a forced evacuation. I've seen what happens to the "unprepared" in real-world disasters and crises... and it's not pretty.

Oh, One More Thing...

If you happen to be someone with an elderly parent or someone else you're responsible for, don't make the mistake of thinking they'll be ready and waiting for you when you arrive to grab them.

I can almost promise they won't be ready!

It will actually even help YOU survive a crisis if you can make sure they're schooled on how to prepare and their supplies are ready NOW instead of trying to pull it all together at the last second.

90 SURVIVAL USES OF PARACORD

As a former CIA officer, I know a thing or two about getting the most use out of everyday items and using them in ways most people wouldn't ever suspect.

It is vital to have this kind of knowledge so that if you're ever in a tight spot, you have the tools and the skills to escape a dangerous situation.

Paracord — a durable lightweight rope about as thick as your shoelaces — a perfect example.

No one will ever give a second thought to the laces in your shoes. But when they are made of some of the strongest paracord material, they could get you out of a jam... even save a life.

Paracord was originally used in the suspension lines of U.S. parachutes during World War II, but once in the field, paratroopers found many other awesome uses for this rope.

And get this... Paracord was even used by astronauts during the repair of the Hubble Space Telescope.

It's all because of the way this stuff is constructed. In each strand of cord, you'll find seven super-strong strings all woven together in a breakthrough pattern. Some paracord can hold up to 550 pounds of tension!

Given my background in the government, I've been through some amazing training. During one particular training event, we were placed into different scenarios and had to use only the tools in our environment to escape.

In one scenario, I was gagged, bound with zip ties and stuffed into the trunk of a car. And just using a length of paracord I had laced my boots with, it took me less than 15 seconds to get out.

If you replace your existing shoelaces with paracord, you can use the paracord to form a friction saw that will set you free from the zip ties.

Simply remove the paracord from one of your shoes and tie a bowline knot around that shoe. Then run the other end of the paracord through the zip tie and tie another bowline knot around your other shoe.

Then move your legs as if you are riding a bicycle. The zip tie should pop right open. It's that easy!

Paracord is incredible stuff. There are literally dozens of other potential uses — some of them lifesaving. Which is why I've put together this report — a comprehensive list of practically every scenario and possible use you can get out of paracord.

Some of these are self-explanatory, while others may need a little explanation. See below for the 90 other uses for paracord.

Hunting/Fishing

1. Use the inner threads as fishing line.
2. If you have some time on your hands, use the internal strands to create a fishing net.
3. Make a trotline for fishing. Remove the inner strands, and then singe the ends of the outer nylon shell. Slide swivels to the shell and tie an overhand knot on either side of the swivel. Use the inner thread to make your drop lines, and then thread your hook.

How-to: **http://bit.ly/2eFGwi7**

4. Weave the inner strands together and construct a gill net.
5. Make traps and snares by tying the inner strands to branches.

How-to: **http://bit.ly/2xa1OiP**

6. Create a makeshift bow by attaching some paracord to a branch. You can create an arrow by shaping and sharpening a stick.
7. Construct a bola by tying a rock to the end of the paracord. Use to hunt birds or as an improvised defense weapon.

Medical Uses

1. Make an emergency tourniquet. Wrap paracord around the injured limb approximately 2–4 inches away from the wound to help slow or stop the bleeding. (Don't apply directly to the wound.)
2. Use the paracord to weave a net between two long sticks or branches to make an improvised stretcher.
3. Make a splint by tying straight sticks around a broken limb.
4. Use the inner threads as emergency suture material.
5. Use it as a sling for an injured arm.
6. Use the inner strands for emergency dental floss.
7. Create a medical ID bracelet by attaching paracord to a medical identification tag. This should include important information such as blood type, contacts to call, name, birth date, etc., in case of an emergency.

Self Defense/Safety

1. Create a tripwire by stringing paracord around your campsite to protect against intruders.

2. An alternative method to the basic tripwire, make a tripwire alarm. If you attach some bells or cans to the paracord, it can also act as an early-warning system.
3. Create makeshift handcuffs.
4. Secure bad guys or intruders to a tree or chair.
5. Make a spear by tying a knife to a branch.
6. Use as an emergency escape rope.
7. Create a makeshift sling with which to throw rocks.
8. Make a gun sling. Loop three strands of paracord through a swivel. Braid the strands and then attach to a second swivel. (For extra strength or a wider string, you can use extra paracord to create a second braid over the first one.) Melt the ends to seal and attach to your weapon of choice.
9. Keep your gun clean by using it as a bore snake.
10. Wrap around a weapon for a no-slip grip and shock absorber.
11. Create a bullwhip for defense.
12. Temporarily lock a door with paracord and a paperclip.

How-to: **http://bit.ly/2gLzxZa**

13. Use it as a rescue line.
14. Tie people together on a trail so that everyone stays together and so no one gets pulled away.

Clothing

1. Suspend clothes off the ground by making a clothesline.
2. Make an emergency belt to hold your pants up.
3. If a belt doesn't work, make suspenders.
4. Replace a broken bra strap.
5. Replace broken or missing shoelaces.
6. Repair or create a zipper pull.
7. Hang tools from your belt.
8. Tie around your neck to hang tools from.
9. Create a neckerchief slide.

10. Replace damaged or missing drawstrings in packs, bags and sweat pants.
11. Use the inner strands for emergency sewing thread.
12. Secure a garbage-bag rain poncho around your body to keep you dry.

General Uses

1. Hang something up off the ground.
2. Secure things to the outside of your backpack.
3. Don't have keys? Use it to unlock your car. Tie a slipknot in the middle of the string, work your way inside from the corner of the door, maneuver your slipknot in place over the lock and pull.

How-to: **http://bit.ly/2w6RZND**

4. Secure your boat or skiff to a tree.
5. Make a towline; double or triple up for extra strength.
6. Use it to secure a tent.
7. Create a makeshift lanyard to hold items like keys, a knife, etc.
8. Rig a pulley system to raise and lower heavy items.
9. Keep rolled-up items secure.
10. Make a sack for carrying groceries or gear.
11. Secure a tarp between trees to stay covered from rain.
12. Tie objects together for easier transport.
13. String together and make a hammock.
14. Create a makeshift ladder by stringing together some sticks or boards.
15. Tie tall garden vegetable plants to stakes.
16. Have a pet? Make a collar.
17. Already have a collar? Make a leash.
18. Hang a bear bag in trees to keep food away from critters.
19. Tie loose items down so they will not blow away in a storm.

20. Identify members of a group using different-colored armbands or bracelets.
21. Use it as a workout aid for pullups or situps.
22. Tie a heavy knot in the middle and let your kids use it for skipping rope.
23. Use it to rappel down a cliff.
24. Tie hair back with a makeshift hair tie or headband.
25. Make yourself a seat by suspending a log off the ground between trees.
26. Tie onto a sled so you can drag it during the heavy snow.
27. Bundle stuff together.
28. Make a tire swing.
29. Use as a pull cord for a chain saw, boat engine, etc.
30. Tie the ends together and keep the kids entertained by playing cat's cradle.
31. Use for barter.
32. Make a bow drill. Get three pieces of wood for the fire board, spindle and handhold, and use your bow to drill slowly over tinder until it starts to smoke.

How-to: **http://bit.ly/2w6M779**

33. Create a makeshift tent by stringing up a tarp to a few trees.
34. Make different-colored armbands or bracelets and use to identify members of a group.
35. Quickly climb trees by using it as a climbing rope.
36. Wrap around hands to create emergency work gloves.
37. Use it as a fire starter.
38. Cut up and use as trail markers.
39. Use for cooking by hanging a kettle/pot over a fire.
40. Make a watch strap.
41. Tie knots through it and pull through a hose to clean.
42. Polish your razor by using as a strop.
43. Bundle around firewood to make carrying easier.

44. Hang a light over designated areas at night.
45. Make an improvised fuse. Paracord burns easy.
46. Wrap around a Maglite to create a handle and grip.
47. Never lose your gloves again. Tie your gloves with paracord and secure to the inside of your jacket.
48. Practice tying lifesaving knots.
49. Secure an animal to a post.
50. Keep kids entertained by using it to make arts and crafts.

I'm sure the list could go on, given a little imagination and creativity.

The fact is paracord has a multitude of uses and could save your life in an emergency. That's why I recommend you keep this miracle string on you at all times. Whether it be on your shoes or on your wrist as a bracelet, you'll get the peace of mind that comes with knowing you're carrying an item every single day that can help you survive the most dangerous situations.

BUILD (OR BUY) YOUR OWN SURVIVAL SHELTER: HAVE A SAFE PLACE TO HUNKER DOWN WHEN THE SHTF

There's an old missile silo in Kansas that's been transformed into a luxury underground survival bunker for the rich and famous. The structure can withstand any natural or man-made disaster.

And with 15 pressurized levels, this bunker boasts every accommodation — from classrooms to a movie theater to a heated pool.

The cost? $1–3 million per room.

Most of us probably lack the funds for a luxury survival shelter, but quality survival bunkers come in a variety of designs at many different price points. Even without all the bells and whistles, these shelters can still provide a safe place for you, your family and your emergency supplies.

Before you consider buying (or building) a survival bunker, you first need to ask yourself this question: Do you want a safe room that is good for a few hours, a storm shelter that could last a few days or a bunker to last for an extended time? Your answer will depend on your surroundings, your family size and your budget.

Let's take a closer look at each of these options.

Safe Rooms

Safe rooms are typically the most affordable option. They are usually aboveground — and they're one of the easiest shelters to construct yourself. There are also a few reliable companies that will install a safe room for you in your home or garage.

If tornadoes are a threat where you live, I highly recommend investing in a sliding door. Strong winds could push heavy objects against the door, blocking your exit and trapping you inside. A sturdy sliding door will be easier to open against debris.

Survive-a-Storm Shelters have a variety of safe rooms in different sizes ranging from $4,000–7,000. Depending on where you live, I recommend the Swisher ESP Safety Shelter. It has a sliding door and can fit approximately nine people.

Survive-a-Storm Shelters: **www.survive-a-storm.com**

Storm Shelters

Storm shelters are usually built underground out of cement or fiberglass, and occasionally steel. Your storm shelter should be close to your home for easy access — under your garage or in your backyard.

A storm shelter under your garage will be well-hidden and easily accessible, but in the event of a natural disaster, debris from your home or garage could block your exit — just ask the Longest family.

Josh and Katie Longest of Oklahoma installed a storm cellar under their garage. In 2015, Josh and Katie fled to their cellar along with their three children during a tornado. The twister ripped through their property, scattering debris. In the chaos, the garage door and rubble from their home fell on their storm shelter, completely blocking the exit.

After the storm passed, a concerned neighbor rushed over

and began removing the wreckage. But once the door was clear, the Longests were still unable to open the door from the inside.

Their particular shelter had a latch on the outside intended to keep the door closed when the shelter is not in use. The storm had closed the latch, preventing the door from opening. Luckily, the neighbor was there to lift the latch and rescue the Longests from their storm shelter.

When it comes to storm shelters, I recommend purchasing a quality underground shelter rather than building your own. Life Pod Shelters are an excellent pre-made option. This company offers a four-person shelter for $4,000 or a nine-person shelter for $8,000.

Lif Pod Shelters: **www.lifepodshelters.com**

A slightly more affordable alternative is the Allegiant 12-person precast concrete storm shelter for close to $3,000. The door has two latches on the inside to secure it in place during a storm.

Bunkers

Bunkers are the superior option when it comes to survival shelters for your family because they are designed for extended survival living. While a storm shelter is great in an emergency, you and your family won't want to stay in one for very long.

Bunkers are typically built underground with plenty of space for sleeping and supplies. I've seen shelters made from fiberglass, culverts and steel. Here's my advice: Don't use culverts. Culverts are designed to transport water — not keep water out — and often, they are merely crimped together. Steel is the best choice in my book, but it carries a few risks.

Bunkers made out of shipping containers seem to be all the rage these days — and they work well if you know what you're doing. Shipping containers are not made to support weight or force from the sides. If you bury a shipping container, it's critical that you install beams to support pressure from the sides. You will also need to find a quality sealant to prevent rust.

As with storm shelters, there are companies that build customizable steel bunkers. Rising S Co. designs, builds and delivers your shelter — which is convenient for people who want to protect the privacy of their survival space. Their standard bunker starts at $40,000, and they offer different options depending on how many people you're putting up and how much storage space you need.

Rising S Co. Bunkers: **www.risingsbunkers.com**

They also have a luxury bunker that can attach to an aboveground safe house. The $8 million luxury bunker can comfortably sleep over 30 people and includes a gym, laundry rooms, a bowling alley, swimming pool, parking, garden space, media room and large kitchen space.

Regardless of the material you use, it's important to have two entrances if you can. Bunkers are made for an extended stay, but you want an extra way to escape from intruders or if one exit is blocked. Make sure the doors are high quality and can be locked from the inside. Avoid doors that are made of cheap materials or doors with exterior hinges. A waterproof shelter won't be worth anything if the door lets water in. You can even find bulletproof doors if that is a concern for you.

If you want electricity in your bunker, make sure you research solar panels or bikes that hook up to battery chargers. Look for ways to control the air pressure and filter the air inside. And don't forget a reliable water system. If your bunker is suited for a six-month stay, you need to make hygiene a priority. Rising S has information on each of these options.

I hope this information helps you decide on a survival shelter that best fits you and your family's needs. However, I still strongly encourage you to do a lot of research before investing in one. You don't want any hidden surprises if one day you have to bet your life on your choice.

PREPPING FOR A FINANCIAL COLLAPSE: THE BEST WAY TO PRESERVE YOUR WEALTH

By Byron King

[Jason's note: My colleague Byron King is a Harvard-trained geologist and former aide to the United States Chief of Naval Operations. This "old rockhound" has made frequent appearances in mainstream media such as The Washington Post, MSN Money, MarketWatch, Fox Business News, CNBC's Squawk Box and PBS' NewsHour. When he talks about gold, I listen. Here's his latest analysis on the fate of the dollar and how you should prepare for an economic collapse.**]**

We'll soon experience profound problems with the U.S. dollar. To prepare you for what's about to happen, Jim Rickards, economic adviser to the CIA and author of *Currency Wars* and *The Death of Money,* has outlined the five-step sequence of economic collapse: Repricing, Acceleration, Transmission, Irrationality and Oblivion.

Of course… bankers and politicians will try to truncate this sequence so that we never get all the way to the final collapse. We'll see several stages of the collapse play out in any event, because central banks are out of room to steer monetary policy outside of a very narrow channel.

This will put increased importance on special drawing rights (SDRs) — a global money created for use by central bankers — and gold as possible tools with which to truncate the next collapse.

I expect that many nations will use SDRs as a method to protect themselves — certainly the U.S. But if you're not a country plugged into the central bank, what's left for us mere mortals?

Your best option is to use gold.

Gold Abides

Now let's apply the example of gold moves during a collapse to the Five Stages model. Begin with repricing. In essence, we'll have a market sell-off. People will sell stocks in an attempt to minimize losses.

Some people will likely sell gold and good-quality mining shares because they want to book what gains are on the table and gold is liquid. Expect gold to reprice more or less along with broad markets.

Then comes acceleration. Repricing becomes even worse as the downside opens up into a canyon of loss. Gold and shares will likely sell down more but then find a floor. This is because there is inherent value in gold — "gold as money" — which overcomes the desire to sell, sell, sell.

Eventually, acceleration can become transmission. The rush to the exits jumps from one market to another and then others. Everyone wants their money back, but the realization kicks in that it can't happen.

When reason leaves the scene, we'll see utter irrationality. This is when people panic. They will sell everything they can. And this is when you'll want to have cash on hand.

You can buy gold and high-quality mining shares for literally pennies on the dollar. Strange as it may seem, gold and good-quality mining shares will begin to creep back up.

At some point, there may be capitulation. It's the last stage: oblivion. People hate the markets, they hate stocks, they hate companies and management teams. It'll be near-impossible to give away shares for many firms. And gold and well-regarded mining shares will begin to resurrect from the ashes.

The Bottom Line

Again, we won't always see every stage play out. Sometimes bankers and politicians will "successfully" stop financial distress from escalating. But... this just pushes the problem further into the future and does nothing to fix the root of these problems. This means that, eventually, we are likely to see a full-blown collapse.

When that happens, you'll want to have physical gold in your possession — 10% of your investable assets to be precise. It will be one of the first assets to bounce back.

HOW TO STASH YOUR CASH WHEN YOU'RE ON THE MOVE

Here are eight ways to conceal cash safely and discretely when traveling:

- Try an ankle wallet. This accessory wraps around your ankle, making it difficult for pickpockets to access. The Eagle Creek Undercover Leg Wallet is one brand that can hold plenty of cash.

Eagle Creek: **http://bit.ly/2xa5hhz**

- The Shacke Hidden Travel Belt Wallet hangs down inside your pants. I've used this gadget, and it makes it nearly impossible for anyone to snatch your wallet

Shacke Hidden: **http://amzn.to/2gG7gzt**

- The Lewis N. Clark RFID-Blocking Hidden Clip Stash Travel Belt Wallet is a small wallet you clip to your pants. Plus, it's an RFID-blocking wallet, so hackers can't steal your credit card information

Lewis N. Clark: **http://amzn.to/2gMd91M**

- Use a hollowed-out ChapStick container to hide extra cash. Roll up a few $20 bills and stash them inside — criminals will have no idea the money is there

- You could also use a small pill container that clips to your keychain. Instead of medication, you can fit a folded $100 bill in there

- If you want to use an "advanced" spec ops strategy, take some money and put it in a ziplock bag. Fold the ziplock bag into a small square and duct tape it to the inside of your leg underneath your clothes

- Here's another advanced strategy: Wrap two of your fingers together with athletic tape as if you'd jammed them. Before you start wrapping, put some money between them. You can easily conceal several bills this way

- Don't forget about your cellphone case! (Even though I don't recommend taking your cellphone overseas, I know many people do.) Just take off your case, put some money inside and pop it back on your phone.

A little bit of cash could get you out of a major jam. Be sure to carry $200–300 — including a $100 bill. Being able to flash a $100 bill will motivate a lot of people to help you out, no matter where in the world you are.

BUGGING OUT WITH PETS

By Dennis Diaz | *Chief Editor, Survival Ready Blog*
We have two cats and two dogs in our house. The issue of what to do with them in case of an evacuation is an important part of our bug-out plan.

Just like in our household, a lot of people consider their pets as family members. The thought of leaving one of your furry friends behind to face whatever is coming is devastating. It would be an impossible choice for some, which is why you need to plan ahead.

Let's assume you are bugging out with dogs. These guys can certainly carry their own weight and walk along beside you. If you have a cat (or several cats), you are probably going to have to carry the little critters — unless they have a mind follow you of their own accord.

If you plan to go to a shelter, you should know that most do not allow pets. You could leave them in the car, but that is rarely a good option. If you decide to head for the hills or if you have an alternative location lined up, you will be fine to take your pets.

Here are some steps you will need to take to ensure a smooth evacuation with your furry friends.

Prepare a Pet Bug-Out Bag

Your pets need their own bug-out bags — or a small section in your bag — to hold their supplies. You can find backpacks or saddle bags that are made for medium to large dogs, so they can carry their own supplies. But only if you will be with your pet to make sure they don't get snagged on a branch or a fence, etc.

Your pet's bug-out bag should contain a small amount of food and their own water rations. A collapsible bowl will come in handy for the food and water. A few treats would be a good idea as well, to summon the animal or settle their nerves. And a blanket is necessary if you'll be sleeping outside.

Have Tags, Leashes and Collars

Before the need to evacuate even arises, you should make sure your pets have collars with up-to-date identification tags. Leashes for dogs will help you keep them reined in. Have a reflective collar on your pet so you can find them at night using a flashlight. Avoid collars with bells or several metal tags. These will alert others to your pet's presence, which might endanger you if you are trying to stay off the radar.

Pet Documentation

It's also a good idea to keep vet records in your pet's bug-out bag. If you do happen to go to a shelter that accommodates pets, you may have to prove they are up to date on their vaccinations. If you decide to board them while you travel, you may also need that proof. If you lose your pets, documentation will also help you prove ownership.

Having your pet chipped will be helpful if your animal is found by someone who has access to a chip scanner. In a true SHTF scenario, this isn't likely, but it never hurts to have your pet chipped. In certain situations, like after Hurricane Katrina when animals were rescued after some time, there's often no way of identifying pets and returning them to their owners. If your pet is chipped, there's a greater chance they will be returned to you.

Photos of Your Pets

Keep a print photo of each of your pets with their documentation. If you lose your pet, you'll want to have a photo to show people as you ask around. This will also help you prove ownership should someone try to claim your pet as their own.

If you pet lands in a shelter and you have no other way to prove ownership, a photo with you and your pet together should be enough proof. Keep in mind the importance of having physical photographs. A photo on your phone isn't going to do you much good if the battery is dead.

Pet Meds

Like humans, pets can get sick. If your pet has a diagnosed condition that requires medication, pack extra to help them stay healthy. Flea and tick control medication or collars will also come in handy, especially if you will be traveling through the wilderness.

A can of Blu-Kote is a vital part of any pet first-aid kit. If your pet suffers a laceration or is wounded while you are evacuating, this spray is both an antibacterial and healing ointment in one.

And don't forget to pack a supply of heartworm medication as well. Being out in the wild increases your dog's risk of being bit by an infected mosquito, which can lead to heartworm.

Pet Carriers

Carriers are typically reserved for cats or small dogs that slow you down. If you're traveling by vehicle, keeping your pet crated will ensure a panicked animal doesn't make driving hazardous. Pets who are used to their carriers will feel more secure when they are tucked away inside.

If you are bugging out in a hurry, you can grab a couple of pillow cases to carry small animals. This will also keep them from seeing what is happening around them. Pets can get just as scared as humans, and you don't want them running off in terror.

Pets can be your companion, your early warning system, your source of comfort and your protector. They deserve to be cared for in the best way possible. Be sure to plan ahead so you can meet their needs — as well as your own — in a survival situation. Man's best friend deserves no less.

DITCH THE DEAD WEIGHT BY TOSSING THESE FIVE NONESSENTIAL TOOLS

A bug-out bag should be unique. Even if you buy a prepared bug-out bag with all the gear included, you should take the time to customize it to fit the needs of the person depending on it for survival.

The reality is there are so many different opinions on what you should and shouldn't include in your bug-out bag. That being said, here is a list of items that, in my opinion, you don't truly need and will add unnecessary weight to your bag:

Flare Gun or Signal Kit — Unless you are bugging out on a boat, you don't need a flare gun to signal for help. Most likely, if you're bugging out, you won't need to signal for help, because you are trying to stay off the grid and find safety. This is a "sexy" item that adds unnecessary weight, and you'll probably never use it.

Tool Kit — Some people carry a small tool kit with screwdrivers, wire cutters, saws, etc. I recommend carrying a multitool such as one made by Leatherman, which serves many of the same purposes as its full-size counterparts. In addition, many survival saws or screwdrivers are cheaply made items from China that will break easily, which is why I suggest spending your money on a quality multitool that will hold up.

Sleeping Bag — Even if you buy a lightweight sleeping bag designed for backpacking, it is still a waste of space. I recommend packing an emergency bivvy. These typically weigh less than 4 oz., take up very little space and keep you just as warm. Plus, if you know anything about wilderness survival, you can cover the ground with leaves, bark and pine needles (duff) to sleep on, which will help you stay warm.

First-Aid Kit — Let me explain this one. A lot of people will buy simple first-aid kits that are tiny and lightweight. The problem is most of these "survival first-aid kits" contain a few bandages and little else you could reliably depend on to save your life. I recommend creating your own first-aid kit. Be sure to include items such as QuikClot and a CAT tourniquet to stop or control bleeding. Please don't bet your life on some $8 first-aid kit you grabbed in the Walmart camping section.

Lanterns — I'm shocked at the number of times people show me the humongous "camping lantern" they've put in their bug-out bag. Look, you really only need a few small flashlights and, of course, extra batteries. But don't go overboard, because these items quickly add up. If you've ever had to move around outdoors at night, then you know your eyes will adjust and you can see pretty well without a flashlight.

FIVE WEIRD SURVIVAL HACKS USING HOUSEHOLD ITEMS

1. Plastic Wrap — One of the best things about plastic wrap is that it is airtight and watertight. Use it to retain body heat and stay dry during a snowstorm by wrapping your legs, arms and midsection.

   Likewise, this is a great way to waterproof your survival gear. Another use for plastic wrap is building a shelter. You just need four posts — like trees — and you simply wrap the plastic around the posts and over the top. Once inside the shelter, you can use a piece of wrap to seal the entrance. It can also be used to cover a wound or as a sling for an injured arm.

2. Soda Can — You can get tons of different uses out of a soda can after you polish off the bubbly beverage. First, a soda can makes an easy lamp. Cut one side of the can and pull it open. Place a small candle in the can and voila! Now you have a lamp. You can also make an oil lamp using a can.

   Fill the soda can halfway with olive oil, and then dip a rolled paper towel into the oil and presto! Now you have an oil lamp. Lastly, using a household polish to buff the bottom of the can, you can turn it into a signaling mirror. If you were stranded in your home and needed to alert rescuers, this hack would come in handy.

3. Bandana — Bandanas are one household item that literally has hundreds of uses. One of the best and most obvious uses of a bandana is as mask. It can protect your face from smoke, dust and other airborne elements.

   Another use is for medical emergencies. You can use a bandana as a sling, tourniquet, bandage or wrap for an injury. Or you could wrap it around the back of your neck to prevent sunburn. You can also use it as toilet paper, a potholder, a rag to clean your eyeglasses or as a sling to throw rocks — also known as a shepherd's sling.

4. Mouthwash — When it comes to survival situations, infections and bacteria are one of the biggest threats you must address. Surprisingly, mouthwash can serve many purposes to reduce these risks. First, you can use it as an antiseptic to clean cuts or wounds. Next, you can use mouthwash to sterilize your cooking gear, as well as a cleaning solution around the house. Finally, mouthwash can kill many common household bugs — even ticks.

5. Pantyhose — If you've served in the military, you may be familiar with some of the many uses of pantyhose. Soldiers have used pantyhose as an added layer of warmth and to protect against bugs. Medically, pantyhose can be used as a tourniquet, as a sling or to secure a bandage over a wound. And you can use it to remove debris from water. Now, pantyhose won't filter out everything, but it can stop large pieces of dirt or other particles that could block a filter.

MASKING YOUR PREPARATIONS FROM NEIGHBORS

It can be dangerous to have neighbors see you prepping — you become a target when something does go wrong, as they will seek you out for help or try to steal from you — you need to appear vulnerable and not draw attention.

So what does this mean?

Operational security.

This is a military term, essentially meaning the security necessary to deny the enemy any useful information about what you are doing. The key is to avoid suspicion. And I have a few tips to help you do so:

1. Mum's the word. Keep your mouth shut. Don't volunteer any more information to people than they need to know. You want to be wary of strangers and be careful not to reveal too much information that could give them any intel.

2. Be cautious of technology. Make sure you watch what you say over text and email. After all, nothing is secure these days. Don't send anything that could be perceived

as incriminating, or that could let on as to what your preparations are.

3. Avoid social media. To an extent, at least. Just because you are prepping does not mean you should be advertising that through photos on Facebook or Instagram. The fact is even if you don't think you are giving away too much information, many smartphones will attach a GPS coordinate to the metadata in the picture. Now your hideaway may not keep you so hidden.

4. Keep the bumper stickers to a minimum. What many people don't think about when they add those cute little stickers symbolizing their family members and pets is that now anyone has intel into the members of their family. And an honor roll sticker? Don't even think about it. While you might be a proud parent, this can give away where your child goes to school and give a little more insight into where you live. Make sure your car has nothing inside or outside that can help to identify you.

5. Keep your home anonymous. Do you tend to leave your garage doors open? Or the blinds to the front windows of your house? These are big no-nos. Not only will the passerby be able to see what's inside, but they can even get a visual on doors and potentially what kind of locks are on those doors. If the drapes are left open, it would make it much easier for someone to map out the layout of your home.

Whether you're dealing with a natural or a man-made disaster — whether you're bugging out or bugging in — you need to have a security plan to protect yourself and your family. When people are desperate, they'll do things you never expected. Like the neighbor down the street who has always been nice to you. What if he knows you have a ton of survival supplies and comes to take them? Always have a way to defend yourself no matter the situation. Both an AR-15 and Remington 870 shotgun are good long guns to have on hand for extreme situations. The next time you are reviewing your emergency plans and survival gear, take the time to go over these dos and don'ts with your family. I would hate for a simple mistake to put you or a loved one in danger.

THE NO. 1 WAY TO STORE EMERGENCY WATER

The water crisis in Flint, Michigan, is a good example of the catastrophic consequences of a contaminated water supply. And while this disaster was the result of greed and negligence, any number of events could disrupt our water supply to devastating effect.

Terrorist groups the world over have long sought to poison water supply systems. There is evidence that as far back as 2002, al-Qaida operatives have been studying plans to poison water supplies in the U.S.

In July 2002, the FBI arrested Earnest James Ujaama after discovering documents on how to poison U.S. water supplies in his possession. The FBI had been investigating Ujaama for months because they believed he was trying to open a terror training camp in Oregon. Thankfully, his capture thwarted all of his plans.

When the Well Runs Dry

Water is one of the most fundamental things you need to survive. Which means it's also one of the most important things you need to stock up on for an emergency.

As a general rule, I recommend storing one gallon of water per person per day. If possible, I would try to store at least 30 days' worth of water in your home. With that being said, it's essential to store water properly. Otherwise, it will be worthless when you need it most.

I have several friends who tell me they store water in refillable plastic bottles. The problem with this method is cheap plastic bottles can leach chemicals into the water over time.

I also have friends who store their emergency water in 55-gallon drums. While these drums can hold a large supply of water, they are impossible to move. If you need to evacuate your home, you'll have to leave that drum behind.

Instead, I recommend storing water in a quality container like the WaterBrick water storage system. These 3.5-gallon containers are made from BPA-free high-density polyethylene (HDPE), a food-grade plastic known for its strength-to-density ratio. They are easily stackable, reducing the amount of space taken up by multiple bottles or large drums. And coming in under 30 pounds when filled, transporting WaterBricks is a piece of cake. (They also have a convenient handle for easy carrying.)

WaterBrick Storage System: **http://bit.ly/2eAPsFg**

Water Storage Tips

Remember to store water in a cool, dry place. If you have a basement storage room, this space would be ideal — it's where I keep mine. But you should always store emergency items in multiple locations. When disaster strikes, there is no telling what will happen. What if your storage room floods or catches fire or a beam collapses?

I'm often asked if it's necessary to treat water for long-term storage. If you are filling your water containers with tap water, then it's already been treated to some degree. But to be extra safe, I recommend adding some type of treatment to your water such as Aquamira Water Treatment drops.

Aquamarina Water Treatment Drops: **http://bit.ly/2w1YykA**

This brings me to the point that even treated water must be rotated or it will eventually go bad. At the very least, you should empty and refill your storage containers with fresh water once a year. When you rotate your water, look for signs that the water has gone bad. Check for signs of algae, cloudiness or discoloration or a foul smell. These are signs you need to rotate your water more often or perhaps that you need to store it in a cooler environment.

Now, let's say you run to your storage room during an emergency, open one of your WaterBricks and a terrible smell wafts out. This is one reason you should be prepared to extract water from other sources. Because WaterBricks are comfortably lightweight and effortlessly portable, it's easy to carry one to a nearby lake or stream to fill up.

The Bottom Line

There are many other reasons why I like the WaterBrick water storage containers. In addition to their supreme functionality in an emergency, you can also take them camping, boating or tailgating. They're strong, compact and versatile.

Remember, our bodies can survive only a few days without water. Don't be unprepared when it comes to water storage.

FOUR EMERGENCY WATER SOURCES IN YOUR HOME

Recently, I had the opportunity to attend PrepperCon in Salt Lake City. For those who aren't familiar with PrepperCon, it's an expo for survival and preparedness enthusiasts featuring guest speakers, product demonstrations and instructional classes.

One of the attendees was José Salvador Alvarenga. On Nov. 17, 2012, Alvarenga set out from the fishing village of Costa Azul, off the coast of Chiapas, Mexico.

Shortly after embarking on what was supposed to a 30-hour deep-sea-fishing expedition, José's 24-foot fiberglass skiff was blown off course by an intense storm, during which he also lost engine power on his small craft.

Fourteen months — or 438 days — later, José spotted land. He abandoned his boat and swam ashore, finally ending his harrowing journey at sea. Clearly, this is an incredible story of survival.

Lost at Sea

This courageous fisherman was able to outlast his ordeal by eating raw fish, turtles, small birds and whatever refuse he could salvage from the ocean. But what about water? Because the reality is you can only survive for about three days without water, and José was adrift for over a year.

Using any container he had on hand, José collected rainwater to drink — which is certainly a viable option if you're desperate. However, it's definitely not my first option when it comes to finding fresh water, because it could be contaminated. If you live near a large industrial plant, for instance, rainwater could be tainted by noxious chemicals coming from the plant.

So — besides rainwater — here are some other sources for finding drinkable water during an emergency:

- Fill 'er Up — If you have time to prepare for a disaster, one of the things I recommend doing is filling your bathtubs and sinks with water. If an earthquake breaks water supply lines or a storm cuts off power to your well, you could be without water for an extended time. But you could use the water from your bathtubs and sinks to survive until you are able to get more

- Pipe Dreams — If your local water supply is no longer safe, you can still use the water already in the pipes. However, the first thing you need to do is shut off the main water supply to keep contaminated water from entering the pipes. Next, go to the lowest faucet in your house (such as one in the basement) and turn the water on. Using a bucket, catch the water left in the pipes to tide you over

- In Hot Water — Another option to consider is the water in your hot water tank. Depending on the size of the tank, you could have 40–60 gallons to use, which could make a huge difference in a survival situation. Lastly, while it's not the most pleasant option to consider, you could also drain the water from each of your toilet tanks. If your water is blue or filled with chemicals, though, I don't advise using it for drinking

- Outside Chance — Finally, if you've been without water for an extended time and used every possible source inside your home, you need to be prepared to leave your house and find water outdoors. Outside sources may include nearby lakes, streams or drainage ditches. Just be sure to filter the water before drinking it.

Here are two final pieces of advice. First, while it's always advisable to have a backup plan, your primary source of water in an emergency should be your water storage. Whether you've stocked up on bottled water, filled a few 55-gallon barrels or invested in WaterBricks (my No. 1 water storage system), you should have one gallon of water per person per day for 30 days.

WaterBrick Storage System: **http://bit.ly/2x7rZqF**

Second, if you do have to tap into the alternate water sources listed above, you need to have a way to filter it so you don't get sick. Illness often leads to dehydration, which is a surefire way to make a bad problem worse. Check out the SurvFilter — this handy device once saved my life on an overseas mission, and I would trust my family's lives with it, too.

SurvFIlter: **http://bit.ly/2iY8gDr**

Water is the elixir of life. If you haven't already started stocking up, I recommend making this your No. 1 prepping priority.

ENSURE YOUR FAMILY'S NOT EXPOSED TO TOXIC WATER

By now you've surely heard about the water crisis in Flint, Michigan. The city's tap water was found to contain high levels of lead, and a state of emergency was declared.

"I just couldn't believe we were paying to poison our kids," declared Flint resident Lee-Anne Walters, expressing the shock and anger felt by all who live in the city.

Fully 6,000–12,000 children alone were exposed to drinking water with high levels of lead, including Mrs. Walters' son, who now has a compromised immune system.

Other symptoms throughout the city include everything from rashes to hair and vision loss, and many now face the possibility of long-term disabilities like mental disability.

How did this happen? And most importantly for you, how can you ensure you and your family never find yourselves in the same position?

A Failure of Government

Flint used to get its tap water from Detroit. As hard as it is to believe, Detroit's tap water was safe and clean.

But in 2014, in an effort to save money, the politicians in Flint switched to getting their water from the Flint River. Almost immediately, local residents began complaining about its taste and appearance, which ran a murky brown from their faucets.

The government insisted everything was fine and that the water was safe for consumption. But as far back as 2011, they knew the water had issues and needed to be thoroughly treated before flowing to residents' homes.

It wasn't until a local doctor showed that lead levels in children had doubled that the government finally admitted they had a severe problem with the water.

Flint's water crisis isn't just a lesson in how corrupt governments are and the lengths they'll go to to hide things from their citizens. It's also a good reminder that all of us should have an emergency water filter for our homes to filter out lead.

Camping Water Filters

There are lots of water filters on the market that are great for hiking and camping. I own several of these filters and keep them in my bug-out bags in my home and in the back of my cars.

One such filter is the Sawyer PointONE All in One Filter. The Sawyer is very compact and can filter up to 540 gallons of water per day, so you never have to worry about clean water. What's more, you can screw the Sawyer filter directly onto a water bottle, making it even more convenient to use.

Sawyer PointONE: **http://amzn.to/2wD9d7q**

Another filter that I use for hiking and camping is the MSR MiniWorks EX microfilter. The benefit of this filter is that it uses a pump. That means you can pump water from hard-to-reach places when you're unable to dip your bottle in a river to get clean water. The MSR will purify 528 gallons of water before you need to change its filter, so it will last for plenty of time.

MSR MiniWorks EX microfilter: **http://amzn.to/2gI08q0**

You just have to keep in mind that as good as these camping filters are, they are not designed to filter out lead. After all, when you're hiking in the mountains and need to purify water from a stream, you shouldn't have to worry about lead in the water!

Not Your Average Water Pitcher

Many of you probably already own a home water pitcher or a filter that hooks up to your faucet — maybe even our health franchise's very own Turapür.

But while these filters are good at turning safe tap water into more healthful water, you should also own a filter that will get rid of lead in the event your water supply becomes contaminated.

For this purpose, I recommend the ZeroWater pitcher.

The ZeroWater looks very similar to other water pitchers, but it is the only pitcher certified by NSF International to reduce lead. (NSF is an independent organization that tests and certifies products.)

The ZeroWater pitcher works by using five different processes to ensure you have clean drinking water.

The first layer is activated carbon that reduces chlorine and other unwanted tastes that are in the water. Next, an ion exchange process removes lead, mercury, and other dangerous toxins.

The three final processes further filter the water to make sure that the TDS level (total dissolved solids) of the water is 000. Basically, the FDA says that TDS levels in purified water must be between 000–010 ppm; otherwise, you can't call it purified water.

ZeroWater Pitcher: **http://amzn.to/2wDLbsS**

I certainly hope you or I won't ever have to deal with lead in our water. But by purchasing the Zero Water, you can rest assured that at least you'll be able to filter it out in the event the government is covering something up in your town.

10 FATAL MISTAKES TO AVOID WHEN STRANDED IN AN EMERGENCY ROADSIDE SITUATION

Life-threatening situations happen in every corner of America, in all types of conditions, in remote areas and metropolitan areas, in all types of weather.

As a former CIA officer, it's my business to be prepared to handle life-threatening situations. And I take my responsibility to protect my wife and three children very seriously.

While violent crimes grab most of the headlines, few people realize you're much more likely to find yourself stranded on the side of the road than you are to be murdered, raped, robbed or assaulted.

Over 30 MILLION Americans find themselves stranded on the road in their cars each and every year. That's more than 25 times the number of victims of violent crimes.

Every time you drive, you are operating in a dangerous environment. It's not just in blizzards or cold weather climates, either. You could be stuck in the desert or on a desolate stretch of highway.

No matter where you are — from the blizzards of Buffalo to the deserts of California or the flash floods of the southeast —

when you are behind the wheel of a car, your life is on the line.

In fact, more than one out of every six licensed drivers will be stranded on the road this year. So it's almost certain you, your spouse, a child, a sibling, a parent or a close friend will be stranded on the road at some point in the next 12 months.

Sadly, hundreds, perhaps thousands, of helpless, stranded motorists die needlessly each year because they're unprepared. If you're serious about doing everything you possibly can to protect your family in an emergency situation, this may be the most important message you'll ever see.

You've taken a wise first step to protect yourself and your loved ones from an unfortunate tragedy that needlessly claims a number of lives each year. There are a few common mistakes you need to avoid in an emergency roadside situation. Making these mistakes has cost thousands of stranded motorists their life. Which is why I've outlined them for you here — so you know exactly what 10 Fatal Mistakes to Avoid:

1. Leaving Your Car

Many people think that the best thing to do while stranded in your car is to get out and look for help. But this couldn't be more dangerous.

Your vehicle is your best protection against the elements, like sun, wind and exposure. The best thing you can do is remain in your vehicle, where rescuers are most likely to find you.

The Los Angeles Times reported a story in August 2016 of what they said appeared to be "the second heat-related fatality in Death Valley National Park" that year.

Las Vegas resident Linda Pi-Wei Hung was on her way to Fort Irwin. After not being heard from for a few days, county and federal search teams used two helicopters and scoured the desert looking for a sign.

Hours later, Hung's vehicle was found along a lonely dirt road. It's been speculated that Hung's vehicle got stuck in the sand, so she left her vehicle and started walking across the hot desert. Rangers speculate that Hung's vehicle got stuck in the sand while she was attempting to turn around, so she began walking across the baking desert to find help.

According to the Los Angeles Times, the high that day was 113 degrees, and Hung appeared to have died from heat exposure.

This is just one example of why you should remain with your vehicle.

Johnathan Doerr, a 19-year-old man from Tooele, Utah, went missing in January 2017. Fox 13 News reports the man was on his way to a job interview but was reported missing after he never showed up. His body was found days later about a mile off the highway.

Johnathan's car was located and appeared to have gotten stuck in the snow. Since he was nowhere to be found, the police speculated that the man had left his vehicle and went to search for help on foot.

According to Fox 13 News, police said it "appears the man died of exposure" to freezing temperatures.

Believe me, it's much safer to stay inside your car than it is to go exploring outside. "Abandon your car only as a last resort. A single person walking through the snow is much harder to find than a stranded vehicle," advises Allstate.

2. Your Car Is Not Visible

This is extremely important to remember. If your car isn't in plain sight, the chances of someone spotting you to help are slim to none.

Husband and wife Cecil Knutson and Dianna Bedwell found that out the hard way. According to The Independent, the pair became lost shortly after leaving a casino while looking for a shortcut to their destination.

The paper goes on to explain how they were ultimately led off the beaten path and became stuck in California's high desert. The couple, both diabetic, were found by off-road drivers two weeks after they had gone missing. Ms. Bedwell was barely holding on, but still alive. Her husband was not as fortunate.

Ms. Bedwell had informed authorities that she and her husband were looking for a shortcut when they got lost in a rough area, their vehicle hidden by trees and surrounding brush. Police stated that "the trees made the car invisible to helicopters that were conducting aerial searches."

You need to make sure that your car is as visible as possible.

How can you make your vehicle easy to find?

Keep a piece brightly colored, reflective ribbon in your emergency travel pack. Hang it from your window, or if you can get to your antenna, tie it to that. Any piece of brightly colored cloth or material that is easy to see will suffice in this situation.

If there is no rain or snow in the forecast, you could also open the hood of your car. This is recognized as a universal distress signal and will help to make you and your vehicle more visible.

Your emergency flashers will also be a good way to signal for help. I would recommend that you only turn on them on if you hear any approaching vehicles or movement outside, in an effort to conserve your battery.

If it gets to be dark out and you can run the engine at night, listen again for movement outside and potential rescuers. You might consider turning on the interior lights, as passersby might be able to catch a glimpse of the glow from a considerable distance.

3. Not Knowing Where You're Going

If you don't know where you are going, you make yourself much more susceptible to getting lost. And if you are lost, your chances of surviving instantly get worse.

Take another look at the story above. Cecil Knutson and Dianna Bedwell got lost trying to take a shortcut home. Had they been prepared with a map or GPS, they might have seen a different outcome.

ABC News reported a similar situation that happened to James and Kati Kim and their family...

The family was seeking a shortcut when the situation got out of control and took a turn for the worse.

James was driving and had missed a turn due to the snow making it hard to see. At a fork in the road, he failed to see a sign that would point him in the correct direction and then turned the wrong way.

Lost and in bad weather, the family decided to call it a night and try their luck in the morning. They parked the car and fell asleep, only to wake up to more snow and their vehicle now stuck.

The family was stranded for seven days when Mr. Kim decided to leave the vehicle and walk to get help.

Help finally arrived to Mrs. Kim and the two children on day nine. However, Mr. Kim was found two days later, dead in a lake 17 miles from the vehicle. (I want to again stress No. 1 on our list — don't leave your vehicle.)

Like Cecil Knutson and Dianna Bedwell, the Kims were just looking for a shortcut on their long drive. Their Saab station wagon got stuck in snow on a side road as they tried to find their way.

It's very important to know where you are going. And if you don't, be prepared with a map or a GPS navigation system and take the necessary precautions. Don't use back roads to save time or avoid traffic unless you're absolutely positive you know where you're going.

Stay on main roads when you can. This way, if anything happens, more people can spot you. Also, main roads are the first areas that rescue workers will reach in emergencies. Don't take shortcuts if you don't know where they lead.

4. Not Having a Backup Battery or Power Source

Nearly everyone has a cellphone these days, which is a great item to keep on you in the case of an emergency. However, a cellphone will only last you so long.

When your battery dies, you will essentially be cut off from any communication with the outside world. You won't be able to call 911 or text someone for help.

That's why it's crucial to have a backup battery or power source in the cabin of your car. Just think of the many ways this small device could save you from hours or even days of desperation. You could recharge the battery on your cellphone in just a few minutes.

And even with a small amount of charge, you could call 911. The GPS function on the phone could help rescue workers pinpoint your exact location and dig you out of whatever sticky situation you are in.

Yet with a dead phone and without a way to recharge the battery, you might freeze to death. Having a battery charger in the trunk won't be much help, because even if you could dig your way to the trunk, it's highly unlikely you would be able to open the trunk, considering it will be buried under several feet of wet, heavy snow.

The battery charger alone could help you escape in minutes, instead of hours. And those critical few minutes could easily be the difference between life and death — especially in subzero temperatures.

5. Not Clearing out the Exhaust Pipe

Carbon monoxide is an odorless, poisonous gas that can kill you. So it's crucial you make sure your car's engine can breathe properly.

Snowy weather is a prime time when a mistake can be made. The Associated Press released a story about an eastern

Pennsylvanian man who was trapped in his running car by a snowplow deluge. Authorities suspect he was trying to dig out his car and was either taking a break in the car with the motor running or trying to get out of the area when a plow came by and buried the car, thus blocking the exhaust and preventing him from getting out.

The man was pronounced dead less than an hour after he was found. He died of carbon monoxide poisoning.

If you find yourself stuck in the snow, it's crucial that you make sure you clean out your tailpipe. However, winter weather is not the only time your exhaust pipe might be blocked.

A story surfaced of five Florida children who were in a truck that was stuck in the mud with smoke billowing inside… the children all unconscious.

WJHG/CNN reported that several hunters were on a hunting trip when they found the truck stuck in a mud hole, the vehicle's tailpipe covered and the children all poisoned by carbon monoxide.

Luckily, the hunters showed up in time and freed the children and performed CPR until paramedics arrived. Aside from being a little shaken up, the children left in good health.

While that story had a happy ending, there are so many more that don't. The ugly truth is that carbon monoxide poisoning can be deadly in as few as five–15 minutes.

If you are ever stranded with your vehicle and the engine is on, make sure your exhaust pipe has a clear path and has room to breathe, or the repercussions could be deadly.

6. Not Having a Blanket or Any Items to Keep You Warm

Freezing cold temperatures can lead to hypothermia — a dangerous condition that can quickly kill you.

So if you are stranded in your car for an extended period in freezing temperatures, you're going to need something to keep you warm.

I recommend a Mylar survival blanket. This waterproof, heat-reflective blanket is constructed of durable, insulating Mylar — a breakthrough material designed by NASA for space exploration. This high-tech space blanket is thin and flexible and could save your life in an emergency situation.

Mylar helps keep you warm in several ways. First, it stops evaporative heat loss. When your sweat evaporates, it uses energy from your body and lowers your body temperature.

Mylar slows down the process of evaporative heat loss by increasing the humidity of the air next to the skin.

The space blanket also reduces convective heat loss. Cold air or wind causes convective heat loss, and the blanket forms a strong barrier between you and the cold air that lowers your body temperature.

Finally, we lose body heat through radiation — the heat simply radiates off your body. A Mylar blanket keeps you warm by reflecting 90% of your body heat back to you.

Plus, Mylar space blankets are super-small and lightweight.

And it's multifunctional, too…

In addition to serving its main purpose as an emergency blanket, it can also be used as emergency shelter by creating a tent or tarp. The material is waterproof, so it will protect you from rain or wet snow.

If you suddenly find yourself trapped in a freak blizzard, you could use it to heat your car by covering the windows of your car to reflect body heat back into the car.

The space blanket can be used to reflect heat either toward you or away from you. If the sun is bearing down on you while you're stranded, you can cover the windows with the Mylar blanket to reflect heat away from the car to keep you cool.

Because the surface of the Mylar space blanket is so shiny, it also creates an excellent distress signal that's easily visible to passing motorists and rescue teams and from the sky.

So the Mylar blanket could keep you warm while also signaling for help.

7. Not Having a Full Tank of Gas

When the weather is bad or you're driving for extended periods of time, make sure you start with a full tank of gas.

In really hazardous winter weather, the effects of the storm can last several days or more. So the more gas you have the better in case you become stranded.

You'll need it to help you stay warm, to make sure your fuel lines don't freeze, to keep your cellphone battery charged and hopefully even to have enough gas left over to leave after the storm, if needed.

You'll want to run your engine and heater for about 10 minutes every hour to keep you warm while also conserving fuel. I'd also recommend keeping a window cracked while the engine is running to get some fresh air and eliminate the possibility of carbon monoxide poisoning.

8. Not Having Light

Darkness is extremely dangerous in an emergency roadside situation. Without light, you'll have a difficult time finding anything after the sun sets.

Another vehicle could collide with your car, causing it to burst into flames. And in the worst-case scenario, you could get run over by an oncoming car whose driver can't see you.

I recommend keeping a flashlight in the car. The one I recommend is the SEAL Torch 2000.

With its XML-T6 LED bulb, the SEAL Torch 2000 is more than 11 times brighter than a traditional light. This allows you see absolutely everything. And that's critical at night during a roadside emergency.

The telescoping lens gives you the power to dial in the accuracy for a super-tight, nearly blinding beam. Or you can zoom back and cast a wide net to assess the entire situation.

And the SEAL Torch 2000 is practically indestructible, too.

It's made from super-strong metal designed to take a beating — not some cheap plastic like ordinary flashlights.

This incredible tool also has an SOS feature that allows you to send a distress signal that can be seen for miles. And with its specially designed muzzle edge, you can break your windshield to escape your car if necessary.

The SOS feature could been very valuable to a stranded motorist. You could shine the light of the SEAL Torch 2000, which would definitely stand out in the dark.

And using the SOS feature at night, it's much more likely someone would see your distress signal and rescue you sooner.

You could even use the SEAL Torch 2000 as a weapon should you encounter anyone who tries to do you harm while you're stranded on the side of the road.

There simply is no other emergency tool quite like this on the market.

SEAL Torch 2000: **http://bit.ly/2wDa4F0**

I want you to be completely prepared for anything that could happen during a roadside emergency, and as you can see, this spectacular piece of equipment can save your life in many ways.

9. Not Being Prepared With an Emergency Kit

An emergency kit could save your life. As you can see in the examples above, you could recharge your cellphone, keep yourself warm or signal for help with the Mylar blanket and more.

It should be small, compact, designed to easily fit in the cabin of your car — not in the trunk — and packed with life-saving items, including:

- A three-foot-long strip of bright orange ribbon to use as a visual distress signal

- A first-aid kit packed with everything you'll need to take care of small scrapes or even bigger wounds

- Duct tape. After food and water, duct tape is so versatile it could be your most valuable asset in an emergency. Use it as an emergency Band-Aid, to tape broken fingers together, to mark a trail (so you don't get lost or so a rescue team can find you), to leave notes to help rescue personnel find you and more

- Rain gear in case you're stuck in a torrential downpour… when you're wet, your body heat drops more than when you're dry

- Waterproof matches so you can start a fire in any situation to provide heat or light or to cook food and boil water

- And all the items mentioned above…

It's crucial you be prepared with an emergency car kit in the event of an emergency. So whatever situation you find yourself in, you'll have the peace of mind knowing you've got all the equipment you'll need to survive until help arrives.

Life-threatening situations happen in every corner of America in all types of conditions, in remote areas and metropolitan areas and in all types of weather. And most people are terribly unprepared for even the most common crises.

You can hope and pray that you and your family never find yourself in an emergency roadside situation without the survival equipment and supplies that could save your life. However, hoping is not a good strategy when your life is on the line.

Especially when you know that more than one out of every six American drivers is going to be stranded on the road at some point in the next 12 months.

If you or a family member is suddenly stuck in an emergency roadside situation, you need to have the survival supplies and equipment that could save your life.

The only responsible thing you can do to protect yourself

and your family from tragedy is to be prepared for unexpected events like these.

By familiarizing yourself with these 10 fatal mistakes and how to avoid them, and by investing in a well-stocked emergency pack, you've taken necessary precautions to keep you and your family safe from sudden tragedy and possibly even death.

YOU CAN'T DRINK GOLD

Four men were chosen for an incredibly important — and dangerous — intelligence mission. The region of the world they were headed to was so hostile to the United States they couldn't fly into the country.

Instead, they had to be dropped into a neighboring country and hike to their final destination. Because they would be hiking for several days and needed a significant amount of gear, a support team dropped packages they could pick up at strategic points along the way.

The men had specifically requested a water bladder (similar to a CamelBak) so they could stay hydrated in the desert they were hiking through. This posed a bit of a problem. The support team was concerned that when the water bladders were dropped they would explode and damage sensitive equipment that was also included in the drop package.

One support team member came up with the bright idea to include gold bullion in the package instead of water. They figured that with the gold the four operatives could purchase all of the water they needed.

What the support team member failed to realize is that these operatives were hiking through the middle of nowhere. It didn't matter if they had thousands of dollars worth of gold bullion — there wasn't anyone around to trade it with. Fortunately, the intelligence operatives ended up OK, but I'm willing to bet that they had some choice words for the support team when they made it back to base.

So here's the bottom line: Yes, it's important to have gold and silver bullion as part of a preparedness plan. But it should come only after you've put together all of your other survival supplies.

You first need to ensure that you have food storage (at least one month), water storage (at least one week) and bug-out bags in your home and in the back of your vehicles.

After all, if a crisis occurs and people are desperate for food and water, they're not going to care that you've got a shiny gold coin. They're going to care about keeping food and water on hand to take care of their family.

So please, don't fall into the trap that you can buy your way out of an emergency situation and that you don't need to bother to prepare ahead of time.

I can tell you as a father of three young children that there's no amount of gold in this world that's going to get me to sell my food or water storage and watch my family suffer.

PAYING, TRADING AND BARTERING IN A CASHLESS WORLD

When the lights go out for a long time, your cash will be worthless to most people.

Just three weeks into a crisis, Bill Gates could stroll into anybody's home with a wheelbarrow of cash and nobody would sell him a thing — not water, not canned goods, not even a few tomatoes growing in their garden.

Cash would no longer have a value. Which is why you will need a store of items that people NEED in order to survive, which you can pay, trade and barter with.

That could mean more tangible forms of payment such as water, gasoline, alcohol, food and more.

So in order to help prepare you for this type of emergency, I've put together this report. Read on for my list of valuable items that you should stock up on in the event your cash will no longer be any good…

Basic Communication and Negotiation

First and foremost, you need to figure out what you want and what you currently have in stock.

Value in a cashless world is typically determined by utility, usefulness and rarity (or difficulty to obtain/make), so keep that in mind.

When determining what you can trade for the item you want, find out what the other person needs — the more in need of something they are, the more it is worth to them, and the more easily they will make the trade. However, the item you are trading with must not exceed the value of the item you're getting in return

It would be inconceivable to assume society as a whole would throw off its sense of justice in a cashless world. Fairly quickly in this situation, some kind of either improvised or variation of an existing justice system would emerge, probably with qualified overseers to settle disputes.

For this reason, it would be foolish to make any transaction without proof of that transaction. All transactions — no matter how small — should be set in writing and dated, with three copies (for you, the person you're trading with and some kind of authority that keeps records). You should also have a neutral third party witness the transaction and sign the agreements with you (not much different than a notary).

The Most Valuable Items to Stock

Bullets: Ammo is easy to stock up on as long as you choose the calibers that are most common, such as the .22, .22lr, .223, .308, 9mm and 12 gauge shells.

Since the government is making it tougher and tougher to buy guns and ammo, get it while you can. It's likely you will be able to sell it to people who have run out.

Bonus if you can make ammo yourself with a press!

Metals: Metals like copper, steel, iron, rebar, etc., are used in multitudes of things, like electronics, appliances, infrastructure and buildings. They are easy to find and will be useful for barter.

Tools and building supplies: Items like wood, nails, hammers, saws and other general fix-it tools will be in high demand after a collapse. You could even use your tools and barter simply with your skills to build shelters or for repairs, etc.

Flashlights: When the lights go out, people are going to be looking for a way to see. And after the sun sets, there will be complete darkness without an artificial light source. Flashlights and lanterns will be a necessity for anyone who doesn't have light.

Batteries: A no-brainer. If you have devices like radios, flashlights and walkie-talkies, you will want to have batteries on hand. And if others have those devices on hand, chances are they will need batteries at some point as well.

Rechargeable batteries: While batteries are a great item to have on hand, rechargeable batteries should have a higher value, because you get more use out of them. I like the Panasonic eneloop rechargeable batteries. These batteries come pre-charged from the factory, so you can immediately put them to use. Also, they can be recharged up to 2,100 times. You could keep these charged and easily sell them for goods and services, even recharging them every so often at a cost.

Water: You need to prepare for the thing that will kill you first. You need water for staying hydrated as well as cooking food to stay nourished and healthy. This will be a high-value item to anyone who has run out, as you can only survive without water for a few days.

Sugar: Stockpiling sugar is wise because it can be used in a variety of different foods and can help you keep your energy up. It will also help you to make comfort foods during hard times, which people might be desperate for in a desperate time.

Rice: Rice is a great source of carbohydrates, is high in calories and protein and has essential vitamins and minerals. Specifically, whole grain rice, as it has a longer shelf life. It's easy to make and makes an easy item to barter.

Clothing: If you're smart, instead of throwing away old clothes (or giving them to charity, which isn't a bad idea, but that's not the point), you can recondition and keep them for after the collapse. With so many preppers focused on food and water, few of them think that that old pair of jeans will ever be useful. It's very likely that clothing factories from China are going to ship them to the U.S. anymore.

Alcohol: This is good to have on hand because it has multiple uses. You can drink it, use it for cooking and even use it for hygienic purposes such as cleaning a cut or wound. Even if you don't drink alcohol, it could be a crucial item in bartering. Knowing how to make it is even better.

Cigarettes (and other tobacco products): Vices are vices. And this one happens to be addictive. Although rather expensive, you can buy these in bulk and be sure that they will be a hot commodity for barter with any nearby smokers.

Medical supplies: This is something you want to put a high price on. Getting meds will be hard if not impossible, so you don't want to just give them away, though that may be the right thing to do. Consider stockpiling the following:

- Ibuprofen
- Benadryl
- Bandages of all shapes and sizes
- Gauze and surgical tape
- Vinyl gloves
- Cotton balls
- Rubbing alcohol
- Aspirin
- Antibiotic cream, etc.

Tip: If you stock up on first-aid supplies to barter with (or simply to hand out freely to people in need), consider the generic name brands as a way to save money. For the most part, many generics do just as well as the more expensive brand names (unless, that is, we're talking about survival gear — a good piece of gear that has a lifetime of use is worth the price paid, specifically if it doesn't break or rip on you).

With the increase in both natural and manmade disasters, improving your first-aid skills should be a priority. To be clear, first-aid preparedness should go beyond just having a first-aid kit. You should have some basic training along with the proper medical supplies. Many local colleges offer first-aid courses that will teach you CPR along with other basic first-aid skills — skills that are essential in any survival situation.

Food: Food, like water, is a necessity for survival. In a survival situation, anyone who runs out of food risks starvation. Food is a great item to store in a barter economy, specifically canned and freeze-dried foods, because they have a long shelf life (especially foods like eggs, which can easily be dipped in wax and kept for years)

Seeds: Gardening is another great skill to hone. You can grow your own food and trade the fresh-grown food. I would recommend planting heirloom or non-GMO seeds — since those seeds can be saved and replanted from year to year. This is the type of skill you should practice now, even if you don't need the food to survive. You never know when that will change, and the experience will be invaluable.

Salt/pepper/other spices: These items, while great for seasoning food, are also very important for preserving perishable food items like meat. Salt is particularly versatile, as it can be used for cleaning and medicinally.

Copper wiring: This is an extremely useful item, as it is used in power generation, transmission and distribution, telecommunication, electronics and electricity. Because of its range of uses, it's a good item to have in place of money

Oil and gasoline: Fuel is a great item to have for barter because it powers essential items such as generators and vehicles.

If someone needs power or is trying to get from Point A to Point B, they will likely put a high value on both gasoline and oil.

Finally, use your skills. Whether it be cooking, home defense, fixing things, medical skills and more… these could always be useful in a crisis for not only you but others. Why not use them to your advantage?

Any of the items listed above will be as good as gold.

Most people think in terms of preparing for what they need… they don't think about what happens when they need to go "shopping" in a society that doesn't trust the value of cash.

That's why I've provided you with the Paying, Trading and Bartering in a Cashless World. So you are fully prepared to survive in an environment where cash no longer has a value.

AN EMERGENCY STOCKPILE EVERY HOME NEEDS

"Your dad's in jail," my mom told me as tears streamed down her face. "I need $1,400 to bail him out, and if I don't get the money within the next two hours, he'll be there for the entire weekend."

I was 7 years old when those words left my mother's mouth, and I remember her frantically making phone call after phone call trying to come up with the money. After all, she got the call from my dad in the evening — the banks were closed, and this was long before there was an ATM on every street corner.

Fortunately, one of our family friends happened to be a rich Italian couple that literally kept thousands of dollars stuffed in their mattress. When my mom called and told them she needed to borrow $1,400 immediately, they said it would be no problem at all. She quickly drove over to their house and picked up the cash, and I stayed there while she and another family friend drove down to the Washington, D.C., jail. Thanks to their kindness, my dad didn't have to spend the weekend in jail.

So why was my dad thrown in jail? A misunderstanding, really. Earlier that day, he and a business partner attended a meeting in D.C. When they got back from the meeting, there was a boot on the business partner's car for unpaid parking tickets.

This partner decided it would be a good idea to try to remove the boot, but while he was doing so, a police car happened to be passing by. When the police stopped to ask him what he was doing, the partner proceeded to scream and yell at them. Obviously, this didn't go over well, and both my dad and his business partner got arrested.

The following Monday, all charges were dropped. But regardless of the happy ending, this is one of the moments in life that I'll never forget.

It's also one of the reasons I believe it's incredibly important to always have a stash of emergency cash on hand. Life is unpredictable. You never know when this emergency cash will help get you or a family member out of a jam, or when it will save your life by keeping you clothed and fed.

Be Your Own Bank

Here's what I recommend:

- Have enough cash on hand to cover one month of living expenses. This is different for everyone— some folks may need $3,000 to survive for a month, while others need $10,000. Determine what's realistic for your family

- Don't keep it all in $100 bills. You want to have a few bills of each denomination, with the majority of your money being in $20s. This will make it easier to spend if an emergency does arise

- Don't keep it all in one place — split the money up in various places around your home. Keep half in the basement and half in the attic, or even half at your office, if that's a safe option.

Get Creative When Stashing Your Cash

Wherever you decide to store the money, it's critical that it isn't easily accessible or identified. Never keep your emergency cash stored anywhere in a master bedroom — that's the first place criminals go when they break into a house.

Instead, get creative. For example, you could keep the money in a small fireproof safe inside a box in your attic that's marked "old clothes" or "sewing materials." If you enjoy camping like I do and have a ton of camping gear stored in a closet, you could use a stainless steel water bottle to store your cash.

Of course, the more creative you get, the safer your cash could be. For instance, I know one fellow who has a gun safe where he keeps an old gun, about $100 worth of cash, and

some worthless jewelry. This is his decoy safe, and he's not going to be too upset if a burglar pops this open.

His real safe full of guns and cash is buried in a floor safe in his home. He uses something similar to the SentrySafe 7250 Waterproof Floor Safe, which I recommend.

SentrySafe 7250 Waterproof Floor Safe: **http://amzn.to/2xLAZ1s**

Another of my favorite options is to hide your cash in plain sight by using a wall safe that's disguised as a picture frame or an electrical box.

However you decide to store your cash is, obviously, up to you, but the most important thing is that you start building up your emergency stash today. If one day you turn on the news and discover the banks are closed and ATMs have run dry, you'll be grateful that you planned ahead.

FOUR COMMON SURVIVAL MISTAKES AND HOW TO AVOID THEM

In this newsletter, we've discussed many, many things you should do in preparation for an emergency, the moment a crisis occurs and in the aftermath of a disaster.

But just as important as the shoulds are the should nots.

So here's a list of four common mistakes that could put your life at risk when disaster strikes. If you ever find yourself in a survival scenario, these are four things you DON'T want to do:

1. Don't rely on social media. While social media is a great tool for sharing photos and funny anecdotes, I wouldn't put too much trust in the accuracy of information people post in a crisis situation.

When someone posts unverified information and three of their friends share it, then three of each of their friends share it and on and on… the spread of misinformation is difficult to stop.

The fact is false intel can get you killed.

Too many people trust everything they see on social media. Always be sure to verify the veracity of what you read online, no matter who posted it.

2. Don't change your emergency plans. If you and your family have an emergency plan in place, stick to it. If you've arranged to meet at your child's school, then head to your child's school when the stuff hits the fan. In my family, not only do we have a designated meeting spot, but we have a backup spot as well.

Unless there's an insurmountable reason — the roads are blocked or a bridge is washed out — you must remain calm and stick to your plan. When disaster strikes, too many people forget all their preparations and just wing it. This puts you and your loved ones in unnecessary danger, so don't abandon your plan.

3. Don't underestimate the situation. Don't be that person who drives through a flooded road because the water doesn't look that deep only to watch your car get carried away. In any type of survival situation, be extra cautious. Never underestimate the strength of Mother Nature, and always err on the side of prudence.

4. Don't just focus on food. Obviously, you need to eat to survive. That said, some people focus so much on food storage that they forget other necessities.

Our bodies can go without food for longer periods than without water. And if you live in a colder climate, warmth is an important consideration. I have many friends that are guilty of this, and I'm always reminding them to be well-rounded in their preparations.

In addition to food, make sure you have water storage, water filters, medicine, medical supplies, clothing and shelter.

Do or Die

Now that we've got several don'ts out of the way, let's revisit some of the dos. Here are the four most important things you should do before and during a survival situation:

1. Do plan and practice. When it comes to survival gear,

people often forget to familiarize themselves with the ins and outs of all their gear so they know how to use it in an emergency. Learn how your gear works and be sure to test it periodically. This may seem basic, but remember, during a stressful situation, you won't have time to figure out your equipment.

Believe me, if you knew all the prep work that spies do before going on an operation, it would make your head spin. After all, if an operation fails, people may die. The same could be said in an emergency, so it's important to know your gear.

A good way to bring the whole family up to speed is to take your gear camping. Once, my family lived off of survival food — you know, the kind that comes in pouches — for an entire week to make sure we liked it and our kids would eat it. The food wasn't too bad, the kids ate (almost) everything and now we all know what we're in for.

2. Do make friends. Use your skills and supplies to help others, because they may also be able to help you. Let's say your neighbor is a paramedic and you have an extensive collection of guns. You could strike a deal to help each other in a crisis, trading protection for first aid.

Basically, people have a better chance of getting through dangerous situations together. I realize that the movies make it seem "sexy" to be a lone wolf. But in real life, you'll be much more successful if you're willing to work with others.

3. Do immediately set up communications. In an emergency, you need to stay on top of the latest information. This why I recommend having an emergency radio and knowing how to use it. A great inexpensive radio for listening to news and weather is the Sony ICF-S10MK2 pocket AM/FM radio.

"People have a better chance of getting through dangerous situations together."

You should also have a two-way radio to communicate with friends and family. A two-way radio allows you to check in with your loved ones and see if they're able to report any useful information. Just be sure everyone knows which channel to use ahead of time.

4. Do maintain security. Whether you're dealing with a natural or a man-made disaster — whether you're bugging out or bugging in — you need to have a security plan to protect yourself and your family.

When people are desperate, they'll do things you never expected. Like the neighbor down the street who has always been nice to you. What if he knows you have a ton of survival supplies and comes to take them?

Always have a way to defend yourself no matter the situation. Both an AR-15 and Remington 870 shotgun are good long guns to have on hand for extreme situations.

The next time you are reviewing your emergency plans and survival gear, take the time to go over these dos and don'ts with your family. I would hate for a simple mistake to put you or a loved one in danger.

NINE SURVIVAL MYTHS THAT ARE DOWNRIGHT DANGEROUS

By Robert Blaze | *Contributor, Survival Ready Blog*

Survival and preparedness reality shows are both good and bad. On the one hand, they bring awareness to important topics such as being ready for disasters. On the other, they propagate a lot of myths to satisfy and delight some of their less informed viewers.

Myth: The most important thing in a survival situation is finding food and water.

Well, it depends. The rule of threes states that shelter is the most important thing. However, I lean more toward the "What's going to kill you first?" approach. For example, if you have a wound that could get infected, then access to clean water and medical supplies is your top priority.

And in situations where there's a chance your core body temperature will be affected, then shelter should be your first priority.

Shelter is more than just unpacking your tent. You also have to find the right place to camp to avoid floods, wild animals and people. You have to build it in such a way that it protects you from the elements and keeps you warm and dry throughout the night.

Hypothermia will kill you a lot faster than lack of food. Your body will last for days, even weeks, without anything to eat. But if you're wet and unable to get yourself dry and stay warm... you won't last long.

Myth: Starting a fire is easy.

The bow drill method, using dryer lint as tinder, using a ferro rod... there are many ways to start a fire. And many of them are depicted in YouTube videos that make starting a fire seem really easy. But is it?

If you're in a damp environment, or if the wood isn't dry enough or simply isn't the right kind, you could end up wasting your time and energy.

Some people might argue that starting a fire is not difficult. Anyone can start a fire with a lighter in seconds, and most preppers have at least two–three in their survival bags, not to mention blast matches and even steel wool and a 9-volt battery. But if your primary methods don't work for any reason, you could be in serious trouble.

Myth: Eating snow will keep you hydrated.

In reality, your body will have to spend a great deal of energy to warm that snow before it can utilize it. It's much better to melt the snow into water and then drink it. You should also filter it with a bandana and purify it if you have the means. Rainwater and water resulting from melting snow is typically safe to drink, but the cleaner the better.

Myth: Water from a cactus is safe to drink.

Water from cacti is very acidic and could cause you to get sick, especially if you drink it on an empty stomach. This doesn't mean you'll die, but it won't make the survival situation any more pleasant for you or your kidneys.

Myth: You need to boil water for X minutes to kill pathogens.

According to the Wilderness Medical Society, which is quoted by a number of survival blogs and articles (including Princeton's website), all pathogens will be killed by the time the water comes to a rolling boil, even at high altitudes.

Myth: Alcohol warms up your body.

Quite the opposite. Alcohol will make you feel warmer by sending more blood to your skin. However, this blood has to come from someplace else, which means your internal organs will receive less blood and your body temperature will drop.

Myth: Drinking your own pee is a good idea.

Don't do it unless you're an astronaut with access to NASA's Water Recovery System or you really, really need to. Just like salt water, urine will dehydrate your body even more.

Myth: Making shelter is all about the roof.

Not really — there's a lot more to it. You need protection from ALL the things that can harm your body one way or another: damp soil, wind, critters. Plus, your shelter needs to keep as much heat in as possible to keep you warm.

For survival purposes, a bivy bag, may make for a better shelter than hanging a tarp over a few branches. You should also consider how to insulate your shelter, whether it's with aluminum foil, leaves, moss or other materials.

Bivy Bag: **http://bit.ly/2wBwbNJ**

Myth: You can suck the venom out of a snake bite.

Not a good idea, even if you're Rambo. You should either have a snake bite kit and the knowledge to use it, or, even better, seek medical attention immediately. Never suck the venom out, because you'll not only further damage the wound, but poison yourself as well.

The big takeaway here is that you can't learn real survival skills from reality television. But the more you read and learn from reliable experts, the better prepared you'll be. Knowledge trumps tools and gear every single time.

10 SIMPLE DIY FIRE STARTERS

By Anthony Urso

Fire is one of the most important components to survival. It provides heat, cooks your food, purifies your water and gives you an overall sense of comfort. Without fire, you would struggle to survive without electricity and the modern conveniences we have become accustomed to.

Because fire is so important, it is crucial you have at least two ways to start a fire in your bug-out bag and emergency survival stash. Fire-starting materials are typically very lightweight and small enough to fit in the glove box of your car, in a pocket of your purse or even in a shaving kit.

"Fire is so important, it is crucial you have at least two ways to start a fire in your bug-out bag."

If you like being crafty or don't want to spend the money on fire starters you buy in the stores, here are some ideas for making your own:

1. Cut up strips of old cardboard you probably have lying around. Dip the strips in wax and let them dry. Pop them in a sandwich bag and add them to your emergency gear.

The coated cardboard will burn nice and slow. This is ideal when you are trying to get a tinder bundle going and don't want it to burn out in a quick few seconds.

2. Put a bunch of your junk mail through a paper shredder. Place the shredded paper in a bag and toss it in your bug-out bag. You can also coat the paper shreds with melted candle wax for added burn time. The next time you burn a candle, save the wax for your DIY fire-starting materials.

3. Buy a bag of cotton balls and a jar of petroleum jelly (Vaseline). Use a knife or ice pop stick to spread petroleum jelly on a cotton ball. Place the gooey cotton balls in a sandwich bag. You can make the cotton balls easier to light by adding a couple drops of lighter fluid to each cotton ball. The petroleum jelly will add several minutes of burn time to the cotton ball, which will give you enough time to get a tinder bundle burning.

4. Save your egg cartons and shred some more of those old bills and junk mail you don't want. Stuff each slot with shredded paper. You can also use old sawdust. Melt candle wax and pour it over each wad of paper or sawdust in the egg carton. Allow the wax to dry. Cut the carton into individual slots and store in a plastic bag.

5. Save your orange peels the next time you buy oranges. Allow the peels to dry thoroughly. Once completely dry, store in a plastic or paper bag. The natural oils in the skin are excellent for starting a fire.

6. Buy a pack of cotton makeup remover pads. Dip each pad in melted wax and allow to dry. When you need to start a fire, tear the cotton discs in half or enough to expose the cotton fibers and light with a match. The wax coating will slow down the burn and give you plenty of time to get a healthy fire going.

7. Create decorative fire starters out of pine cones. Wrap twine or use candle wick material around the base of the cone. Put the cone in small bowl so that it is standing upright. Melt wax in a double broiler and pour the wax into the bowl, covering the bottom portion of the pine cone. Wait about five minutes for the wax to harden and then pull the cone out of the bowl. The pine cones will burn nice and slow for several minutes. These are best stored away in your home's emergency supplies.

8. Fill a small jar with rubbing alcohol and drop in used corks. You can often find corks at thrift stores or in bulk at various craft stores. When you are ready to start a fire, put your cork in the tinder bundle and light a match. The alcohol will immediately spark, and the cork will burn for about a minute. You can remove the corks from the alcohol solution after a few days and store in plastic bags or old medicine containers to keep in your bug-out bag.

9. Dry bundles of herbs from your garden. You can transform your fire starter into something pleasant and aromatic. Place a few of the herbs on a piece of newspaper. Roll the newspaper up and around the herbs. Twist the ends to form what resembles a piece of wrapped candy. Put the newspaper bundle in the middle of a pile of twigs and light it.

10. Combine cedar shavings (which you can buy at any pet store) with cupcake liners. You can pick up a bag of old candles at most thrift stores to waterproof your fire starters. Use a cupcake pan and line each slot with a paper liner. Fill the liners with shavings. Melt down the old candles and pour the melted wax into each cupcake liner. Allow the wax to dry and you have quick fire starters for under $10.

PROTECT YOUR DIGITAL MEMORIES FROM A BLACKOUT

Almost every facet of our modern society depends on electricity being always available. If you've been prepping for any stretch of time, then you've probably heard of an EMP, or electromagnetic pulse. These large releases of energy are caused by solar flares that are discharged by the sun but can also be triggered by detonating a nuclear weapon in the atmosphere.

A strong enough EMP could wipe out all electronics that haven't been shielded. Supply chains would fail, food would spoil, we wouldn't be able to purify or pump water on a large scale, and many other electricity-dependent systems would falter.

The solution to protecting your electronic devices is to build what's called a Faraday cage that has enough layers of protection to negate the effects of an EMP and protect your devices. Fortunately, a Faraday cage is relatively affordable for anyone who wants to play it safe and protect, say, their hard drive full of family photos, a flash drive full of professional documents, and so forth.

Here's how you can build your own Faraday cage and save your treasured electronics.

Required Materials:

- Heavy-duty aluminum foil
- Plastic wrap, such as Saran, or plastic bags for each electronic item
- Pieces of cloth for wrapping items
- A cardboard box (the amount you'll need depends on what all you're protecting)
- A galvanized steel trash can (optional: for storing a large amount of items).

How It's Made:

1. Wrap an item that you want to protect in cloth. This keeps the item from making contact with the aluminum foil and prevents sharp corners from piercing the foil.

2. Wrap the device in plastic wrap or place it into a plastic bag.

3. Wrap the plastic-covered item with at least three layers of foil. Ensure that the device is covered well by each layer.

4. Put the foil-wrapped device into your cardboard box.

5. Wrap the entire cardboard box in two layers of aluminum foil. (Having more layers means having more protection.)

6. Store the wrapped box off of the ground.

7. (Optional: Line your galvanized steel trash can with cardboard and then place your wrapped items into it. Be certain that the foil is not touching any metal and that the lid fits tightly to the can.)

Power Your Essential Devices After an EMP

The aftermath of an EMP is a frightening picture to imagine. The devices that still work after an EMP will eventually lose their charge, and with the entire electric grid annihilated, it will be hard to keep vital communications devices, and possibly your freezer, running.

Only a generator that is powered by a free, highly available type of fuel will keep your power running indefinitely. That's why we've researched and designed the perfect solution: the Power Whisperer, a quiet, portable, solar generator that is resistant to EMPs.

Power Whisperer: **http://bit.ly/2wBChxw**

[Jason's Note: For more from Lee, visit **www.independentlivingnews.com]**

MY TOP MUST-HAVE SURVIVAL TOOLS

By Cade Courtley | *Former Navy SEAL*

In the SEAL teams, if you don't have the right gear — you don't come home.

It might be as simple as the extra pair of AA batteries wrapped in tape that made all the difference on a mission in Iraq. Or that one extra quart of hydraulic fluid that kept my teammate's heavily damaged helicopter airborne until he was able to safely land it in Afghanistan. Then there's the 5 oz. self-applied tourniquet that has saved thousands of lives over the last decade.

The right tools make all the difference. But what are the "right" tools?

Well, they vary — depending on your geographic location, the operational environment (hostile/permissive), local laws, weather and the situation.

I understand that's quite a lot of factors to consider when equipment shopping. So where should you start?

Here are five pieces of gear I never leave home without. You'll notice there are a few common elements between these items. They are all:

1. Small and lightweight.
2. Durable.
3. Capable of performing multiple functions.
4. Easily carried on the body.

I've had to rely on each of these tools in many different situations, and I can personally attest to their efficacy and life-saving abilities.

Not only do I cover how each of these tools comes in handy in critical circumstances, I give specific recommendations for the brands I carry. Take a look below.

1. Watch With GPS: My preference is the Garmin fenix,  a rugged, multisport timepiece with GPS navigation, altimeter, compass and barometer — in addition to all of the basic functions of a watch. The extra features help you navigate in unfamiliar territory. This watch also has a great "back track" feature. If you get lost, you can simply follow your path back to where you started.

The altimeter is a great tool for knowing your position and telling others where you are, and the barometer will keep you ahead of the game if the weather starts to change. The light on the watch can be used for signaling when attached to a small piece of rope and spun over your head. In the SEAL teams, we called this move a "buzz saw" and used it for signaling aircraft.

2. Tactical Rigger's Belt With D-Ring Buckle: I wear the Elite Survival Systems Cobra Tactical Rigger's Belt. More than just keeping my pants up, this belt has a heavy-duty quick-release buckle that allows me to remove it quickly and use it as  a weapon. The D-ring can be used for emergency descent from a high point, used to anchor someone else or as an attachment

point to keep someone close in a low-visibility situation.

3. Multitool: You get a lot of bang for your buck with a good multitool. You can cut with it, make repairs with it, even fight with it. I prefer a more robust set of pliers than the needle nose variety that comes on many brands, including the collapsible "fist pack" size, which is why I carry the Gerber Flik Multi Tool everywhere I go.

4. Water Filter: You can go weeks without food, but you will only survive a few days without water. In a survival situation, you can't always expect clean water to be easily available, which is why I recommend the SurvFilter 300. This device uses nanotechnology to filter approximately 300 gallons of pure water — directly from streams, puddles, lakes and more — before needing to be replaced. Independent testing proves this filter effectively removes 99.9999% of contaminants — including viruses and chemicals.

SurvFilter 300: **http://bit.ly/2hNPjxE**

5. Butane Lighter: There are several reasons you may need to start a fire — to keep warm, cook a meal or perhaps signal someone — and you can't count on a disposable lighter when

that time comes. I carry the Ultimate Survival Technologies Delta Stormproof Lighter. It's waterproof with the cover closed, and the flame is capable of withstanding winds of up to 80 miles an hour without going out.

By amassing this quintessential collection of gear, you will be more prepared to handle any crisis situation and make it home alive. So pick these items up today and be a survivor, not a statistic.

FROM GETTING LOST IN THE WILDERNESS TO ECONOMIC COLLAPSE, A QUALITY KNIFE COULD SAVE YOUR LIFE

In 1985, two friends by the names of Joe Simpson and Simon Yates decided to climb the Siula Grande, a harrowing, ice-covered, 21,000-foot mountain in the Andes.

They successfully reached the top of the mountain and began their descent feeling as though they'd accomplished their goal — until a horrible blizzard set in. To ensure they didn't lose each other, they tied themselves together with a rope and began the treacherous descent.

As they were carefully making their way down the mountain, things went from bad to worse. Simpson fell and shattered his leg bone into several pieces. Not willing to leave his friend, Yates was determined to get both of them to safety. He attempted to lower Simpson over the edge of a cliff, since Simpson was unable to rappel down himself. However, due to the brutal snowstorm, things didn't go as planned and Simpson found himself hanging in midair as Yates anchored him from above.

After multiple attempts to lower Simpson down, Yates began to lose strength and knew that he would soon be dragged over the cliff to his own death. At that moment, Yates did the unthinkable and cut the rope that was holding his friend. In what can only be called a miracle, Simpson survived the fall into an ice crevasse and was able to hike several miles on his broken leg back to base camp.

Later, when the friends united, Simpson told Yates that he'd made the right decision and he would have cut the rope too.

This is an incredible tale of survival. Beyond the sheer bravery it took, if the men hadn't been prepared with a knife, they both could have ended up dying.

While I realize you probably won't be scaling an ice-covered cliff anytime soon (I know I won't) I'd like to share with you the key qualities you should look for when choosing the factors that make up the ultimate self-defense and survival knife.

After all, you never know when you'll need to rely on a knife, whether it's during a natural disaster or in the midst of some type of urban crisis such as an economic collapse. And the fact is if you do find yourself in a critical situation and you don't have the right knife on hand, you may not make it out alive.

This is why when push comes to shove, the knife you have with you needs to include the following...

1. **Fixed Blade** — Every day, I carry a folding knife clipped to my pants pocket. I use this knife to open the mail and to open all of the boxes I get from Amazon. But other than these purposes, I would never want to put my life in the hands of a folding knife. This is because a "folder" is not built for prying or for intense force, and it will snap off at the pivot point under significant pressure. A fixed-blade knife is much stronger and more reliable.

2. **High Quality** — For certain things in life, I'm very cheap. But not when it comes to my survival gear. After all, I'd never want to find myself stranded in the woods with a $20 knife I purchased at Wal-Mart, because, as the saying goes, you get what you pay for. A quality fixed-blade

knife is going to cost a few hundred dollars and is worth every penny if it gets you safely back to your family.

3. **Tang** — You want the steel of the blade to run from the tip of the knife all the way through the bottom of the handle. This is called full tang. In cheap knives, the blade stops where it enters the handle, which is why you can find certain knives with hollow handles. The problem with this is the same problem of having a folding knife, in that, under duress, the blade will snap off at the handle.

4. **Size** — Paul Hogan's famous line in Crocodile Dundee as he draws his huge knife in front of a potential attacker is "That's not a knife… THAT's a knife!" While big knives look cool in the movies, they are not ideal for a survival situation. First, a huge knife isn't easy to conceal, so you'll have a hard time carrying it without drawing attention to yourself.

Also, big knives weigh a lot more, so if you have to carry it while hiking several miles, it won't exactly be comfortable. The ideal size knife is 8–10 inches in overall length, which allows you to do a number of tasks without running into problems because the knife is too big or too small.

5. **Straight Edge** — You want your knife to be a straight edge and not serrated. Believe me, I know serrated edge knives look cool, but they have very few practical uses and are much tougher to sharpen.

6. **Steel** — Knives are made of numerous types of steel, which is why some knives cost $20 and others are hundreds of dollars. Because the type of steel determines the strength of the blade, the ability to hold an edge, and how easy a knife is to sharpen, you only want to go with a quality steel. These include steels such as S35VN, D2, and AEB-L.

7. **Torture-Tested** — I want to make sure any knife I may

have to bet my life on has passed a series of torture tests. A few such tests include slicing through a tire, being hammered into a cinder block, cutting through a piece of metal, and how far it can slice through a piece of beef. If a knife fails these tests, it's better to find out now than when it really counts.

8. **Ease of Use** — In a crisis situation, you never want to complicate things. In other words, you don't want a knife with a ton of bells and whistles (built-in flashlight, fish-hooks, etc.) that can get in the way or slow you down. You want a knife that you can easily deploy and quickly use if the need ever arises.

9. **Sheath** — No knife is complete without a quality sheath. The fact is if you can't draw your knife from the sheath, or if the knife falls out because the sheath is flimsy, it doesn't matter how good of a knife you have. I personally prefer plastic injection-molded sheaths that hold the knife snug but also allow for quick draws. In addition, I like sheaths that are versatile and can be worn vertically, horizontally, inside the waistband, and outside the waistband on the hip.

I certainly hope you never find yourself in a survival situation, but if you do, you'll be glad you have a knife that meets the criteria above.

SEVEN WAYS YOUR BELT CAN KEEP YOU ALIVE

Unless I'm swimming, I always have a belt on. In addition to supporting the firearm I often carry, a good-quality belt has a number of uses:

1. Make a tourniquet. If there's an active shooter situation and somebody has been seriously injured, you can use a belt as a tourniquet. Just make sure to pull it very tight. Another medical use for a belt? Use it as a sling for an injured arm.

2. Secure doors. In an active shooter situation, a belt can also be used to tie and secure doors shut so nobody can access a room or hallway.

3. Defend yourself. The belt I wear has a heavy buckle made of solid brass. It can be used for self-defense. I've even used it to break a car window.

4. Sharpen a knife. If you carry a knife and need to sharpen it, you can use a leather belt for stropping the blades.

5. Build a shelter. A belt can be used to make a shelter by securing pieces of wood together.

6. Carry important items. Certain belts have pockets in them where you can carry matches, a utility blade and money, among other things.

7. Give a lift. A belt can be used as a towrope in emergency situations. (Yes, I've personally used a belt to tow another car.)

HOW TO SURVIVE NORTH AMERICA'S MOST DANGEROUS ANIMAL ATTACKS

By Cade Courtley | *Former Navy SEAL*

As a lover of the great outdoors, there's hands down no place I'd rather live than the United States. From the lush forests of Appalachia to the frozen tundra of Alaska, this is a vast land of incredible geographical diversity.

You can be hiking in the desert heat of Arizona's Apache Wash Trail on Monday morning… and seeking shelter from a blizzard at 11,500 feet in a cave on Mount Rainier, Washington, on Friday afternoon. And no matter where you hang your hat, you're never more than a few hours' drive from sleeping beneath the stars… pristine hiking trails with sweeping views from a time before man… or one of the 59 National Parks that cover more than 84 million acres of land across the United States and American territories.

In fact, it's so easy that some folks forget that these are still wild spaces, filled with wild animals who consider this land their territory (and rightly so). Most are more than happy to steer clear of you. But if they feel threatened or they feel the need to protect their young, they will attack.

If that happens — and you find yourself unarmed in a life-or-death situation —you need to know how to react.

General rule for wild animals: If they are with their young, they are extremely dangerous. Steer clear and under no circumstances approach an unattended baby animal.

I'd like to tell you that there's one catch-all technique that will allow you to escape any animal attack. But the reality is that every species is different, and what will work against a brown bear will get you killed if you're dealing with a black bear.

Fortunately, there are straightforward techniques for dealing with most wildlife threats — it's just a matter of knowing them and putting them into action. Listed below are the strategies for surviving America's most dangerous animal attacks — including techniques for defending yourself against a wild animal being sighted more and more in human neighborhoods and against the most dangerous nonhuman mammal in the U.S.

Read on…

Black Bears

Black bears are the smallest of the North American bears, but the males can still weigh in at almost 500 pounds. They are swift — reaching speeds of 35 mph over land — and are powerful climbers.

Until recent years, the North American black bear posed little threat to your average camper or homeowner. Their population had been severely diminished by habitat loss and overhunting, so face-to-face encounters were rare.

But in the last decade or so, the population has rebounded and continues to grow. There's now an estimated more than 800,000 bears across the United States, Canada and even stretching down into Mexico.

As the bear population booms — and their habitats continue to shrink — homeless bears are moving into human-populated areas in search of new territory. We're already seeing more of these bears — in and out of their natural habitats — and attacks are increasing.

Just yesterday morning — as I was putting the finishing touches on this very section of your special wilderness survival guide — a 19-year-old boy was dragged out of his sleeping bag by a black bear in Boulder County, Colorado.

The bear sunk his teeth into the teenager's skull and dragged him 12 feet away before he was able to pry himself free. Experts say this was a predatory attack, and the bear was intent on killing and eating him. Luckily, the young man was a wilderness survival teacher and knew exactly how to deal with a black bear.

Identify: Black or dark-brown fur with light-brown fur around the muzzle. Tall, rounded ears. No shoulder hump.

Avoid: Despite their size and strength, black bears are easily startled and would rather avoid direct conflict. If you are in black bear country and suspect they are close by, make noise. Bang pots, blow a whistle or shout out. This will usually get them to clear out before you approach.

If you spot a bear that doesn't see you, especially if it's rummaging through a garbage can or eating, give it a wide berth.

When camping, make sure your foodstuffs are secured away from your tents. Black bears can climb trees, but if you suspend food supplies in a satchel tied to a thin branch, they won't be able to reach it. If you are camping with dogs, make sure you place bells on their collars. It'll make it easier to keep track of your dog and the constant noise is a great way to keep bears away.

Survive: If you come face to face with a black bear, don't

run or try to climb a tree. Black bears will easily out-climb you and you'll be trapped. Instead, keep a calm demeanor and move slowly and confidently.

Pick up small children and animals so they don't make for easy targets. Stand as tall and squared off as possible to show your size. If you are in a group, move together to make a pack with arms in the air and yell. Be loud and wave your arms about. Make sure the bear has an escape route so it doesn't feel trapped and forced to fight.

A bear will test you and make a false start to see if it can make you run. Stand your ground. If the bear thinks for a moment that you're going to flee, it will charge.

When you're hiking or camping in bear country, you should always have a canister of bear-repellent spray within arm's reach. I recommend Counter Assault Bear Deterrent. This is a concentrated pepper spray, supersized and highly compressed to reach greater distances. Bear sprays are designed to be carried in an easy-to-wear holster on your belt and should not be buried deep in your backpack.

Counter Assault Bear Deterrent: **http://amzn.to/2x6TGjr**

It's worth noting that there are some drawbacks to bear spray, but it is without a doubt the most effective way to repel a bear attack. Some folks recommend spraying the bear when it's about 40–60 feet away, but if you shoot it at the bear from too far away, you'll only make it angrier.

Depending on weather conditions, the repellent can disperse at this range and not affect the bear. Wait until it's about 25 feet away and then spray a six-second blast in its face. This will maximize the effects of the spray and give you enough time to readjust for wind and get off another blast before it reaches you.

Note: Be careful not to spray downwind. This is a good way to spray yourself and have to fight a bear blind.

Of course, with black bears moving into more populated areas — scrounging in suburban garbage cans and bird feeders — it's becoming more and more likely that you'll encounter one of these bears somewhere you don't expect it... and you won't have any bear repellent with you.

In this instance, if a bear attacks, your best chance of survival is to fight back. Use anything you can get your hands on as a weapon — rocks, sticks, fists, even biting. Aim your blows at the bear's eyes and snout. It might seem hopeless, but if a black bear sees that their victim is willing to fight to the death, they'll usually just give up and flee.

Brown Bears

Brown bears — including the subspecies of grizzly and Kodiak bears — average between 500 and 800 pounds, but the males can weigh up to a thundering 1,700 pounds. This puts them comfortably among the largest land predators on the planet.

The brown bear isn't as prevalent as the black bear and tends to avoid heavily populated or urbanized areas. They have been known to raid barns and garbage dumps when food is low — a dangerous trend because they can associate humans with food and lose their natural fear of people — but you're most likely to encounter a brown bear in the wilderness of Alaska or northwestern Canada. There is also a small percentage of brown bears in Montana, Yellowstone National Park, Utah and some parts of Washington.

While the majority of fatal black bear attacks are executed by hungry males in search of food, most brown bear kills are carried out by mothers protecting their young (as mentioned earlier). Thanks to their size, strength and powerful claws, a brown bear can easily disembowel a fully grown man in a direct confrontation. So you'll need a completely different strategy to deal with them.

Identify: Medium to dark-brown fur. Distinct shoulder humps. Short, round ears. Long, pale claws.

Avoid: Talking, singing or wearing bear bells on your packs will signal to bears to steer clear of you. Given enough notice, a bear will want to avoid an encounter as much as you do. If you accidentally sneak up on a grizzly — and they haven't seen you — it's time to beat a stealthy retreat. The last thing you want to do is surprise a mother with her cubs.

Survive: While brown bears are larger and more unpredictable than their black cousins, bear-repellent spray is still effective. In fact, it's even more effective than a firearm. According to researchers in the U.S. and Canada, bear-repellent spray is effective 92% of the time, compared with 67% for guns. That's a big enough difference to keep me reaching for my spray every time.

If the bear continues to come at you, hit the dirt, leave your pack on and play dead. Lay on your stomach with your hands clasped behind your neck. Spread your legs to make it harder for the bear to turn you over. Remain still until the bear leaves the area. Most brown bear attacks are defensive and they will leave you alone if you assume a submissive position. Fighting back usually increases the intensity of such attacks.

The bear can linger nearby for as long as 20 minutes. During this time, attempt to conceal your hyperventilation and control your body so you're in a state of complete stillness.

If the bear continues to attack after you submit, you are the victim of a rare predatory assault. Your only option is to fight for life. Use whatever you have at hand to hit the bear in the face. The same goes for a brown bear that attacks your camp or stalks you — it's likely they're starved, desperate and hunting you for food.

The Bear Survival Motto: If it's black, fight back. If it's brown, lay down.

Important: When camping, make sure you place any food with odor well away from your campsite in a bag that is suspended from a tree.

Mountain Lions

Mountain lions — also known as pumas or cougars — are primarily nocturnal predators with a diet of mostly deer and elk. But if you've ever worked on a farm in mountain lion country, I'm sure you've seen what one of these fellas can do to your livestock.

Chances of seeing a mountain lion in the wild are slim. They operate at night and move silently. They have an aversion to humans, but it's wise to stay aware of a predator that can leap upward of 18 vertical feet.

Identify: Tawny to light cinnamon in color. White chest and underside. The backs of the ears and the tip of the tail are black. Much larger than a bobcat or lynx.

Avoid: Mountain lions stalk their prey, waiting for the ideal moment to pounce. Travel in groups of two or more and make a lot of noise. Lions are more likely to attack you if you're hiking solo. Do not let small children or animals wander on their own. A mountain lion will identify this as easy prey straying from the pack.

It's good practice when hiking to "watch your six." Look behind you every six steps and even the stealthiest predator will have a hard time sneaking up on you.

If you encounter mountain lion kittens, leave the area

immediately. The same goes for a fresh animal carcass. Mountain lions will often return later to feed on their kill.

Survive: If you encounter a lion, face it and appear as large as possible by raising your arms or holding objects that make you appear large like an open coat. Don't take your eyes off the animal, expose your back or run. This will trigger their predatory instincts to pursue and attack.

If the cougar starts to act aggressively, shout, wave your arms, throw things. Like most wild animals, mountain lions will only get in a fight if they know they can win (or they're protecting their young). They won't know what to make of unexpected behavior like this and will likely retreat. Give the lion an escape route. If it thinks it's trapped, it will have no choice but to attack.

If you are attacked, stay on your feet and protect your neck — lions recognize this as a vulnerable spot and will deliberately attack it. Fight back aggressively with fists, sticks, rocks — anything you can get your hands on. Lions have been known to retreat when their prey fights back. If a lion has you in its grip, strike at its eyes. This will cause the lion to loosen its grip.

Alligators

Florida is home to an estimated 1.3 million of these fearsome apex predators. The average size of an adult male is about 11 feet, but gators continue to grow as they age. A grandfather alligator can  grow up to 15 feet and there have been instances where they've grown to a full 19 feet.

Gators are ambush hunters, remaining camouflaged in the water with only their eyes peering above the surface. They lie in wait until something swims or walks by and then lunge forward at high speed. Using their powerful tails, gators are capable of launching their bodies up to 5 feet out of the water, extending their kill range to beyond the water's edge. Once a gator pounces, it drags the prey underwater to drown it before resurfacing to feed.

The good news is that most gators have no interest in killing humans and don't consider them prey. But they can oftentimes mistake humans and small children for their usual prey when swimming in murky waters.

Identify: Alligators can stay submerged for 20–30 minutes at a time, making them extremely difficult to spot. Sometimes you'll see a loglike shape with a small pair of eyes just above the surface of the water… but chances are they'll see you before you see them. That's why it's important that you stay vigilant around inhabited waters.

Avoid: Make lots of noise. If alligators know humans are ashore, they'll be sure to stay away. Keep small children and dogs away from the edge of the water — alligators might mistake them for their natural prey. Don't swim in low-visibility conditions like brackish water or at night. Stay well away from the water's edge in unfamiliar areas and gator-infested waters.

If you spot an alligator, do not approach or feed the alligator. This will teach the alligator to not be afraid of humans and put others at risk.

Survive: If you encounter an alligator, your first instinct should be to run. Most humans can easily outrun a gator on land, and at a distance of about 25 feet, they're no longer a threat.

If the alligator grabs you in its jaws, thrash about violently and make as much noise as you can. Splashing and screaming can disorientate the animal and force it to let you go. Gators are not used to grabbing something as big as you. If you put up a big struggle, you can force the gator to let you go and retreat.

If you survive an alligator attack, seek medical attention immediately. Their bites are extremely dangerous due to the reptile's sheer bite force and risk of infection. Even with medical treatment, an alligator bite may still result in a fatal infection.

Wolves

The American gray wolf is typically nonaggressive toward humans. They instinctively fear us and 99% of the time would rather steer clear of us entirely. They are, however, a danger to livestock and small animals and have been known to attack when starved, desensitized to humans or rabid.

Often, predatory attacks are preceded by a period of cohabitation with humans. If humans feed the wolves — intentionally or by leaving food unattended outdoors — wolves gradually lose their natural fear. Once this happens, an attack can come at any time. The problem is usually isolated to the wolves in a local area. After a successful attack, they will continue their attacks until all the desensitized wolves have been exterminated.

The majority of victims of predatory wolf attacks are children under the age of 18 or, in some cases, small women. The victims are repeatedly bitten on the head and face and are then dragged off to be eaten somewhere safe.

Because of their size and strength, wolves with rabies are far more dangerous than other animals with the condition. Bites from rabid wolves are 15 times more dangerous than that of a rabid dog, and wolves are capable of traveling large distances and infecting many animals and people in a short amount of time.

Identify: Grizzled gray coats. Large nose pad. Much broader and blockier than a coyote. Low-pitched, drawn-out howls (a coyote's howls are short and sharp). Tracks are almost identical to your average dog tracks but almost twice the size.

Avoid: Hike in groups to avoid being outnumbered by a large pack. Keep dogs leashed at all times. Don't leave food out for wolves or attempt to feed them in any way. If you spot wolves who seem comfortable around humans, report them to authorities immediately.

Survive: Recognize the signs of aggression — barking, howling, raised tail. Stand confidently, stay calm and make yourself as large as possible.

Do not run. Back away slowly. Try to put a large rock or tree at your back so the pack can't circle you. If one of the wolves attacks, fight with all your strength. Demonstrate that you're a dangerous target and the pack will no longer see you as prey and move on.

Dogs

You might be wondering what "man's best friend" is doing on this list of deadly wild animals. Your dog is probably a well-trained, affectionate and loyal creature. But I'm afraid this isn't always the case.

With 89.7 million dogs living in the United States, they can't all be "good boys."

The truth is you're far more likely to be attacked by a dog than any of other animals on this list. Dog bites send more than 350,000 victims to U.S. emergency rooms annually. That's more than 950 per day on average. In 2016, 41 of those attacks were fatal.

I am a true believer in the old saying that "there are no bad dogs, just bad owners." Most dog attacks occur because of inadequate training and poor containment. However, the overwhelming majority of fatal attacks (77%) are committed by just two particularly dangerous breeds — pit bulls and Rottweilers. Pit bulls killed 254 Americans between 2005 and 2016 — about one death every 17 days.

Insurance companies will often raise a homeowner's premium if any of the following dogs — regardless of the dog's individual temperament or training — are known to be on the property: Akitas, Alaskan malamutes, bulldogs, mastiffs, chows, Dobermans, German shepherds, huskies, Presa Canarios, Rottweilers and pit bulls.

Dogs & Children: It's estimated that someone is bitten by a dog every 75 seconds in the United States. More than 80% of the time, the victim is a child. Sometimes dogs who were thought to be dependable and safe have been known to react aggressively toward infants.

Dogs have been a part of our culture for so long that it's easy to forget they were once wild animals — just as wild and dangerous as any of the other animals on this list. Since their domestication, they've lost their fear of humans — but at their core, they are still guided by their primal survival instincts.

Nearly all canine species — including dogs — abide by a pack rule of hierarchy and dominance. They follow a dominant leader, are deeply territorial and are loyally devoted to the pack. Because of their size, children are rarely considered leaders to be feared or followed. For this reason, small children should never be left alone with any breed of dog. And their play should be monitored carefully.

Avoid: Never purposely aggravate or tease a dog. Dogs that are regularly chained and confined are usually more aggressive and should be avoided. It's unwise to assume that only certain breeds are dangerous. Just about any dog can cause injury.

When approached by a potentially dangerous dog, don't look it in the eye, as it may consider this a threat. Do not smile — the dog will think you are baring your teeth aggressively at it. Control your fear. Stand firm, remain calm and do not move suddenly. Do not run, as this will activate the dog's prey-chasing instinct.

Observe the animal's body language. A growl or bared teeth are obvious signs of aggression. But a more subtle indicator is the position of the dog's head. Low is submissive, high is on alert. But if the head is level with its body, then it is preparing to attack or fight.

It is best to turn sideways so that you are not directly facing the dog and watch the dog through your peripherals. If the dog is still approaching, loud commands, such as "down" and "stay" could halt its approach. But don't point your finger or expose your hands.

Slowly back away from the animal, making no sudden movements or changes in posture. Once a sufficient gap has been established, get to a place out of the sight line of the animal.

Survive: If the dog attacks, you must gain immediate control of the encounter and subdue the animal. The most effective way to do this is to get the dog on their back.

When they bite, dogs will grip tightly with their teeth and try to tear flesh by shaking their head aggressively. You'll want to protect your face, throat and chest. If you have time, wrap a jacket or extra layers of cloth around your arm and offer that to the attacking dog. It may sound counterintuitive, but once the animal has you in its grip, you can easily use this to your advantage.

If you don't have time to prepare, keep your vulnerable areas, inner thighs and groin protected. Try to kick the dog in the throat, nose and the back of the head. This will stun the dog and give you time to get away. If the dog is going to bite, best that it gets a hold of your outer leg, where the skin is thicker.

If the dog sinks its teeth into you, turn on the animal and drop your full weight onto its body. Slam your knees — or crash down with your elbows — directly onto its body. Try to land on its ribs — which break easily — and strike at its head, especially at the back of the neck or at the base of the skull.

If you have one at hand, use a towel, coat or shirt to cover the dog's head, which will subdue them and give you time to escape. If available, a blast of cold water from a hose or even a bucket of cold water thrown into its face will disorient the dog.

If you're attacked by multiple dogs, don't try to subdue each dog with your body weight as you would during an attack from a single dog. Dogs work in packs, and this will make you more vulnerable. Instead, attempt to strike at each approaching dog's nose or eyes, or grab one of their limbs. If the dog pack senses a more formidable adversary from the onset, the dog pack's instinct will often make them back off and retreat.

After the attack: You'll need to determine whether an attacking dog has rabies or a history of aggression. Call the police or the local animal control unit and try to find out who owns the dog and its history of inoculations.

Seek medical attention for your wounds. Dog bites tear the skin and often require stitches. A dog's mouth — contrary to popular myth — has a lot of bacteria that can cause serious illness if a wound is unattended. If you haven't had a tetanus shot in the past five years, you may require additional preventative tetanus treatments.

America is home to some of the world's most deadly land predators... but that shouldn't stop you from enjoying everything this country's incredible wilderness has to offer.

Keep in mind the tips provided in this guide and remember — they want to avoid conflict just as much as you do. Travel in groups. Make some noise. Stand tall and confident.

AIRLINE SURVIVAL GUIDE

When faced with the worst, It's not just the gear you have that matters. It's your willpower.

In 1971, a 17-year-old girl and her mother were on a Christmas Eve flight to visit family. Suddenly, a bolt of lightning struck their plane, causing it to spiral out of control toward the ground. When the plane crashed, it killed 91 people. The sole survivor was the 17-year-old girl.

Alone deep in the jungles of Peru, this young woman refused to give up, despite the fact that she had several broken bones. Fortunately, her father had taught her several survival skills, which she used during her 10-day ordeal in the jungle until she was rescued.

"While gear is incredibly important, the No. 1 factor in survival is your will to tough it out no matter what."

Thanks to these skills, she knew to pour gasoline on her maggot-infested wounds to bring the maggots to the surface so she could more easily remove them. She also knew to find and follow a river, which led her to a remote village where three men helped save her. Years later, her remarkable story was turned into a documentary called Wings of Hope.

A lot of people believe there's no hope in surviving a crash, but there are definitely things you can do to prepare ahead of time to give yourself the best possible odds of surviving.

For instance, the Federal Aviation Administration (FAA) has discovered that the people most likely to survive a crash sit within five rows of an emergency exit. A lot of people die from fire and smoke inhalation after a crash since they can't get to an exit quick enough.

Luckily, most airlines allow us to book our flights on the internet and select our seats. When booking your flight, be sure to select seats within five rows of an emergency exit.

The FAA also uncovered that most plane crashes occur during the first three minutes of a flight and the last eight minutes of a flight. This means you should keep your shoes on and the headphones off during takeoff and landing so you're as prepared as possible in the event something horrible does occur. But even if you're 100% alert and sitting in the exit row itself, you could survive the crash and end up stranded in a remote wilderness.

If that happens, the gear you have could mean your survival. The last time I flew, I had in my pocket my cellphone, Tactical Pen, paracord key chain with my keys on it, lock pick set, credit cards, cash, bobby pins, hair barrettes, steel wool, and a small tactical flashlight. In a crash, you've got to assume the only gear you'll be able to access is the gear on your body.

The batteries in the flashlight and in the cellphone can be used to start a fire. Touch the two ends of the battery with a gum wrapper or steel wool, which will ignite. You could also light the cash in your pocket to get a fire gang. To help build a shelter, you could use the paracord from the keychain or your shoelaces to tie sticks together. The Tactical Pen — a self-defense tool suitable for taking on planes — could be used for self-defense if you came across some unfriendly critters while attempting to make your way to safety.

Tactical Pen: **http://bit.ly/2gH9dPI**

And while gear is incredibly important, the No. 1 factor in survival is your will to tough it out no matter what. When I was with the agency, I saw guys who were a lot stronger than I fail because they didn't have the mental toughness to keep going. You've got to dig deep and not give in no matter what. If the resilient 17-year-old girl had given up on day nine, she hadn't kept going, she would never have been rescued on day 10.

The bottom line is to put the odds in your favor of surviving a plane crash, choose the right seat on a plane, have some gear on your body, and promise yourself that you'll never give up.

HOW TO SURVIVE WHEN DISASTER STRIKES ON THE WATER

Tens of thousands of boats go under every year — this number includes at least four large ships every week. So before you decide to cast off, there are several things you should do to ensure your safety and increase your chances of surviving a nautical emergency.

Before You Head Out

I truly believe that the key to survival is preparation! This couldn't be truer when it comes to boating activities. As always, situational awareness is key:

1. Inventory safety equipment. Are there enough life vests and/or life preservers so that everyone on board will have access to one? Are they in proper working order or have they seen better days? Water (especially salt water) is very tough on ALL equipment. You DON'T want to find out the life vests are totally worthless when you most need them. Additional items that should be on every boat are fire extinguishers, flares or some kind of signaling device

and a VHF marine radio. And I always say IF it takes a battery, it's going to take a sh*t exactly when you need it, so have backups.

2. Locate the emergency supplies. Are they under seats or in compartments? Are they easily accessible? Are you on a larger vessel that has lifeboats or rafts? Where are they located? You should identify at least two locations for these lifeboats, preferably in different parts of the ship to give you options if you can't get to one of them.

3. Know your exits/evacuation route. If you are on the interior of a ship, be sure to plan your evacuation route. Again, have at least two options, preferably in opposite directions. Realize that one of the most dangerous and common boating accidents is an engine fire. Since the engines are located at the stern (rear) of the boat, avoid going that direction when you evacuate.

It Happened: You Are Taking on Water or the Boat Is on Fire

Time for a "threat assessment." Immediately abandoning the vessel you're on isn't necessarily the right answer:

1. Do you think you can keep the vessel afloat by plugging the breach? Often, this will be enough to get you back to shore/dock. This can be done with patch kits or you can improvise using wetsuits, life jackets, etc. Your only goal is to stop the leak or at least slow the flow of water so you can remove it (manually or using bilge pumps) faster than it is entering the vessel. This is key because most shipwrecks (nearly 64%) take place within sight of a dock or land.

2. If there is a fire, can you extinguish it rapidly? Remember that boats have fuel on board and this situation can turn very bad very quickly.

3. If abandoning ship is the best option, remember that you are now going to be dealing with issues like possible drowning, exposure (hypothermia or heat stroke), dehydration and starvation on the open water. Not to mention wildlife.

You've Decided to Get Off: Before Hitting the Water

Before you jump into the water, there are several things you should do to improve your chances of survival:

1. Ensure you have properly donned your life jacket. ALL straps should be buckled or tied.

2. Try to communicate to anyone you can reach with the VHF marine radio about your situation. In U.S. waters, channel 16 communicates directly with the Coast Guard as well as other boats in the area to send out a MAYDAY. Give the following information. Repeat it THREE TIMES:

   - Who you are
   - Where you are
   - The condition of the vessel
   - And what you plan to do.

3. Get any supplies that are buoyant and will not hinder you in the water, including bottled water and signaling devices — basically, anything that will aid your survival efforts.

Abandon Ship

Once you decide to leave the ship, you should first attempt to do so in a life raft or boat. Your priority is to get away from the sinking vessel as quickly as possible. A large, sinking ship creates powerful downward suction that has the ability to pull you under if you are still nearby.

If you are going into the water and a life boat isn't an option, be sure to:

1. Put on several layers of clothing, which will provide additional thermal protection.

2. Find a clear landing zone. If you can, enter upwind to keep clear of smoke, fumes and fire.

3. Keep your feet and knees together, cross your arms over your chest and tuck your chin.

And most importantly... never enter the water headfirst!

WHAT DO YOU DO WHEN A BOMB EXPLODES?

It's tough to wrap my head around it at times, but the fact is we live in a time when — without hesitation — a terrorist will detonate a bomb at a concert filled with children.

You can never take your safety for granted, and you need to know how to react if, heaven forbid, you find yourself in a situation like the one that just took place at the Ariana Grande concert in Manchester, England, 2017.

So here are some quick tips if you ever see that day…

- Whenever you go to a big event, always identify two exits upon arrival. This takes only about 30 seconds to do, but very few people make the effort to do this. This way, you have an alternative escape route if something happens that blocks one of your exits. For example, at the Ariana Grande concert, the bomb went off near the arena entrance, which meant you didn't want to head in that direction. Instead, you would quickly move to the second exit you previously identified to get out of the area as quickly as possible

- If an explosion goes off in your vicinity, quickly scan the room. While the inevitable panic ensues, you need to keep your wits about you and take a second to make sure the exit you're heading to is safe. You don't want to be rushing to a place where a guy with an AK-47 is waiting to mow people down. I realize keeping your cool is difficult to do when you're scared and confused, but it's crucial that you can immediately assess whether you're heading in a safe direction

- Most of the time, it's not a good idea to follow the crowd. If the bomber has a secondary device, they're going to place it at the most likely exit people will be rushing toward. So if you see everyone running in a certain direction, you probably want to head the other way. Think about crowd mentality — people will blindly follow the herd without thinking. This is another reason why following the crowd is often a bad idea. Most people have no idea why they are going where they're going, except for the fact that everybody else is headed that way

- In the event you suffer a serious injury and are bleeding, be sure to apply pressure to the wound and seek medical attention as soon as possible once you've gotten to safety.

While these tips may seem simple, they can and have saved lives. Whenever you're out and about — at a shopping mall, concert, marathon or night club — please be vigilant.

MAKING YOUR OWN BUG-OUT BAG COULD SAVE YOUR LIFE

Your phone rings and startles you awake. You look over at the clock… it's 2:37 a.m.

When you pick up the phone, the caller confirms your identity with a predetermined challenge question and, upon hearing your correct response, tells you to be on-site in 10 minutes.

You immediately roll out of bed and hurry over to your closet to grab the bag that you always keep packed and ready in case you receive this type of call. As soon as you're dressed, you rush out of the house and begin to drive to the airfield.

The entire way there, you try to keep your cool. There's no way of knowing if this is a training exercise or if you're about to head overseas because of a terrorist event. The only thing you do know for sure is that the bag sitting in your back seat has critical items to keep you alive for a few days in case this turns out to be a real mission.

Upon your arrival, you quickly find out this is not a training exercise — rather, a foreign country has taken hostile action towards a U.S. target. You're sent overseas, and as soon as you touch down in the foreign country you get to work and are able to eventually complete your mission and gather vital intelligence for your country.

None of this success would have been possible if you weren't prepared with the right gear and were able to vacate your house in 10 minutes or less.

This scenario is something that most members of the CIA, NSA and DIA are familiar with. Even if the stakes in everyday life aren't quite as high, I'm a firm believer that everyone should have a "bug-out bag" in their home that allows them to vacate in no more than 10 minutes.

A Universal Lifesaver: The Bug-Out Bag

A bug-out bag is a bag full of gear that allows you to survive for at least 72 hours during an emergency situation. Some people call it a "72-hour kit" or an "escape bag" or a "get out of dodge bag."

It doesn't matter what you call it as long as it contains the proper gear to keep you alive.

After all, you might not be getting a call from headquarters to be on site in 10 minutes, but you may hear of a fire or other natural disaster barreling down on your home and you need to get out fast. If you do find yourself in such a dire situation, here are the items I recommend you keep in your bug-out bag.

Before we dive in, a note: Keep things as simple as possible. You don't need 749 different items for your bag, and you definitely don't want your bag to weigh a ton, since you don't know if you'll be carrying it on foot.

Ideally, you want your bag to weigh 25 pounds or less.

The 10 Necessities

Let's take a look at the most important items to include in a bug-out bag.

1. Three days' worth of clothing. This means shirts (include one with long sleeves), socks, underwear, a pair of pants and a jacket.

2. Clean water and a filter. The DATREX emergency water pouches work well. You'll want to put at least four of those in your bag. As for the filter, consider the LifeStraw or the Sawyer PointONE All-in-One filter.

3. Quick and easy food. I recommend adding one of the Datrex 3,600 calorie emergency food bars. They'll last you for five years, and I can tell you from personal experience they actually don't taste that bad. In addition to the food bars, I would throw in at least two of the MET-Rx Big 100 meal replacement bars, which will definitely fill you up if you have to rely on them.

4. Emergency tube tent. Now we're getting into the "survival" territory. If you can't find a building in which to take cover, you'll need to provide your own shelter. Look for a tent that doesn't weigh much and won't take up much space in your bag. Coghlan's makes a great tube tent that comes in a pouch as small as a poncho. You can get it for under $10 on Amazon.

5. High-quality poncho. When you're in a dire situation, you could use a poncho for shelter. Make sure it's high quality — don't spend 99 cents on a plastic poncho that will easily get holes torn in it. Instead, spend a few more bucks (about $12) and get something along the lines of the Frogg Toggs Ultra-Lite Poncho.

6. Fire starters. Get a Bic cigarette lighter from a gas station, and also include some Swedish FireSteel. FireSteel was originally developed for the Swedish military. It can produce a spark over 5,000 degrees Fahrenheit and can be used in any type of weather at any altitude. If you have

the FireSteel along with the Bic lighter, you'll be all set if you need to build a fire to stay warm or cook some food.

7. An encrypted USB drive. This will allow you to safely store copies of your driver's license, passport, bank account and stock information. The USB drive I use is the IronKey, but there are several companies that make encrypted drives.

8. Extra cash. You'll also want to have some cash sealed in a Ziploc freezer bag. At a minimum, I'd have $100 in cash in $20 bills but if you have $300 in $20 bills even better.

9. Tactical flashlight. Get a small tactical flashlight from a quality brand such as SureFire or Fenix.

10. Quality fixed-blade knife. Unless you're going somewhere where it's illegal, you always want a good knife with you and the one I use is the NOC Knife.

These are the necessities for a simple bug-out bag that includes what you need to survive.

You can certainly add more luxury items and get as creative as you wish, but don't get carried away — remember, "Ounces equals pounds, and pounds equals pain." Even if all you include are the contents above, you'll be good to go in a crisis situation should you have to vacate your home in minutes.

TOMAHAWKS: AN UNDERRATED SURVIVAL TOOL EVERYONE SHOULD HAVE

I carry a lot of survival items with me, but one of the most important is often overlooked. It's not food, water, a compass, or even a gun.

It's a small tool that I once used to free my family from a snow bank after a vehicle crash. On another (and less serious) occasion, I used it to chop through drywall in my new house, allowing my wife to see a priceless fireplace that the previous owner had covered up.

The trusty tool I'm talking about is a tomahawk. The reason I love the tomahawk is because it's so versatile. It can be used for cutting up wood for kindling (starting a fire), self-defense, and even hacking your way out of a vehicle.

Because of its variety of uses, Special Forces soldiers are known to carry a tomahawk when they deploy overseas.

My three favorite tomahawks are the American LaGana Vietnam Tactical Tomahawk, the Browning Shock N' Awe Tomahawk, and the Micro Hawk. But for everyday use, I'd recommend the Micro Hawk, which is the smallest of the three. I carry it in my car at all times, and it's so compact I can store it in my glove box.

American LaGana Vietnam Tactical Tomahawk:
http://amzn.to/2eFMumI

Browning Shock N' Awe Tomahawk:
http://amzn.to/2eFEKRM

Micro Hawk: **http://bit.ly/2eBbx6D**

You see, different sized tomahawks have different applications. I like the Micro Hawk for everyday use because it weighs less than 12 ounces and it's only 7 inches long. The size and weight make it an ideal tool for camping or hiking, but also for self-defense purposes.

CHAPTER 7:

EMERGENCY MEDICINE: THE BASICS OF FIELD MEDICINE

DOCTOR'S ORDERS: 10 MUST-HAVE MEDICAL ITEMS FOR YOUR BUG-OUT BAG

By Dr. Omar Hamada | *United States Special Operations Physician*

72 hours.

In the event of a disaster, that's how long emergency services say you should be prepared to wait for help. It could be more, it could be less. But if your bug-out bag has enough food and water to last you 72 hours, you should be in good shape...

That is, of course, unless you or a loved one is injured.

When push comes to shove, you could probably go a day or two without food or water. But if a falling sheet of metal punctures your leg — and you're bleeding out — you don't have 72 hours for someone else to come to the rescue.

You need to act fast... and you need the right equipment to do it.

I've seen too many bug-out bags where first aid is treated as an afterthought. I'm talking about back-crippling 50-pound bags, packed with everything but the kitchen sink... and a $5 first aid kit thrown on top.

As a husband and father of four children, I value preparedness above all else. I've created a survival pack — fully equipped with the necessary medical supplies — for each of my family members. I know the importance of being properly prepared and can rest easy knowing that my loved ones are safe when a disastrous event strikes.

Don't get me wrong, I understand the need to save space in your bug-out bag. But a Band-Aid and a cleansing wipe just aren't going to cut the mustard when there's a broken limb, open wound or the threat of serious infection.

That's where the tools listed below come into play.

Proper first aid is an integral part of your bug-out bag. A potentially lifesaving kit will take up minimal space and weigh just a few pounds extra — packed right, you'll barely notice it.

Below are my **10 Must-Have Medical Items for Your Bug-out Bag** and where to find them...

Trauma Kit

Use this trauma kit to quickly control bleeding at the scene of the accident. Each kit comes with bandage materials, bleeding treatment supplies, duct tape, a triangular bandage, wound care and instructions for trauma and accident management. The package is durable and waterproof — perfect for outdoor survival situations.

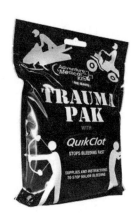

$20–40; **http://amzn.to/2xLzIYn**

Tourniquet

I recommend including a high-quality tourniquet you can apply with one hand. One of the best and easiest to use is the SWAT-Tourniquet. It can be used as a pressure dressing or all-purpose wrap, but is primarily used as a tourniquet to control heavy bleeding. And it's easy to use:

Simply stretch the tourniquet out, wrap it above the wound and tuck it into itself.

$12–20; **http://amzn.to/2w21bCZ**

SAM Splint

The SAM Splint provides comfortable support for any fractured or injured limbs. It's made from a thin core of high-quality aluminum alloy positioned between two layers of closed-cell foam. The product is versatile due to its moldable nature, can be reused and is 100% waterproof.

$12; **http://amzn.to/2wDvf9W**

Sunblock

Sawyer's sunscreen lotion features a nongreasy "breathable matrix" formula that penetrates deep into your skin. This guarantees optimal all-day sun protection from a single application — perfect if you're stuck on a roof in hot weather or exposed to the elements. It's waterproof and sweat resistant, so it's ideal for any excessive physical activity.

$7–10; **http://amzn.to/2w1NjsE**

Insect Repellant

Ben's Repellent Spray protects you from harmful insects such as mosquitoes, ticks, fleas and even chiggers and midges. The product's formula provides lasting 10-hour tick protection and

13 hours of mosquito protection. The spray is unscented and a must-have for every camper, hunter or backpacker.

$8; **http://amzn.to/2vHF7lQ**

Skin Glue

New-Skin is an antiseptic liquid bandage for hard-to-cover cuts and wounds. It dries rapidly to form a water-proof protective cover. It keeps out dirt and germs while sealing in moisture and letting your skin breathe.

$7–23; **http://amzn.to/2iZ3Hc0**

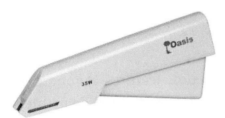

Suture

The Oasis Skin Stapler drastically reduces surgery time in an emergency. Its slim, light-weight design handles like a well-balanced, precision instrument, but it's suitable for even the tightest of budgets. Easy to use and constructed with high-quality materials, the stapler comes preloaded with 35 sterile staples.

$15; **http://bit.ly/2xLy5Ki**

Bandages

The Lifeline 121-piece kit is a real first-aid kit. Stocked with a comprehensive assortment of 121 pieces, including bandages, gauze pads, towelettes, adhe-

sive tape and cotton tip applicators. Everything is stored in a hard-shell foam case with clear plastic pockets, making it easy to find what you need in an emergency. The package comes with a carabineer ready to be clipped on a backpack or belt.

$30; **http://amzn.to/2wBlgnp**

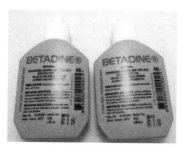

Betadine

Betadine Solution is an invaluable tool for defending against topical infections. Its active ingredient (10% povidone-iodine contained) fights a broad spectrum of pathogens. You can count on it for effective protection against bacteria, viruses, fungi, spores, yeasts, and protozoa.

$10; **http://amzn.to/2gIp4xn**

Survival Saw

Sumpri's pocket chain saw is lightweight, versatile, flexible and compact. It can cut through a three-inch branch in less than 10 seconds and is perfect for quickly creating an improvised splint or walking stick. It's made of strong, heat-treated steel and comes

with a compact belt loop pouch to store your chain saw.

$13–20; **http://amzn.to/2gHha7B**

Always remember, preparation is the No. 1 factor for survival in an emergency situation.

Bolster your bug-out bag with these 10 medical items and you'll have the tools to deal with life-threatening wounds and injuries — quickly and easily — and get the time you need to reach a fully equipped medical facility.

HOW TO STAY CLEAN AND HEALTHY WHEN THE SHTF

By Dr. Omar Hamada | *United States Special Operations Physician*

In the course of my medical career, I've seen many people who don't take very good care of themselves because they feel fine — until they don't, and then it's too late.

It's the same thing in survival. So many people don't prepare for disaster while things are going well — they have running water and electricity, stores are full of food and the pumps are full of gas. Then suddenly there's no water or electricity, store shelves are empty and pumps are dry and people panic as they realize that the infrastructures they once depended on so heavily are gone.

Believe it or not, one of the most difficult things to manage in times of disaster is hygiene — unless you are proactively prepared. Luckily, this preparation is pretty simple and only requires minimal supplies:

- A shovel
- Lime/ash
- Unscented bleach
- Bladders or jugs
- Soaps.

With regards to survival hygiene, I recommend focusing on three primary things: waste disposal, water and personal hygiene.

Easy as 1, 2, 3

If plumbing is down and you lose access to running water, it is very important to go to the bathroom away from your living space. Find a place about 50 yards from your living quarters and far from your water supply. Bury excrement in a shallow hole using your shovel and top it with lime and/or ash to control the smell and speed up decomposition.

To obtain water for drinking, washing and other personal uses, it is best to find running water (like a stream or brook) and use a quality water filter. If you cannot find running water, use whatever body of water is available.

If there is a lot of sediment, let the water settle for an hour or two before filtering to help preserve your filtration system. Make sure your filter is capable of filtering out most bacteria, parasites, protozoans, viruses and fungi.

Today, most filters you find at reputable outdoor stores are sufficient. However, for extra protection, consider adding a one-quarter teaspoon of bleach per gallon of water or boiling it for 10 minutes. You could also add iodine, with the understanding that iodine makes water look and taste awful.

Finally, when it comes to personal hygiene, remember that it is hard to smell yourself. If you are cohabitating with others, be considerate and bathe or shower at least twice per week. Remember though that hygiene is not only for the benefit of others, but it also helps prevent disease and keeps you healthier.

One Sin to Avoid

One thing that has taken our world by storm that I'm not too crazy about is hand sanitizer. Although it's good to have some around, don't go overboard with it.

Your immune system, just like your muscular and cardio-vascular systems, needs to be worked out daily. If your hygiene is over the top and you overuse hand sanitizer constantly, you are practically killing your own defenses. It's perfectly OK to let your body exercise its ability to fight off infection by not using hand sanitizer — except in certain instances.

As I've said before, the most important aspect of survival is staying healthy. If you take care of your body by practicing good hygiene, your body will take care of you.

SURVIVAL A TO ZZZZ

By Dr. Omar Hamada | *United States Special Operations Physician*

I'll sleep when I'm dead!

That was how I used to respond when people questioned how hard I worked.

Now we know that sleep is essential to living — and living well. It is during the seventh and eighth hours of sleep that the brain functions best to repair and rehabilitate.

Without enough sleep our immune system weakens, our memory fails, our emotions become more fragile, our thinking gets muddled, our reaction time slows and our fine motor skills suffer.

Recently, I was talking to Jason and Cade about this — we've all got our stories.

On a protective detail while seriously sleep deprived, Jason saw threats that weren't there. He began to question whether or not he should engage and shoot these hallucinations. He also recalls once seeing a tripwire on the ground after hiking for hours on end — but there was no wire.

During Hell Week, Cade remembers being so utterly exhausted that he began to hallucinate visions of three 747s crashing into San Diego Bay while rowing around in his 250-pound Zodiac.

His six boat mates — who all had experienced their own sleep-deprived hallucinations — laughed when Cade tripped out and began screaming that they should row over and help out the crashed aircraft.

As a doctor, I also experience sleep deprivation. However, at 50 I can't handle it as well as I did when I was 25. Back then, it would take a couple of days of little or no sleep before I felt "off." Now, after one three-hour night, I'm sluggish, irritable, slow and clumsy.

My point is this: The No. 1 thing you can do to improve your odds of survival — whether on the interstate or off-road in the wilderness — is to make sure that you get an adequate amount of quality rest on a regular basis.

If you're having trouble falling asleep or sleeping through the night, talk to your doctor. Your life really does depend on it.

HOW TO BEAT THE HEAT AND AVOID DEHYDRATION

By Dr. Omar Hamada | *United States Special Operations Physician*

The most important aspect of survival is... staying healthy.

Without your health — your ability to breathe, eat, move freely and enjoy life — you aren't living, you are merely existing. And without your health in a survival situation, you will most likely succumb to the situation you are trying to survive.

Believe it or not, the single most important part of maintaining your health and surviving is staying hydrated.

Bodies of Water

Our bodies are 60% water. It's in our cells, our blood vessels, our bones, and it surrounds our brain and spinal cord. Water is essential to life for the proper functioning of all our systems.

The problem is that it is VERY easy to become dehydrated, because so few of us drink the amount of water we need. In fact, most of us live in a continual state of mild dehydration because of all the soda, tea and coffee we drink.

Without proper hydration we get headaches and walk around fatigued, grumpy and irritable. It's amazing what good water does for you.

In order to tip the balance in a positive direction, it's a good idea to drink approximately one ounce for every kilogram of body weight every day. An easy way to estimate that is to take half your weight in pounds and subtract 10%.

Let's say you weigh 200 pounds. One half of that is 100. Subtract 10% and you've got 90 kg. So ideally, you'd want to drink about 90 ounces of water a day.

In a stressful survival environment, your hydration needs will increase. A good rule of thumb here is to drink enough water that your pee stays clear. The darker your urine is, the harder your kidneys are working to concentrate urine so your body holds onto precious fluids. And remember, by the time you're thirsty, you are already dry.

Do As I Say, Not As I Do

Here's a slightly embarrassing personal story. You know, we're all "invincible," right? We're hard and we keep pushing through any barriers or obstacles.

Well, when I was with 20th Special Forces Group, we were doing a land navigation exercise at Redstone Arsenal, Alabama, in July. It was HOT. And I was young and stupid.

The older guys told us to make sure we had water before we started the exercise. But I figured I was smart and in shape and would complete the course in no time since I had "superior" land navigation skills.

I bet you can guess what happened. I got lost. I thought I was dying of thirst. I didn't know how to get back. I had no water. I saw a dirty stream and actually thought for a second about drinking a little water after filtering it through my shirt (this is not a good idea).

Thankfully, I wasn't as lost as I thought — I was just hot, tired and dehydrated. Soon I was able to pick up my bearings again and finally get back to base.

Lesson learned.

So remember: ALWAYS take water. ALWAYS have a good water filter with you. And ALWAYS stay hydrated.

ENSURING YOU & YOUR FAMILY WOULD SURVIVE AN 8-WEEK QUARANTINE

Dr. Ian Crozier walked into the room wearing a Tyvek suit, mask, rubber boots, goggles, and multiple layers of gloves. He was surrounded by people on death's doorstep with blood and vomit littering the floor. Each day, he'd try everything he could to save his patients, but the mortality rate was incredibly high.

One day, the doctor began feeling sick himself. Tests showed that he too had contracted the Ebola virus he had been fighting. He was immediately flown from Sierra Leone to Emory University Hospital, in Atlanta, where his chances of survival were slim.

Incredibly, after spending 40 days in the hospital, Dr. Crozier recovered, although long-lasting symptoms of the disease plague him to this day. He's one of the few people who've been on the brink of death yet survived the virus outbreak that killed an estimated 12,000 people and infected thousands more.

The fact is the majority of these deaths occurred in West Africa. We are very fortunate to live in the United States, where pandemics such as the bird flu or Ebola don't usually affect us. Our top-notch medical care and sanitation keep diseases from quickly spreading.

However, pandemics have affected the world since the beginning of time and all of us need to give some thought to how we can protect our family if an outbreak does come to our town. The best way to do this is to ask yourself the following question: Will I be able to shelter in place for up to eight weeks if a pandemic hits my area?

By "shelter in place," I mean quite literally to survive in one place, most likely your home. Believe me, I know the thought of having to stay locked in your house for eight weeks isn't very appealing, but if your town is getting ravaged by a virus, you'll do whatever you need to in order to survive. And quarantining you and your family in your home will likely give you the best chances of making it out alive.

Of course, you've got to have the correct supplies in your house to survive for eight weeks. Let me share with you the short and simple list I use for my own family.

First, you need enough food and water for two months. Even if you're not worried about a pandemic, I think it's a good idea to have several months of food and water on hand for any type of crisis situation.

I get my food from the LDS Cannery because this food comes in No. 10 cans and has a 25–30-year shelf life. There are plenty of other places online where you can get long-term food storage, so choose whatever suits you best.

LDS Cannery: **http://bit.ly/2w2c2wE**

As far as water, I use the 7-gallon Aqua-Tainers to store two months of water in my basement. I know plenty of people who use the 55-gallon water drums, but I prefer the 7-gallon containers because they're easier to move around.

Aqua Tainers: **http://amzn.to/2eYOF1s**

In addition to food and water, you'll want to get a box or two of N95 respirator masks. Although you shouldn't be leaving your house in the event of a pandemic, you may need to go into your yard, and every time you leave your house, you definitely want a mask on.

You'll also want to get a box or two of Nitrile surgical gloves. If you plan on touching anything that may have a chance of containing the disease, you'll obviously want your hands protected.

Don't forget to stock up on antibacterial soap so that your family can wash their hands several times a day. Also, have plenty of bleach on hand so you can constantly sanitize surfaces.

Other items you should seriously consider having at home include plastic sheeting, so you can create an isolation room in your home if a family member becomes infected, and duct tape to seal the plastic. Also get Tyvek suits for family members, goggles, prescription medications, and lots of contractor-grade trash bags for waste removal.

As I mentioned above, this is a simple list and is, obviously, not all-inclusive. You can certainly add convenience items such as board games or toys to keep people entertained. But if you only have the list above, which isn't terribly hard to assemble, you'll be leaps and bounds above everyone else if a deadly virus does end up crippling the United States and the city you live in.

50 SURVIVAL USES OF
A MYLAR BLANKET

By Dr. Omar Hamada | *United States Special Operations Physician*

During my 14 years in the U.S. Army, I learned a thing or two about staying alive when things go south — and the importance of having the right equipment in an emergency situation.

For 10 of those years, I served as a flight surgeon and diving medical officer for the world's most elite fighting force — the U.S. Army Special Forces.

My men and I had access to the highest-quality equipment on the planet: top-of-the-range night-vision goggles... bleeding-edge weaponry... a vast web of communication channels...

But one of the most valuable tools in our arsenal was a low-tech item carried by all my combat medics on every mission — the Survival Blanket.

You might laugh, but this blanket is a versatile, lightweight piece of equipment with dozens of uses in a combat or emergency situation. In fact, most folks who own one of these don't realize even half of the potentially lifesaving applications it has.

Let's say that you're an operator on the ground in Afghanistan, spending days at a time roughing it in harsh mountain territories. There are no Humvees... no mess tents... and no cot to lay your head at the end of a long, hard day. The hot mid-day sun is a baking 90 degrees F on average. And overnight, it's not uncommon for temperatures to drop to below freezing.

I don't need to tell you how dangerous exposure to these extreme temperatures can be. But if you have a mylar survival blanket you'll be a step ahead of the game.

At night, by simply wrapping yourself in your blanket, you can easily create what's known as a "passive warming system." It may be thin and flexible, but it's lined with a layer of vapor-ized aluminum — making it an excellent thermal reflector. It traps and returns 90% of your body heat, keeping you warm for hours without batteries, fire or any other source of heat.

During the daytime, an inside-out blanket makes for ex-cellent shelter. You won't want to actually wrap yourself in the blanket — because it will form an airtight seal and conserve unnecessary heat — but rigged to a couple of branches with some paracord or duct tape, it will reflect heat better than any tarp or canvas.

But a mylar blanket does much more than just regulate body heat. In fact, it's not uncommon in an emergency situa-tion to use two or three blankets at once — maybe creating a waterproof shelter with the first, while lining your boots and gloves with another for an extra layer of insulation.

That's the beauty of these blankets. They are so light and small, carrying six of them won't increase the weight of your rucksack by more than a pound. So why wouldn't you always carry at least one?

In my experience, the old saying "No plan survives contact with the enemy" has proven to be true time and time again. That's why you need to equip yourself to deal with the unex-pected. And when weight and space matters, you want to get the most practical uses out of every piece of gear you can. And I'm not just talking about military missions.

If you've ever taken a camping trip with the family only

for it to rain nonstop for the entire trip... got lost while hunting and found yourself in the woods after dark... or spent a cold winter night at home without electricity... then you know what I'm talking about.

In each of these situations and many more like them, your Special Forces Survival Blanket can be used in dozens of ways to make you more comfortable and safe, and to use in potentially life saving ways.

Shelter

1. Use your blanket as a sleeping mat or ground sheet. It will keep out the damp on those cold nights and prevent loss of heat through a dirt floor.
2. Create a waterproof shelter. With some paracord or duct tape, you can suspend the blanket between two branches and shelter yourself from the rain.
3. Shade yourself from the sun. The reflective properties of the blanket make it much cooler underneath its shade than in the sun.
4. Use as insulation in a makeshift shelter. A structure of sticks and branches lined with the blanket will have increased protection against wind, water and sun.
5. Boost a light source. For extra light, position the blanket behind candles or lanterns to reflect the light back into a room. You'll be surprised how much brighter you can make it with this simple trick.
6. Make your own cord. By cutting your blanket into strips and twisting them together, you can create a piece of cord with a higher tensile strength than a single strip. You can use this cord to lash together your shelter.
7. Hang the sheet behind your campfire. Its reflective surface will reflect the excess heat back toward you and keep you warm on even the coldest night.

Communication

8. Signal for help. The blanket's reflective properties make it the ideal signaling device. It can be used as a giant signal mirror. Or you could string it up — not too tight, not too loose — so it flutters and shimmers in the wind.

9. Turn your blanket toward the sky and it becomes a rescue beacon alerting airborne aid to your location. Cut the blanket in three and use the pieces to spell out SOS.

10. On the move? Cut the blanket up into strips, tie them to branches and use the easily spotted, reflective pieces as trail markers.

11. Leave a message. If you have a permanent marker, you can tear off a small square of your blanket and leave a message that won't be washed away in the rain.

Medical

12. Make a sling. For a simple, durable sling, simply cut a long, wide strip from the blanket. Gently loop it around the broken arm and tie behind the neck.

13. Use it as a tourniquet. Cut the blanket into even strips and twist to make a durable piece of cord. Tie it above the wound, closer to the body than the joint.

14. Make a splint. In the event of a broken finger, use a strip to tie the injured finger to a healthy one. Broken limbs can instead be lashed to a sturdy, straight branch.

15. Make a compression bandage. A strip of the blanket can help stop bleeding by tightly securing an absorbent piece of cloth or fabric over the wound.

Food

16. Catch rain. Thanks to its waterproof qualities, the blanket makes an excellent rain catcher. Dig a small hole in

the ground and place your blanket over it to collect rain to replenish your water supply.

17. Catch fish. Cut off small pieces of the blanket to create a shiny lure for catching fish. Small rocks can be wrapped in pieces of the blanket and tied to a makeshift line to weigh it down.

18. Cook food by creating a DIY solar oven. Using soil or rocks, build a semicircular mound facing the sun and drape the blanket over it, with part of the blanket lining the ground in front. Place small pieces of food on the blanket in front of the semicircle and leave until well cooked. Slivers of meat rather than chunks will cook more quickly and thoroughly.

19. Cook food over the embers of a fire. Thanks to your blanket's heat-resistant properties, you can use it as a foil to cook food on, once the flames have died down. Mylar melts at 254 degrees C (489 degrees F), so there is no fire danger.

20. Use it to make a bear cache. Wrap your food in the blanket, tie it off with a piece of rope or paracord and toss the rope over a high branch. Hoist it up high, out of the reach of bears and other critters, and tie it off.

21. Protect your survival garden. Keep your garden healthy and productive by draping the blanket on top of it in extreme conditions to combat heat or frost.

22. Keep the birds away from your veggie patch. Tie small strips of your blanket to your bushes. The shimmering reflections and constant movement will keep birds off your vegetables and fruit bushes.

23. Use it for hunting. Tear the Survival Blanket into strips and braid a net with the pieces. Use the net to trap rabbits, birds and fish.

24. Collect drinking water from snow. Place small amounts of snow in a divot on the blanket. The sun reflecting off

the surface will melt the snow, which can be collected with a funnel for drinking water.

25. Boil water. Line a hole in the ground with the blanket and fill with water. Heat rocks over a fire and drop carefully into the water. The heat will be transferred from the rocks into the water and boil it.

26. Cut into 10-inch squares and then tie off the ends to make small pouches to carry nuts, berries or other small items.

Clothing

27. Keep your legs insulated and dry. Cut up the blanket to make makeshift gaiters. Wrap the piece around your legs and secure with duct tape.

28. Create a makeshift poncho. Cut a hole in the center of the blanket, stick your head through and wear it to stay dry.

29. Evade thermal imaging. Covering yourself with your Survival Blanket will prevent thermal imaging devices from picking up your heat signature.

30. Make waterproof shoe covers. If it's raining and you don't have proper footwear, cut the blanket in half and tie it around your shoes to prevent wet feet. Use duct tape or a piece of cord made from strips of the blanket to tie off the shoe covers.

31. Dry your damp clothes. After washing and drip-drying your clothes, lay your Survival Blanket on the ground and place your damp clothes on top. The blanket will reflect the sun's heat into your clothes and dry them faster than a traditional clothesline.

32. Use as a windbreaker. If you have a broken jacket zip or find yourself in the elements without a jacket, wrapping the blanket around you will cut the chill and keep

the rain and wind out. The blanket is so thin it can even be worn under your jacket for extra warmth.

33. Repair your clothes. Patch holes and tears in your gear with small squares of the blanket.

34. Fight off frostbite. Cut off pieces of the blanket to line boots and gloves. This can be a critical move in an extreme low-temperature emergency situation. Your fingers and toes are the most susceptible parts of the body to frostbite. Hesitation could mean losing them entirely.

35. Keep your pants up. If you're stuck in a survival situation for a prolonged length of time, you may find yourself losing weight… and your pants falling down. Make a belt by twisting some strips of the blanket together and looping it through your pants.

36. Keep your gear dry when you're on the move. If your pack isn't waterproof, line the inside of it with the blanket to keep your clothes and supplies dry.

37. Make a DIY wilderness refrigerator. You can easily cobble together a makeshift refrigerator by wrapping food inside the blanket, tying it off and then placing it in a cool stream or creek.

Comfort

38. Keep the sun off your neck. Affixing a strip of the blanket to the back of a baseball cap or hat will keep the hot midday sun off your neck and stave off sunstroke.

39. Build a windshield. Your Survival Blanket isn't just waterproof; it's also wind resistant. String it up to use as a shield to keep the wind off your shelter, keep a campfire lit or give you the elbow room to do tasks that require a steady hand.

40. Wrap yourself up and stay warm. This is one of the most common uses of the Survival Blanket, but its value

shouldn't be underestimated. Your Survival Blanket's incredible heat-saving properties have saved countless lives. Note: It's important to remember that the blanket doesn't create heat, only conserves it, so the sooner you wrap up, the more heat you'll conserve.

41. Make a pillow. Stuff your blanket with soft items such as clothing or leaves and ball it up to use it as a pillow. Your neck will thank you in the morning.

42. Stay safe and warm while you sleep. Layering the blanket in your sleeping bag will add an extra layer of warmth and prepare you for those sharp temperature drops in the middle of the night.

43. Keep the kids warm. If you have young kids in cold temperatures, it's a good idea to line their car seats with the blanket to give them an added layer of protection and warmth. Remember your car seat may be heated, but theirs isn't.

Miscellaneous

44. Make a flotation device. Your blanket is waterproof. If you tie off the ends and fill the blanket with air (like a parachute), you can create an improvised flotation device in a fix.

45. Make a backpack. Turn your blanket into a horseshoe pack by rolling up your equipment inside it and tying it off.

How-to: **http://bit.ly/2x7aeHW**

46. Make rope. The tensile strength of this blanket is surprisingly strong. Cut it into strips and braid into a rope. It's a little slipperier than regular rope — so don't go rappelling down any cliffs with it — but is strong enough to be a valuable tool in a survival situation.

47. Clean up. In a fix, you can cut a small piece of fabric

from your blanket and use it as a rag to clean up.

48. Drop anchor. You can turn your blanket into an anchor simply by filling it with sand, snow or dirt and tying off the end.

49. Protect your devices from an electromagnetic pulse (EMP). In the event of an EMP, which would shut down all electronics in its blast radius, devices stored in a bag made from your Survival Blanket would be protected.

50. Use as dry storage. During a hurricane, snowstorm or even rain shower, you can wrap up your supplies and clothes in the blanket and keep them dry until the bad weather passes.

These are 50 of the ways your Special Forces Survival Blanket can come to the rescue in a survival situation. But this is just the beginning. I'm hearing reports of new and incredible uses every day.

Is it any wonder that the Green Berets carry this lifesaving medical tool with them everywhere they go? It's no exaggeration that this device could save your life or the life of a loved one.

I recommend that every single American keep at least one of these Survival Blankets in their house — preferably in their bedside drawer for easy and rapid access.

Personally, I keep one in my bug-out bag and a spare in my car. That way I'm prepared for emergency wherever it happens.

FOUR STEPS TO SURVIVING A GLOBAL PANDEMIC

By Dr. Omar Hamada | *United States Special Operations Physician*

The Hong Kong flu. The Asian flu. The swine flu. The bird flu. H5N1 influenza. Ebola.

These are scary, life-threatening diseases you hope you only ever read about but never experience. Unfortunately, these are all recent pandemics that have ravaged communities and killed tens of millions of people.

Every year, doctors stress the importance of getting a flu shot, but — for one reason or another — 50% of us don't. We think the shots will give us the flu (they can't), or that they don't cover the right strains (sometimes that's true) or that they contain unsafe heavy metal additives (the single-dose vials don't).

Up to 20% of Americans will get the flu every year. Approximately 200,000 of us are hospitalized with the flu annually, and up to 50,000 people die from flu-related complications every year.

People over the age of 65 account for 90% of these deaths.

An Ill Wind Is Blowing

The severity of viral illnesses goes in cycles. Over the past few years, we've had relatively mild cases of the flu, and the numbers above reflect these milder variants.

Now, I don't mean to scare you, but we're due for a much worse cycle — a worldwide pandemic that could circle the globe in a matter of hours. Think of the movies Contagion, Outbreak or I Am Legend.

How do prevent you and your family from becoming a statistic? I recommend following this four-step process:

Stay Healthy — To keep your body in optimum shape, focus on the easy-to-remember concept of the three-legged stool:

- Get enough sleep every night
- Eat a vegetable-based, Mediterranean-style diet
- And maintain an active lifestyle — one where you are getting at least 150 minutes of vigorous exercise every week (amounts to 30 minutes a day, five days per week).

Other things you can do to keep disease at bay are to make sure the "big three" are running on all cylinders. This means maintaining your immune system, limiting oxidative stress and promoting anti-inflammation. If you take care of your body, your body will take care of you.

Get Your Shot — Let me be clear: You can't get the flu from the flu shot. It's impossible. The flu shot uses a "killed" virus. If you come down with flu-like symptoms, that is simply your immune system reacting to the vaccine as it builds the antibodies that will protect you against the real thing.

Avoid Infectious Exposure — If you don't want to get the flu, NEVER touch your face unless you've just washed your hands. You may also want to consider wearing a mask in public places where you might encounter large numbers of possibly infected people. If you have to fly, consider using a personal space air purifier. Look for one that uses the same technology

NASA used in the space shuttle program and currently uses on the International Space Station — like this one from Vollara.

See Your Physician — Visit your doctor and get on an antiviral as soon as you notice any symptoms or have a known or suspected exposure. If you think you may be getting sick or if you have a known exposure, you have 48 hours to get on the antiviral drug Tamiflu to reduce the severity of the disease. If you move too slowly, this medicine won't be able to change the course of your infection, because the life cycle of the virus in your body will have progressed too far for the drug to be effective. So the key is to act fast.

If you follow these four steps, your body will be much better prepared to fend off the flu or bounce back quickly if you do indeed contract the disease.

Here's to your best health!

HOW TO AVOID TICKBORNE DISEASES

By Dr. Omar Hamada | *United States Special Operations Physician*

There are over 800 species of tick, and these nasty little bloodsuckers make excellent carriers of many dangerous diseases.

If a tick bites you, you may end up with Lyme disease, Rocky Mountain spotted fever, ehrlichiosis, babesiosis, relapsing fever, Q fever, tick paralysis, tularemia, Colorado tick fever — even a red meat allergy! And that's not all. There are many other illnesses and viruses that can be transmitted to humans and animals by ticks.

Here are some interesting tick statistics:

- Less than 2% of ticks actually carry disease

- Less than 50% of people who come down with a tick-borne illness can recall being bitten

- And a tick must usually be attached for at least 24 hours before transmitting infection. In summary, ticks are bad players that you need to stay away from if at all possible. This means:

- Avoid wooded and brushy areas — especially April–September. If you are hiking, stay on the trail

- Wear long-sleeved shirts with long pants and tuck your pant legs into your boots
- Treat your skin with repellant that is at least 20% DEET
- Treat your clothing with permethrin
- Conduct a full-body tick check before you turn in for the night
- Lastly, wash your clothes in hot water and dry them in a hot dryer.

If a tick has bitten you, don't be overly concerned. If you're worried, consider prophylactic treatment with doxycycline. If you develop a fever and a rash, seek immediate attention from your physician.

THE VIABILITY OF VETERINARY MEDICATIONS

By Dr. Omar Hamada | *United States Special Operations Physician*

You may have heard that one very effective way to procure and stockpile prescription medicines for the rainy day is to use veterinary medications meant for horses, cattle, dogs, cats and fish.

Well, you heard right.

These meds are relatively cheap, readily available and easy to find at your local co-op, Walmart or veterinarian.

What I'd like to do in this article is give you a down-and-dirty guide to help you prepare for the possibility of being unable to get your prescription and over-the-counter (OTC) medications during a crisis.

Take Two and Call Me in the Morning

Before we get started, allow me to briefly discuss the differences between medications that are packaged for human use versus those that are labeled, "For veterinary use only. Not for human consumption."

First, focus on the generic or common name of the drug — not the trade or brand name. The various formulas of a given drug may differ a bit in the delivery systems, binders and additives, but the actual active drug is pretty much the same regardless of the formula or supplier.

The main differences you need to pay attention to between drugs labeled for human use versus veterinary drugs are the dosages and quality control standards to which the drugs are produced.

Quality controls determine the purity of the active drug, the actual amount of the active ingredient in each pill or capsule versus what is stated on the packaging and the sterility or cleanliness of the production process. Veterinary processes are quite a bit looser than the processes used in production of drugs for human use. That's one reason for the price differential.

However, in general, there shouldn't be that much of a difference in topical medications (those placed on the skin), drugs that are orally administered or those that are administered in the form of a suppository. Where I'd be careful is with injectable drugs or those you put in your eye.

So let's divide this up into three sections — OTC medications, your daily prescription medications and prescription medications to be used as needed. Make sure to store whatever medications you want to stockpile in a cool, dry, dark place in order to maximize the life of the medication. I recommend replacing your stock within two years of the expiration date.

OTC meds are easy. Go to your local pharmacy or grocery and buy supplies of

- 200 mg ibuprofen (Motrin, Advil, Nuprin)
- 500 mg acetaminophen (Tylenol)
- 25 mg diphenhydramine (Benadryl)
- 325 mg acetylsalicylic acid (aspirin, Bayer)
- 2 mg loperamide (Imodium)
- Bisacodyl (Dulcolax)
- Melatonin

- Steroid creams
- Yeast medications
- Whatever else you think you may need.

To procure an extra store of your regular prescription meds, ask your physician for a prescription for your second home, a stockpile or a long trip you wish to take. Most doctors are fine providing this with the understanding that your insurance company probably won't pay for it.

If your doctor isn't comfortable writing an extra prescription, in the event of a crisis, consider cutting your dose in half temporarily to double the time you'll have at least some medication available. (Even better, do your best to get healthy and see if you can wean off any of your medications by losing weight, exercising, improving your diet, etc.)

The other thing you might consider is purchasing and stockpiling veterinary equivalents of the same medications you take. Just know that not everything is available. For example, you are going to have a hard time finding statins for animals, but you should be able to get blood pressure medications, insulin, seizure meds and select others without too much of a problem.

Finally, here are some prescription meds that are always good to have on hand in the event of an emergency: Tamiflu, antibiotics, antifungals, non-narcotic pain medications. Sometimes, as above, you can get your physician to write you prescriptions for these without too much trouble.

If not, you can look for appropriate veterinary equivalents. One example that seems to be all the rage is fish antibiotics such as Fish Mox. Just remember, if you are allergic to the human form of amoxicillin (which is a semi-synthetic form of penicillin), you will be allergic to the fish form of amoxicillin — it's the same drug!

As we wrap up, I also suggest considering alternative, holistic, naturopathic remedies — such as essential oils, herbs and the like — for certain conditions.

CHAPTER 8:

SURVIVAL AND SPY TRAINING: THE NEXT LEVEL

FOR EVERYDAY GEAR, LEAVE THIS PIECE BEHIND

They look cool. But when it comes to survival gear, should a bulletproof vest make the cut?

As I learned while I worked for the government, when it's 100 degrees outside, the last thing you want to do is wear a bulletproof vest. They're heavy, and in the heat you feel like you're baking inside. But it's a much better alternative to getting shot.

In fact, I remember one instance when I had to draw my gun and convince the fellow staring at the wrong end of my barrel to do exactly as I said. Thankfully, he listened, but I was still grateful to be wearing a vest that protected my vital organs that day.

These days, I rarely wear a bulletproof vest unless I'm going to an extremely dangerous country.

In my regular day-to-day life, you won't find me wearing one. However, I often get questions from people asking if they should buy a bulletproof vest to have on hand for home defense or some type of end-of-the-world scenario.

Honestly, I'm not a huge fan of bulletproof vests for home

defense. During a home invasion, things happen quickly. You will rarely take the time to put on a vest. Instead, you should be spending the precious seconds grabbing a gun and getting your family into a safe area of the house.

However, I am a fan of having a bulletproof vest for bigger crisis such as an economic collapse. In a crisis event, you may have to go get milk or gas — if looters are doing crazy things, you may not want to leave the house unless you're protected.

If you do decide to get a bulletproof vest, I recommend a Level IIIA. The National Institute of Justice (NIJ) rates the different protection levels of vests, and Level IIIA means the vest can stop up to .44 Magnum. In other words, it stops pistol rounds but not rifle rounds. In the U.S., almost every police officer is wearing a Level IIIA vest, and you can easily buy them online from places such as BulletBlocker and Infidel Body Armor. If you do wish to get a vest that stops rifle rounds, you'll want a Level III, which you can also get from the companies above.

7 TIPS TO ENSURE YOUR NEXT INTERNATIONAL VACATION IS CAREFREE

The ground beneath me started to shake and I thought my heart was going to burst from my chest. I started running like my life was on the line — because it was.

I turned to look back and finally saw the 2,400-pound beasts emerge from around the corner. I kicked it into high gear as I felt them getting closer.

Suddenly, someone elbowed me and another person shoved me and chaos ensued, as nobody wanted to get mowed down by the animals.

I was able to fight my way out of their path, and ended up pinned against a concrete wall as the bulls rushed past me.

It was an incredible adrenaline rush.

Running with the bulls in Pamplona, Spain, had been on my bucket list for a long time. However, now that I've done it, there's not a chance in you-know-where that I'll do it again.

In fact, the day after I ran with the bulls, a Frenchman was gored to death — one of 15 people killed since 1910.

Because this is such a dangerous activity, I did a significant amount of research before heading to Pamplona.

I read almost every book and article imaginable. I knew the best places to begin the run and the places to avoid. And I knew exactly what to do if I tripped and fell to the ground during the run. (Lie flat on your stomach and cover your head. Never attempt to stand up, because that's when people get gored.)

In addition to all of the planning and research I did to ensure my wife didn't end up a widow, I also made sure I was properly prepared to travel internationally.

Even if you have no desire to fly to Spain to run with the bulls, there are a few vital things you should do every time you travel overseas.

Make sure you have a valid passport. According to the State Department, only 36% of Americans do. My wife and I always ensure our passports are up-to-date, just in case.

I certainly don't plan to flee the country (and I hope my wife doesn't, either), but a passport is a good form of "insurance" that everyone should have, even if you aren't planning on going overseas anytime soon.

Also, don't forget to memorize your passport number. This eliminates the need to pull out your passport when you are required to fill out paperwork and reduces the chance of a criminal seeing your American passport and targeting you.

Once the details of your trip start coming together, scan all of your important documents onto an encrypted flash drive. (I use the IronKey flash drive — **http://amzn.to/2vHKTE3** for details.)

This includes copies of your driver's license, passport, travel insurance information, hotel and airline reservations, and emergency phone numbers for family as well as the U.S. Embassy wherever you are going.

Having these documents on file ensures that you will be able to contact your loved ones and get home safely in the event that you are robbed or a more serious emergency takes place. Make sure to continually add documents to this flash drive as you further plan your trip.

"I always spend the extra money to stay in a decent hotel overseas to ensure that I'm in a safe environment."

Be careful when it comes to choosing your hotel. Do plenty of research, and don't be cheap. Here in the U.S., you and I can stay at a Motel 6 and it's no big deal (if you don't mind bedbugs).

But if you stay in a dumpy hotel overseas, you could be putting yourself in serious danger. I always spend the extra money to stay in a decent hotel overseas to ensure that I'm in a safe environment.

I'd also recommend using a website like hotels.com to read reviews and see pictures of any hotel you're considering.

Airbnb has become increasingly popular lately, but I'd personally advise against it. Remember, Airbnb is not a hotel, and unlike checking into a Marriott, you're never 100% sure what you're going to get. Your safety is far more important than to take this type of risk, so avoid apartment-sharing companies and spend a little extra money to book at a real hotel.

Check the State Department website (**http://bit.ly/2gBEq30**) for any current travel warnings that may impact your trip. There, you'll see a box on the right side of the page that allows you to enter the name of the country you are traveling to.

You'll also find contact information for the U.S. Embassy and Consulates in the country you're visiting. Definitely write this information down and add it to your encrypted flash drive.

Most of us do plenty of research on the places we want to go when travelling to a new city or country. But it's just as important to spend some time researching the places you should avoid.

You need to know if you shouldn't leave your hotel at night, or what sections of the city should be avoided after dark. One good place to find such information is the "Stay Safe" section of Wikitravel.org. Simply type in the place(s) you plan on visiting and scroll down toward the bottom of the page.

Be particularly aware of pickpockets, which are a thousand times worse overseas than they are here in the U.S. Never carry money in your back pocket, and be sure to get a special travel wallet.

I don't recommend using a wallet that hangs around your neck. Those are too obvious and thieves deal with them all the time.

Instead, I recommend getting a travel wallet that wraps around your ankle or your thigh. There are also options that secure to your belt and hang down inside your pants. (Check out the Shacke Pocket Vault, as an example.)

Shacke Pocket Vault: **http://amzn.to/2xLJCJy**

Also, don't keep all of your eggs in one basket. I realize some people may think it's overkill, but I always carry two different travel wallets in two different places for an added security measure.

Don't carry a purse. In a lot of places in Europe, criminals will cut the purse strap and be off and running with your purse before you know it. These criminals often work in two-man teams. One person will come to distract you — by offering to sell you something or offering to help you read a map — and the second man will come by and cut the purse strap or pick your pocket. Instead, use a travel wallet like the ones I described above.

Be careful when it comes to taxis. Never, ever take a "ghost" taxi. What I mean by that is an unmarked car that's not sitting at the taxi stand. Often in foreign countries, drivers will offer to help "save you money" and skip the taxi lines, but they can't necessarily be trusted. Stick to officially marked cabs, even if they're more expensive.

I'd also warn against using Uber. (Personally, I advise against Uber even in the U.S. — just Google "Uber attacks" and you'll see why.) Instead, have the hotel you're staying at call a taxi for you or ask them to recommend a taxi company. When the taxi comes, you should already have your route planned out so that you can tell the taxi where to go. That way you'll avoid being ripped off by taking the long way in an unfamiliar city.

I know this checklist might sound intimidating, but it's the best way to ensure that a trip overseas goes well and that you and your family remain safe.

Most of us live in safe and comfortable areas where we don't have to give much thought to our everyday travels. Going overseas requires proper planning, but doing so pays off.

If you follow this advice and have good situational awareness, you shouldn't have any issues at all.

THE ART OF SUCCESSFULLY BRIBING THE POLICE IN A FOREIGN COUNTRY

I was in a foreign country, standing in front of two police officers with my hands on the back of my head, fingers interlaced.

And I was sweating.

I was traveling with someone who had just gotten us in a jam. I was furious — I could have killed them for doing something so stupid — but I had to remain calm.

Then one of the officers grabbed me and told me he was taking me down to the police station.

Needless to say, going to jail in a foreign country is pretty much the last thing you want to do. But by following the exact same advice I'm about to share with you, I was able to get out of the jam and leave the area safely, even though my wallet was left a little lighter.

Before I continue, I want to make it clear that I'm talking about using bribery, but only in the direst circumstances. I would never condone bribing the police here in the U.S. because it would not end well for you — in fact, you'd likely go to jail.

However, if you're in Mexico and you have to bribe the police in order to keep yourself out of a Mexican prison, then I'm all for using a well-placed bribe in order to keep you safe.

The scenarios in which you may have to bribe the police overseas can vary. Maybe you're legitimately pulled over for a moving violation. Or maybe some corrupt cops see that you're an American and simply want to hassle you. Whichever situation you find yourself in, here is…

The "Right" Way to Bribe the Police

Even though we're talking about bribery, you would never, ever say anything like, "Officer, what's it going to cost me to get out of this?" You would also never whip out a huge wad of cash and start peeling back bills while looking at the officer.

While some officers are absolutely corrupt, they'll still be royally ticked off if you make it clear you are trying to bribe them. Instead, what you want to do is play the dumb and apologetic American.

Be as nice as you can be, and apologize over and over for your mistake. Then say the following key words:

"I am so sorry, and I'm sure there's a fine I have to pay for this. How do I go about paying it?"

This is exactly what I did in my situation. The police officer told me there was a $50 fine and I could just take care of it with him. So I handed the officer $50 and was able to go on my way. Little did he know I would have paid a heck of a lot more than that to get out of there.

The good news is even if the police officer won't take any cash from you, it won't appear as if you're trying to bribe him. If you ask him if there's a fine to pay and he says yes and tells you that you have to go to the courthouse or somewhere else to pay it, then at least you'll know what you have to do.

Hopefully, you never find yourself overseas in a situation that requires you to "pay a fine." But if you do, you now know what to say to get on your way and keep yourself out of any foreign jails.

FIVE TIPS FOR A SAFE TRIP OVERSEAS

Imagine you're on your dream vacation basking in sunshine and admiring the view of a beautiful lakeside resort. Needing to go back to your room, you grudgingly tear yourself away from your spouse with the promise that you'll be back in five minutes.

Arriving at the door to your room, you insert the key card and turn the handle. It doesn't budge. You give it another go, but it's still locked. Confused, you try several more times, but no luck. Then you head down to the front desk and explain something is wrong with your door. The receptionist tells you there's nothing they can do to help you get back into your room. They're powerless.

Sound far-fetched?

Well, it's exactly what happened to guests at the luxurious Romantik Seehotel Jaegerwirt in Turrach, Austria.

Total Takeover

It all started when the hotel received an email one morning demanding a ransom of $1,800 to be paid by the end of the day or the amount would double. It turns out hackers had infected the computer system that controls the electronic door locks with ransomware.

Guests started to complain that their key cards weren't working and — with the hotel at full capacity — the manager decided to pay up. The ransom was paid in Bitcoin, making it virtually untraceable. The hacker made off with the money scot-free.

According to the Justice Department, ransomware attacks averaged 4,000 per day in 2016. This number will continue to increase because the crime is so difficult to prevent. And since enough people choose to pay the ransom, it's worth the minimal effort for hackers.

The criminals behind these attacks usually don't ask for large amounts of money. But they're smart and they know that a service business, like a luxury hotel, would be willing pay a few thousand dollars to keep their guests happy.

While it doesn't sound like the guests themselves at the Seehotel Jaegerwirt were in any danger, it's easy to see why criminals target hotels for all sorts of nefarious activity. Tourists stand out and frequently make easy targets for con artists.

Checking In?

Next time you plan a hotel stay, remember these specific safety measures to help you avoid being a victim:

1. Research the hotel. I don't mean you should check if the hotel serves a complimentary breakfast or has a fitness center. What I mean is if you were at home when disaster struck, you would (hopefully) have a plan to defend yourself or flee if needed. When you stay in a hotel, you should familiarize yourself with the hotel and the surrounding area ahead of time in case of an emergency.

Always carry important contact numbers for family and local law enforcement — and the U.S. Embassy if you are traveling abroad. Also, never stay at a cheap motel, especially overseas. In the U.S., a cheap hotel may get you bedbugs, but overseas, it may get you kidnapped or killed.

2. Always get an extra key. When checking into a hotel, always request two keys — even if you're by yourself. Criminals will often hang out in hotel lobbies looking for easy victims to attack or rob. If they overhear you say you only need one key, they'll know you're alone. This is especially critical for women who travel solo.

3. Stay between the third and sixth floors. Always book a room on or above the third floor and on or below the sixth floor. Most crooks target lower floors because they're easier to rob and make a quick escape. If a criminal has to run down dozens of flights of stairs, their chances of getting caught increase.

If you stay higher than the sixth floor, you might end up stranded if there's a fire. In the U.S., most firetruck ladders don't reach past the sixth floor.

4. Keep your plans to yourself. When checking in, don't talk about how you will be gone all day sightseeing or how you are going to spend a fortune on a once-in-a-lifetime experience. The last thing you want to do is broadcast if your room will be empty or if you have a lot of money.

Once, a buddy of mine went over to Russia to fly a MiG fighter jet. He told everyone he met about his exciting excursion. Later, he realized he was being followed by a couple of unsavory Russian characters and had to hire two bodyguards for the rest of his vacation.

5. Never trust a hotel safe. Don't leave jewelry, passports, money or any other valuables in the safe in your room. These safes usually have combination locks, and you never know who has access to the combination. In fact, most hotel safe

thefts are inside jobs, so keep your valuables with you or find a better place in the room to hide them.

One trick you could use: Bring Gorilla Tape with you and tape your valuables to the underside of the couch or nightstand. You could also take off the cap of the curtain rod and hide your valuables inside the hollow part of the rod.

Staying in a nice hotel should be a relaxing experience for you and your family. By implementing these five safety tips, you will be better protected wherever you may be staying — at home or abroad.

TRAVEL ADVISORY: LEAVE THESE ITEMS AT HOME

Finland's version of the CIA — called Supo, short for Security Police — recently advised its citizens not to take cellphones, tablets, laptops and other devices when traveling overseas.

Frankly, I'm surprised more governments haven't done the same.

When I travel overseas, I never take my cellphone. Instead, I buy a cheap flip phone and an international SIM card that allows me to make calls all over the world. I never take my laptop either. Instead, have a cheap notebook that I can use to send and receive email.

The reason you don't want to take your devices overseas is because foreign governments love to steal Americans' information any chance they get.

The French government, for example, is notorious for sneaking into Americans' hotel rooms and copying all of the information off their devices. The Russian and Chinese governments, to nobody's surprise, also do the same.

And you can't trust hotel room safes because government employees have the keys to those and can easily access them when you're not in the room.

So if you have any important information on your phone or your computer — or even just personal information you'd like to keep private — don't take these items with you when you travel.

HOW TO SELL LIKE A SPY

Whether you're looking for a raise or need to convince your spouse to let you buy a new TV, these four tactics can help you out.

"Armando" sat across the restaurant table from his target. Both men were dressed in fine Italian suits and were enjoying a meal that would end up costing around $1,000 for just the two of them.

But Armando didn't mind the price. He'd been working the target for months and knew the man had vital information that would benefit the U.S. government. Armando had decided he'd offer the target money in exchange for information. If things went wrong, Armando could be exposed as a spy and could end up in prison, facing torture and even death. But if things went right, Armando would secure a highly prized foreign asset that could provide the U.S. with vital intelligence for years to come.

As the meal wound down, it was time for Armando to make his move. He looked the target directly in the eye and thanked him for his friendship over the past several months. Armando stated he'd like to learn more about the target's profession and that he'd like to give the target some money for his help. He told him to spend the money on his beautiful mistress.

You see, Armando knew the target didn't have much money and had a mistress that required a lot of upkeep. As soon as Armando said these words, a smile came over the target's face and he reached over to accept an envelope containing $3,000 in cash. From then on, the target continued to provide Armando with very sensitive information about his country.

Armando would end up being one of the most successful intelligence officers ever. He never got caught as a spy, and he never had an asset turn him down.

So how did Armando obtain such a perfect track record? In the intelligence business, it's called the "art of elicitation."

In the workaday world, it's simply referred to as sales.

Four Tricks to Getting What You Want

When you are a spy trying to get an asset to give you information, what you're really doing is trying to sell them on the benefits of working with you.

All of us sell, in one way or the other, every day of our lives. Even if it's not in your job, you are "selling" every time you try to convince someone of something.

So here are a few tips and tricks that spies use to make the ultimate sale:

- Spies do deep research to find a target's vulnerability. They spend months researching and getting to know the person before making any type of pitch to them. A really good spy will know the target better than the target knows himself. It's important to know what angle will make the target bend to what you want. When selling something, make sure you know exactly where your target's weakness lies

- Spies know how to control their emotions. You have to

be able to look a terrorist in the eye, agree with him and smile. That could be because you know that he's low on the food chain and you're really trying to get to his leader. You've got to pretend to be his friend in order to get to the person you're really going after. The same applies in everyday life. Don't let your emotions or your opinion of someone get in the way of what you want. If they can get you there, work with them

- Never forget the words "Give to get." There's a reason Armando was taking the target to a $1,000 meal that night, and had taken the target to several meals before that. Armando wanted the target indebted to him. In the end, the target felt as though he owed him something because Armando had been so generous in paying for all of their outings. Don't be afraid to go out of your way to help someone out if you think they could help you down the line

- Always develop a reason to meet again. When trying to recruit someone, you certainly don't pitch them on the first outing, just like you don't ask someone to marry you on the first date. To build a solid relationship, you always need to plan ahead and find an excuse to get together again. If you've done your research and know their hobbies, play to those — ask, "How'd you like to go fishing next Saturday?" If someone views you as a friend, they're more likely to help you.

In the spy world, these tactics are used in manipulative ways for the benefit of our country.

In our world, I hope you're not manipulating anyone but instead using these tactics for good. For instance, you can do deep research on someone to truly get to know them and understand them better. You can give things to a person to do something nice for them without seeking something in return.

If more of us spent the time to do this, I imagine we'd be happier and have more successful lives.

YOUR CRASH COURSE IN AIR TRAVEL SURVIVAL

Although air travel is widely considered the safest way to travel (based on miles traveled), it is estimated that 30% of those who have died in airplane accidents did so because they failed to respond better.

What has killed more SEALs than anything else (by a wide margin) are helicopters — I often thought it was the most dangerous part of the job.

Think about it: A team of men in full gear... crammed into a small space... flying around in a machine that has a ton of moving parts... only to slow down like the giant target it is when it's most vulnerable (during takeoff and landing).

Unfortunately, helicopters are a necessity of war. Just like commercial airliners are a necessity of travel.

Here is a checklist you can use before boarding your next flight that may save your life:

Pre-Flight

- What to wear: Wear long pants, a long-sleeve T-shirt and sturdy, comfortable, lace-up shoes

- High heels will slow you down, and they are not allowed on the evacuation slides
- You can cut your feet on glass or get flammable liquids on or in your shoes if you wear sandals or flip-flops — so don't.

Where to Sit

- Most often, the initial impact of a plane crash is survivable. The key to staying alive is how quickly you can get out
- When you book your flight, get seats as close as possible to an exit
- Passengers in the tail of the aircraft have 40% higher survival rates than those in the first few rows.

On the Plane

- Make a mental note of every exit as you pass it
- Once you get to your seat, immediately identify the two closest exits. Study the door and make sure you know how to open it
- Make your evacuation plan, visualize it — even rehearse it if you feel the need. DO NOT open the exit doors during this rehearsal.

Be Ready

- Whenever the plane is below 10,000 feet (normally during the first five and last 10 minutes of the flight) you should be in "full alert" mode
- Press pause on the movie you're watching, take out your earbuds and pay attention. You need to be prepared to respond quickly to any emergency condition.

Impact — Brace Yourself

- If you know the plane is going to crash, brace yourself. The sudden deceleration will cause you to be thrown forward. If you're already in contact with whatever it is you'll hit, the possibility for injury is greatly reduced
- The secondary brace function is to stop your limbs and head from flailing about, hitting things during the violent motion of the crash. This is why you wrap your head in your arms and tightly clasp your hands together
- If there is not a seat in front of you — or it is not within reach — lean forward, place your chest on your thighs and put your head between your knees. Grab each ankle with the opposite hand, or place your hands behind your head to protect the back of your neck
- Your feet should be flat on the floor and farther back than your knees to avoid sustaining any injuries. You'll need your feet to be intact to aid in your swift evacuation.

Post-Impact — GET OUT

Congratulations, you survived the impact! But it ain't over 'til it's over...

Fire — and more commonly smoke and noxious fumes — is responsible for a large percentage of crash fatalities. This is why you need to be ready to spring into action. It's time to enact your evacuation plan:

- Exit the airplane as quickly and calmly as possible. If there is fire or smoke, you will have no more than two minutes to save your life
- The closest exit may not be the best — it could be blocked with debris or there might be a fire waiting outside. If this is the case, move to the second exit you identified earlier
- DO NOT TRY TO GET ANYTHING YOU BROUGHT

WITH YOU! Always life before property

- Secondary explosions are likely so once you are outside, move swiftly away from the plane. You want to gain the greatest possible distance from the crash site, preferably 500 feet upwind, and wait there.

It's important to remember these critical safety tips the next time you book a trip. I want you to reach your final destination as a survivor, not a statistic.

THREE TRAITS TO LOOK FOR IN A PERSONAL PROTECTION AGENT

by JAVELIN | *Ex-CIA Operative*

Recently, I went on a two-week trip with a group of seven individuals. Unfortunately, this was not a vacation for me. I was hired as a bodyguard to protect this group during their travel.

This was no ordinary protection gig. Five out of the seven members of the group were teenagers. To make matters even more challenging, three of the teens were female, which makes for an obvious target when traveling in Europe.

The reality is this job would typically require three bodyguards — but that wasn't an option in this case.

A One Man Show

During our European excursion, the group visited some of the finest restaurants and shopping establishments I've ever seen. The teenagers wanted to have an enjoyable vacation with lots of shopping and sightseeing. They never wanted to stay in one place for very long (which is why it would have been ideal to have two more protection agents working with me).

Since I was alone, I made sure always to remain behind the group, following at a safe distance — not too far, but just far enough — so that I could keep my eyes on everyone. I was also constantly scanning our entire surroundings for anything out of the ordinary that would indicate a threat.

While shopping one day, a man approached the group as we were walking and tried to grab one of the teenage girls. I had seen him coming and before he was able to lay a finger on her, I grabbed his wrist and twisted it downward while shoving him against a wall.

His eyes widened and he immediately said, "Oh, sorry, sorry..." as he backed away and hurried off. I returned to the group and we continued down the street.

Take the High Road

I'm sharing this experience to point out that this is the type of situation where some bodyguards would have beat the guy up or caused a scene resulting in the arrival of police.

Don't get me wrong — of course I wanted to kick the crap out of this guy. But when it comes to providing personal security, you can't just go around throwing punches. This was one of those times when I determined the best course of action was to resolve the threat quickly and quietly and move on with my group.

After all, the touchy-feely guy could have been a diversion — criminals abroad often work in pairs. As a one-man operation, I needed to neutralize the first threat as fast as possible so I could make sure there wasn't another threat ahead.

But thankfully, the rest of the trip was rather calm, and I made sure everyone returned home from their European jaunt safely.

The Right Person for the Job

Now, I realize most of you won't be hiring a personal protection agent anytime soon, but you never know. And if you ever find yourself in need of some muscle, you should know there are certain character traits that make an effective bodyguard.

Here are three things I recommend you look for in the person you're trusting to keep you and your loved ones safe:

Street sense — Bodyguards must know how to blend in and handle themselves tactfully in any environment, as well as be smart with their actions. Like in the story above, you want someone who can see, hear and feel the danger before it happens. They should also have the ability to defuse the situation with a variety of tactics.

Government training — A bodyguard always needs to be a step ahead of the criminals. This is why, ideally, you should look for a bodyguard who was trained by the government and has worked in the field. In other words, you want someone with training in skills such as counter surveillance and rapid threat assessment — even someone who has been trained to handle kidnappings. Obviously, I am biased, but I believe former CIA officers make the best protective agents.

Combat skills — Since there are a lot of places where you can't carry a gun, you need security who is trained in multiple forms of self-defense. For example, I couldn't carry a gun while in Europe; however, I always had a knife on me (sometimes two knives, depending on where we were going). And I'm very skilled in the martial arts.

Even if you never have the need to hire a bodyguard, I recommend strengthening some of these attributes in yourself. You probably can't join the CIA, but you can work on your street sense and learn a few combat skills so you're better able to protect yourself and your family.

HOW TO SURVIVE A RIOT

What should you do if a riot erupts in your town? How do you protect yourself if you suddenly find yourself surrounded by angry rioters?

Here's how to make sure you make it back to your home safe and alive:

1. Always carry some type of weapon on you. Most rioters are cowards. So if they approach your car and start rocking it or try to drag you out, you'll want to be armed and prepared to preserve your life.

   My weapon of choice is a gun. Rioters attempting to carjack you will likely have a change of heart when they find themselves staring down the barrel of a gun.

   It's important to note you should draw your gun only if you are in fear for your life. But if 50 people were surrounding your car trying to drag you out, I'm pretty sure you would be.

2. Pretend to agree with the enemy. I think it's fair to say that rioters are punks. But it might save your life to pre-

tend that you support their cause. Because the worst thing you can do is start mouthing off to a large crowd of rioters when you're outnumbered 100-to-1.

In the intelligence business, sometimes you have to work with the enemy to get to the boss who's higher up the chain of command. I remember one time a buddy of mine working with a terrorist told me, "I would smile and agree with him, but I really wanted to put a bullet in his head.

3. Don't end up by yourself until it's safe. When mob mentality takes over, the crowd tends to attack anyone who is alone. Why? Because — similar to what I discuss above — the pack assumes that a person who is by themselves is against them, or otherwise they'd be rioting too. So don't immediately separate from the group... unless you're sure you can get to safety without being cornered.

4. Keep a 72-hour kit in your trunk. Riots are unpredictable. You never know if you'll have to leave your car or vacate your home and flee to a remote area. This is why I recommend that everyone have a simple 72-hour kit stored in their trunk. If you ever have to escape without warning, you'll have three days of food and water on which to live.

5. Don't show your wealth. I'm a big believer in living below your means and not flaunting your wealth by showing off material possessions. I myself live in a modest house and drive a 2009 truck with 170,000 miles.

Concealing your affluence is especially important if you ever find yourself in the middle of a social breakdown. People driving Ferraris or wearing Rolexes or showing any opulent sign of wealth will have huge targets on their back.

6. Always have a paper map in your car. You and I both know we live in a world where most people are completely dependent on technology. But wireless systems, including navigation, can easily go down, leaving you stranded in a bad situation. You should always keep a physical map in your car as a backup. It could come in handy if you are looking for an alternate route to escape a riot and get home safely.

Remember, every instance of rioting is different. In some cases, it might be appropriate to draw your gun to defend yourself. In others, you may need to pretend to join the masses for a bit, until you can safely get out of Dodge. And sometimes it makes most sense to run like wind.

In any case, if you take a few of these simple precautions and keep a level head, you will be better prepared than most to stay out of harm's way in this violently unpredictable — and increasingly common — situation.

FOUR REAL-LIFE NINJA SKILLS YOU CAN USE TODAY

By Jeff Anderson

A lot of people dismiss the ninja as some fantasy warrior BS that's only for Hollywood.

Big mistake.

The ninja were not a myth — they really did exist, and still exist today.

In fact, I've known a few real ninjas in my life and trust me, there's a LOT more to their skills than just sinking a throwing star into someone's forehead from 100 yards away (which is a myth by the way).

They're skilled at everything from surviving in the wild (alone)… to hand-to-hand combat… bladed weapons… even psychological warfare!

You see, "Nin-Ja" actually means "enduring person", or "one who endures" — in other words, a ninja is an elite survivalist of the highest order, one that could teach the rest of us a thing or two.

Here are four real-life ninja skills you can use today:

Become Invisible

The ninja didn't walk down the middle of the street dressed in a mask and full black bodysuit (actually, they didn't wear black to begin with, but more on that in a minute).

Instead, they would study the dress, walk, mannerisms and even talk of the people they were hiding among — the "grey man" if you will — and you'd never even know they were right next to you because true camouflage is really about blending into your environment, right?

So how are YOU blending in these days?

Do you blend into your surroundings (even urban)?

Or do you wear "tactical" clothing... gun-focused t-shirts... an NRA or "Infidel" hat... a "We Don't Dial 911" sign on your front door... or have a firearms-related bumper sticker on your truck?

If so, you're telegraphing to others your level of preparedness... and should re-think how you project yourself.

Better to be a silent warrior. (Speaking of...)

Walk Silently

The ninja were masters at moving without their enemies even knowing their presence.

They understood how the human body interacts with its environment to create sound that could give away (or hide) their presence.

Likewise — even in your own home — if you were to get out of bed to investigate a bump in the night, do you know how to tread so lightly that you won't be heard if there's actually someone in your house?

First, it helps for you to test this out in the middle of the night (when everything is quiet) and walk through your home, taking note of any creaks and bonks you may not have noticed before.

Plus, the ninja used a "stealth walk" where they put their

weight on the outer edges of their feet to muffle the sound.

Practice this step in gravel or sand to really get it down... and then in your own home at night.

Blend into the Night

Not only were the ninja able to blend into the local population in broad daylight, but at night, they were masters of being a true shadow warrior and as invisible as the darkness itself.

Hollywood dressed them in black, but in reality, the color black tends to stand out more in darkness.

Instead, dark blue clothing becomes virtually unable to view at night because of the way the eyes pick up specific colors — blue being the hardest.

Personally, I carry a super lightweight dark blue windbreaker in my EDC "bag of tricks" (it literally zips inside of itself to only six inches and weighs nothing).

Whether I want to travel unnoticed at night or if I felt I was being tailed, I can quickly pull out my windbreaker... throw it on... and instantly I've not only changed my disguise, but also made myself invisible in darker shadows.

Train in Secrecy

Because so much of the existence of the ninja's skills depended on no one noticing their presence or intentions, they would train in complete secrecy.

Likewise, I personally like to train very realistic and have a private range I go to for my firearms training where I can pretty much do anything I want — without anyone looking at me with my shotgun or AR-15 and thinking I'm some kind of nut job.

Same goes for all my other training — I like to keep my skills unknown to others around me.

Frankly, this mystery tends to make my friends think I'm way more "badass" than I probably am...

...and I like it that way!

AVOID FALLING FOR THIS DEADLY PRANK CALL

I will slit your throat from ear to ear if you do not listen to every word I say.

Do exactly what I tell you. Do not hang up the phone. Do not go to the window.

I know where you are, and if you do not cooperate, I will kill you.

This may sound like the beginning of a movie starring Colin Farrell, but it's exactly what happened to a Utah man named Bob M.

Bob was recently in Chihuahua, Mexico, on a business trip when the phone in his hotel room rang. When he answered, the person on the other end said they had a gun. They said they knew what hotel room Bob was in and threatened to shoot him if he tried to run away. The criminal told Bob they would torture, dismember and kill him unless he listened to every word they said. Then they began making demands.

For the next 18 hours, Bob spoke with the criminal and followed their instructions to the letter. At one point, they ordered him to leave his room and go purchase a disposable cellphone from a nearby store. While he was going to the store, Bob noticed a man sitting in the park across from the hotel that he believed was one of his captors.

Eventually, Bob was freed by Mexican police and was able to drive to El Paso, Texas, where he flew home. When he was interviewed, Bob was quoted as saying, "The whole thing could have been a movie."

A Very Real Threat

What Bob endured is becoming more common throughout the world — especially in Mexico — and it's called virtual kidnapping.

Here's how it works: Criminals attempt to extort a ransom from you without actually taking a hostage or even seeing you face to face. In Bob's situation, he never saw his kidnapper, even though he was on the phone with them for around 18 hours. But they had clearly done surveillance on Bob and knew enough information for Bob to be concerned and take their threats seriously.

In September, a woman in Farmersville, Texas, sadly fell victim to a virtual kidnapping and actually paid the ransom.

Sally Council received a phone call from a man she didn't know, who claimed to have kidnapped her daughter. Sally heard screaming in the background and what she believed was her daughter's voice yelling, "Mom! Please! I've been kidnapped, and they're going to kill me!"

The man on the phone told Sally that unless she did exactly what he told her, they would kill her daughter. While she stayed on the phone with the kidnappers, Sally drove to an ATM and withdrew an undisclosed amount of cash. Then she drove to a Western Union and wired the money to a Mexican address.

After Sally paid the ransom, she was told to wait in the

parking lot of a Daylight Doughnuts until her daughter arrived. While she was waiting in the parking lot, Sally called her daughter's cellphone and realized the kidnapping was fake. Thankfully, her daughter was safe.

A week later, a husband and wife from Torrance, California, wired $3,000 to a Mexican number after receiving a phone call from a man who asked, "Did you kiss your daughter today?" This man claimed he was part of the Mexican mafia and ordered the Torrance man and wife to do exactly as instructed or they would never see their daughter again. Meanwhile, their daughter was in class at the local college — perfectly safe and oblivious to her parents' panic.

In early October, Wendy Mueller of Leesburg, Virginia, received a similar phone call from a Mexican number. These criminals claimed they had abducted Wendy's daughter and demanded ransom. They scammed her out of $10,000 before Wendy received a text from her daughter and realized that she was safe all along.

Setting Up the Con

Each of these instances shows a common method of executing a virtual kidnapping scam: calling someone and claiming to have kidnapped a loved one. The victim is instructed to make a ransom payment immediately by wire transfer. Often, the criminals will use threats to keep you on the phone with them until the payment has been made so you don't contact the person who was supposedly kidnapped and expose the scam.

The caller might also tell you they are a member of a drug cartel — or even a police officer — to scare you out of contacting local authorities. The callers try to instill fear and panic in you, which they hope will lead you to make a hasty decision and pay the ransom without question.

Clearly, criminals who attempt these types of kidnappings

are intelligent enough to research their victims — even use surveillance. In Bob's case, we know they had someone watching the hotel from the park. Who knows why they picked Bob to extort (fancy clothes, fancy car, fancy watch?), but I'm sure it had something to do with being an American businessman in Mexico.

In the case of Sally Council, she believes the criminals knew about her and her daughter because she had been recently involved in a car accident and shared personal details with the other driver. All these thieves need is a little bit of information — and they can turn it on you in a hurry.

In fact, many criminals learn about their victims through social media, where it's easy to gain enough intelligence that people will believe what they say. Be careful of sharing information about your loved ones on social media — that information could be used against you in a virtual kidnapping.

Separating Fact From Fiction

If you ever receive a phone call like the one Bob (or Sally or Wendy or the Torrance family) received, here are a few things to keep in mind.

First, is the call coming from a strange area code? According to the FBI, many of these phone calls come from numbers in Mexico, Puerto Rico and foreign countries.

Second, does the caller insist on keeping you on the line? If so, try to find another phone and call the loved one whom they claimed to have kidnapped. The best thing to do is try to verify that your loved one is safe while keeping the kidnappers happy.

Third, and one of the most important things you should do, is tell the kidnapper you want to speak to your loved one. Demand proof of life or you will not pay the ransom. I know this sounds like something straight out of a Hollywood movie, but if your loved one were actually kidnapped, wouldn't you want to know they were still alive before paying a ransom?

If the criminals allow you to speak to the kidnappee, ask them questions only your loved one would know. For example, you could ask the name of the last movie you saw together, or what present you gave them last Christmas. Try to ask as many questions as possible to verify you're actually speaking to your loved one. Don't ask anything a third party could easily find out from social media or a quick Google search.

Unfortunately, criminals are always coming up with new scams and new ways to steal from us.

They know that using the people close to us is an easy way to fool us into making an emotional decision. If you ever find yourself in a virtual kidnapping, stay calm, pay close attention to the voice on the phone and take the steps discussed above to verify if it's an actual kidnapping or just a scam.

SIX TIPS FOR STAYING SAFE DURING THE HOLIDAY SEASON

1. Keep a 72-hour kit in your trunk. Many people travel long distances by car for the holidays, so make sure you have at least one 72-hour kit in your trunk. If you get stuck in the snow or the mountains, you'll want a minimum of three days of food and water to give you time to stay alive while you're waiting to be rescued.

2. Install a VPN client on your portable device. If you're on an airplane or in a hotel, don't get on public Wi-Fi without using a virtual private network (VPN). A VPN encrypts your information so you can surf the internet without the fear of being hacked. Check out TunnelBear, which is the VPN I use.

3. Avoid overcrowded places. In other words, don't intentionally put yourself in a potentially dangerous situation where fights are likely to break out. Yes, that means the mile-long line for a Black Friday sale. The latest Pokémon toy is not worth getting trampled for, no matter how much your grandkids will love it.

4. Never give out personal information over the phone. If

someone calls you asking questions, hang up and find the company's main number and call them to verify if it was a legitimate person who reached out to you. Scams increase significantly during the holiday season because people are in a more generous mood, and criminals know to take advantage of this.

5. Don't post travel plans on social media. Don't broadcast where you're headed for Thanksgiving or Christmas or how long you'll be gone. Criminals browse Facebook to ascertain who won't be home for the holidays. If they know your home is going to be empty for several days, it makes a perfect target for a break-in.

6. Be aware of your surroundings. This is true in any season. Make sure you're not being followed when exiting the shopping mall with your hands full of expensive gifts. Criminals case the entrances to malls and will follow you to your car to rob you — or worse. When you leave the mall, keep your head up and on a swivel, scanning your surroundings. If you see anyone behaving suspiciously, wait for them to leave or ask security to escort you to your car.

WHY THE U.S. SHOULD TAKE NORTH KOREA SERIOUSLY

by JAVELIN | *Ex-CIA Operative*

One of the last top-secret projects I worked on was out of Asia. My mission was to gain intelligence on one of the most secretive nations in the world: North Korea. My cover was as the CEO of a boutique travel agency that catered to wealthy people who wanted to travel to North Korea.

What made this operation especially challenging was that I couldn't risk entering North Korea myself. So I tracked down North Korean refugees in Japan who could help me gain the intelligence I needed regarding the North Korea's weapons capabilities.

I ended up working with a North Korean freedom fighter with Japanese papers who could enter North Korea via the Chinese border. The North Korean-Chinese border is somewhat of a no man's land where drug smugglers routinely cross back and forth, which is why my source was able to traverse it.

It didn't take this freedom fighter long to figure out that I wasn't just a travel agent, but he understood the information I needed from him and was willing to help me.

Based on the intel we gathered, we learned that North Korea has possessed nuclear weapons capabilities since 2002. They acquired the necessary information from Iran, China and Russia by proxy through Cuban operatives.

So when you hear reports that North Korea is getting close to having the ability to launch a nuclear weapon, that's a bunch of crap. We know they've had the capability for the past 15 years. However, North Korea lacks a delivery method for launching a nuclear weapon, which is the purpose of their recent tests.

A Disturbing Lack of Intel

As I've mentioned before, past presidential administrations have been reluctant to help intelligence operatives successfully gather information on our enemies, so some of our knowledge regarding the North Korea's capabilities is outdated.

In fact, very little intelligence work has been carried out in North Korea since my last operation, which was a number of years ago. Frankly, the Democrats have destroyed our ability to collect intelligence information, so we are stuck playing catch-up.

The scary thing, in my opinion, is North Korea probably has the capability to deliver a nuclear weapon to the West Coast of the United States (not just Alaska), although I believe the chances of this happening are low.

You see, Kim Jong Un isn't a maniac like most people assume. He's a smart, educated man. He wants a relationship with the U.S., but he doesn't want to look weak. He wants the U.S. to come to him and build the relationship on his terms, but he is clearly going about it the wrong way. If Kim Jong Un attacked the U.S., our government would respond with massive military force and annihilate North Korea's capital in addition to blanketing the country with Tomahawk missiles.

Why So Serious?

The question I've been building up to is why should we take

North Korea so seriously?

First, while I believe North Korea could strike the West Coast, the fact is they probably couldn't do so accurately. They may aim for a major city, such as LA, but the missile could end up in the desert hundreds of miles away. I believe we have the defensive capability to shoot down any long-range missile from North Korea, but that's not a theory I'd like to test.

Second, there is no question North Korea could successfully strike Seoul, South Korea, with the basic weapons and artillery they have near the border. Who knows what can of worms an attack on their southern neighbor would open.

Americans should remember that even if the chances of a nuclear attack are slim, everyone needs to be prepared. These preparations should include water and food storage, as well as a bunker or safe house in case of a nuclear missile strike.

The reality is one mistake during a missile test — or even errant artillery fire from the North Korean border — could lead to a major military conflict. While it's probable that North Korea lacks the guidance systems to accurately deliver a nuclear attack, we are dealing with a leader who may not care where the missile lands as long as he gets the attention he wants.

PLAY IT COOL WITH THESE SUMMER SAFETY TIPS

There's nothing quite like exploring the American wilderness in the summer. But it's important to stay safe even when you're enjoying yourself. Remember these simple safety tips to avoid ruining your fun in the sun.

- Share your plans. Whether you are going on a three-day hike or a walk around the block, you should tell someone you trust where you are going and what you are doing. That way, if something goes wrong and you don't return as expected, they can raise the alarm and get you help. This is especially important if you are going on an extended trip.

- Drink up. When spending time outdoors, try to drink water every 20 minutes. This is critical if you are hiking or doing any kind of strenuous activity. Also, watch out for signs of heat stroke if someone in your group isn't feeling well — dizziness, lack of sweating, muscle weakness and hot, dry skin. And don't forget to carry a quality water filter with you in case you run out of water and have to drink from a pond or stream.

- Check your car. Before you embark on a family road trip, always make sure your car is mechanically sound. This includes checking the tires, belts and hoses and making sure you have a fully packed survival bag in the car for each member of your family. Even if you never need to use your survival supplies, you should be prepared in case of an emergency.

- Be wary of scams. During the summer, you see an increase in the number of door-to-door salesmen. While some of these people may be from legitimate companies, be extra cautious. Never invite a stranger into your home. If you aren't interested, say so through the door — don't even bother opening it. Often, these people are actually criminals looking to case your home.

- Clean up your yard. The thing about summer is that kids are out of school, and frankly, they are bored. So whether it's bored kids or a career criminal, when your trees aren't trimmed and your yard is strewn with tools and toys, people will take that as a sign that no one is home. So — while it's not the most fun summer activity — clean up your yard and eliminate places for bad guys to hide.

SEAL SURVIVAL SECRETS FOR THE ROAD

By Cade Courtley | *Former Navy SEAL Sniper*

It's not a matter of if, but when…

There are more than 200 million vehicles on the road in the United States, all operated by individuals with varying degrees of alertness and skill. The chance of getting into a car accident at least once in your life is estimated to be over 95%.

Approximately 43,000 Americans are killed on our nation's roadways each year, and another 100,000 become permanently disabled due to car accidents.

The work I did in Iraq involved a lot of high-speed driving. We rarely wore seat belts, because the idea of having to quickly evacuate the car and getting caught up in the seat belt was a nightmare. Hell, with all of the gear we wore, it was hard enough to get out as it was.

But when I learned that the leading cause of injury in the crew I was working with was from automobile-related accidents, I went against the "trapped" fear and started making my men strap in anytime the speed of the vehicle was over 35 mph. It paid off and saved lives.

Ride or Die

Here are some other driving safety tips you should regularly employ to stay safe on the road:

1. Be mindful of the airbag. In early car models, airbags were so strong that they could cause decapitation if they malfunctioned. Airbags are designed to sense sudden deceleration and impact and inflate at a speed of 200 mph — as fast as a shell fired from a sawed-off shotgun.

   Today, airbags are still powerful, but they are far more sensor-regulated.

   Because accidents aren't planned and an airbag is deployed on impact, I recommend driving with your hands at the 4 o'clock and 8 o'clock positions on the steering wheel, rather than the standard 2 and 10. This will provide a clear path for the bag to release without sending your arms and hands into your face. Also, do not place any object on top of the air bag enclosure, or you may end up eating it

2. STAY AWARE. Multitasking while driving should be illegal. Period. So many auto fatalities could have been avoided if the driver was simply paying attention

3. Respond quickly. If you see that your car is about to be hit, try to respond with decisive maneuvers, but do so as smoothly as possible. You don't want to 360 the steering wheel or slam on the brakes, which may result in the car going out of control.

   The goal is to access the options rapidly and make a decision that will minimize damage. For example, avoiding a head-on collision might require you to veer off the road or accelerate. Every scenario is different, but if you remain calm and focused, you will make the best decision

4. Control braking. There are certain braking techniques that are proven to help you maintain maximum control. Most cars these days have an anti-lock brake system (ABS) that regulates brake fluid and prevents the brakes from freezing up if pressed firmly.

   If your car lacks antilock brakes, then pumping the brake pedal will prevent lockup and allow you to retain control of your vehicle. Slamming on the brakes will cause your car to skid, and the result of the accident is far more likely to be a less favorable outcome

5. Steer smoothly. If you jerk the steering wheel quickly, even when driving at normal speeds, it will also cause the vehicle to skid, and it will often spin in the opposite direction

6. Speed up. Sometimes you may need to accelerate while you weave through obstacles or steer out of the path of an oncoming car to avoid an accident

7. Follow the skid. In the event you blow a tire during the incident, do not slam on the brakes. If the car begins to skid, your instincts will falsely tell you to turn the steering wheel in the opposite direction. In fact, it's best to turn the wheel toward the direction of the skid to regain control

8. Always leave yourself an out. This is sure easier said than done when you're in gridlock on the 405 in Los Angeles, but always try to maintain a "buffer" of distance between your vehicle and the next. A good rule of thumb is you should be able to see the back tires of the car in front of you. This will give you the option if you need to take an aggressive defensive action to escape the situation

9. Arm yourself. I recommend is keeping a Glock .40 and canister of bear spray in your driver's-side door panel.

It's amazing how these items can de-escalate a road rage scenario.

If you keep these nine safety tips in mind, you'll feel much more confident behind the wheel, and you'll be more likely to walk away from an accident.

Remember, I want you to be a survivor, NOT a statistic.

HIT THE ROAD SAFELY WITH THESE IMPORTANT REMINDERS

According to the Harvard Health Watch, the average American spends an hour and 41 minutes driving every day. Because we spend so much time in our cars, here are seven safety tips to keep you from being vulnerable in your vehicle:

- Always carry a bug-out bag or 72-hour kit in your vehicle. Whether you become stranded in a snowstorm, require a first-aid kit when you're out and about or need to flee unexpectedly, having this gear readily available could save your life.

- Don't leave anything personal or identifiable in plain sight. Be aware that passersby can see everything in your car. So don't leave papers with your name on them or hang your work badge from the rearview mirror. Criminals will look for information they can use to steal your identity — or, perhaps worse, stalk you. And obviously, don't leave anything expensive in plain sight, like a GPS or a guitar case. That's like painting a big, fat target on your car.

- Remember that movement saves lives. When you get in

your car, don't sit there and rifle through your purse or check your email. Instead, you should immediately begin driving. People who sit in their vehicles not paying attention are sitting ducks.

- Pay attention to vehicles following you. When you leave work or a shopping center, always be aware of who's behind you. Sometimes criminals watch people get into their car with valuables and follow them home to commit a home invasion. If you are suspicious of a vehicle behind you, make a few turns to see if the car continues to follow you. If you are indeed being followed, don't go home. Drive straight to the nearest police station.

- Always lock your doors. No matter where you are or how long you will be away — or even if you're standing right next to your vehicle but aren't in it — always lock your doors. Increasingly, criminals are stealing items while people are pumping gas. They'll usually distract you by asking a question while their accomplice grabs things from your car.

- In parking garages, park as close to the payment booth as possible. These areas usually have more surveillance cameras and more people around, which helps deter criminals. Thieves prefer to avoid being seen doing their dirty work.

- Make your car look protected. In the same way I encourage you to get an alarm system for your home, I also recommend getting one for your vehicle. And if you don't have a car alarm, buy security stickers to put on the window. This will convince a criminal to look for an easier mark.